First World Hunger Revisited

Also by Graham Riches

FOOD BANKS AND THE WELFARE CRISIS

UNEMPLOYMENT AND WELFARE: Social Policy and the Work of Social Work (*co-edited with Gordon Ternowetsky*)

FIRST WORLD HUNGER: Food Security and Welfare Politics, ed.

Also by Tiina Silvasti

TALONPOJAN ELÄMÄ. TUTKIMUS ELÄMÄNTAPAA JÄSENTÄVISTÄ KULTTUURISISTA MALLEISTA
Peasant life. A Study of Cultural Scripts Organizing The Farmers' Way of Life

TOISTEN PANKKI: RUOKA-APU HYVINVOINTIVALTIOSSA (co-edited with *S. Hänninen, J. Karjalainen and K. Lehtelä*)
Another Bank: Food Aid in the Welfare State

MAATILAN VARJOSSA. RAKENNEMUUTOKSEN ANATOMIAA
In the Shadow of the Farm. Anatomy of Structural Change

First World Hunger Revisited

Food Charity or the Right to Food?

Second Edition

Edited by

Graham Riches
Professor Emeritus of Social Work
University of British Columbia, Canada

and

Tiina Silvasti
Professor of Public and Social Policy
Department of Social Sciences and Philosophy
University of Jyväskylä, Finland

First edition published 1997
This edition published 2014 by
PALGRAVE MACMILLAN

Palgrave Macmillan in the UK is an imprint of Macmillan Publishers Limited, registered in England, company number 785998, of Houndmills, Basingstoke, Hampshire RG21 6XS.

Palgrave Macmillan in the US is a division of St Martin's Press LLC, 175 Fifth Avenue, New York, NY 10010.

Palgrave Macmillan is the global academic imprint of the above companies and has companies and representatives throughout the world.

Palgrave® and Macmillan® are registered trademarks in the United States, the United Kingdom, Europe and other countries.

ISBN: 978–1–137–29871–3 hardback
ISBN: 978–1–137–29872–0 paperback

This book is printed on paper suitable for recycling and made from fully managed and sustained forest sources. Logging, pulping and manufacturing processes are expected to conform to the environmental regulations of the country of origin.

A catalogue record for this book is available from the British Library.

A catalog record for this book is available from the Library of Congress.

This book is dedicated to the memory of
Kwong-leung Tang
谨以此书纪念邓广良教授

Contents

Foreword

When I visited Canada in May 2012, it was the first time I had conducted an official mission to a developed country as UN Special Rapporteur on the Right to Food. The previous missions I had undertaken were to a range of countries in Sub-Saharan Africa, the Middle East, Latin America and Asia. On each of these occasions, it had come as no surprise, to myself or to those following the missions, that hunger and malnutrition were pressing issues on the political agenda. As such, there was little controversy in a UN official coming to analyse the situation.

The mission to Canada was different. Immediately a range of actors, from the news media to Canadian political figures, questioned the very premise of the visit. What was a UN human rights expert doing examining food systems in the developed world while millions were starving in poor countries? This question underlined not only the challenges of conducting such a mission, but more broadly, the difficulties of conveying a highly counter-intuitive truth: namely, that hunger can and does exist amid plenty.

Public discourse slips too easily into Manichean visions of well-fed and underfed countries, in the same way as it slips into a simple vision of food security in terms of net calorie availability. It is only when we shift from talking about food security in blunt terms to talking about the right to food, in its many interconnected dimensions, that we will be able to grasp the fact that pockets of hunger and undernutrition remain rife in the wealthiest countries in the world, and it is only then that we will grasp the reasons why.

The assumption that severe poverty has, and must have been, eradicated in rich countries is, in fact, the measure of how well our societies have managed to keep the uncomfortable reality of food poverty firmly out of public view and public discourse. The two-track economic processes that have mired some communities in disadvantage have in fact marginalized them far enough as to make them invisible to the rest of society.

Indeed, it has taken a steep and highly visible reemergence of food banks in Europe and North America, in the throes of the current financial and economic crisis, to remind the rich world that these are real and pressing issues, and to give credence to the warnings sounded for years by social workers and civil society groups working in these countries, who were all too aware of the fine line between many people and severe food poverty.

Access to food is in fact a key indicator of broader socio-economic inequalities. Food insecurity hotspots generally correlate not only with poverty, but also with a series of factors that marginalize people and particular population groups. Poor communities may lack local fresh grocery stores providing alternatives to the foods high in saturated fats, sugars and salt sold by local retailers. They may cut down on food expenses first, because the costs of rents are incompressible. This can take the form of profound decreases in food expenditure, and switching to cheaper and less nutritious calories.

Now that the debate has reemerged onto the political agenda, it must not stop at food banks. While food banks can provide some relief to those in poverty, they can only offer basic subsistence from day to day – and not a route out of poverty. They cannot therefore be used as a substitute for real measures to address underlying poverty and inequality, and the food insecurity they generate.

Our attention must shift onto the layers of the social safety net lying above food banks, and through the cracks of which many are now falling. Current social safety nets are either not extensive enough or not generous enough, in the context of rising inequality across OECD countries. Indeed, this inequality has now become so extreme that even where social safety nets are extensive, they cannot catch people who are so far below being able to meet the costs of an adequate diet and a decent life. Social protection systems, not least unemployment and child benefits, must be recalibrated to take into account the real cost of living and ensure adequate food for all, without compromising on other essentials.

Nowhere should governments be allowed to escape their obligations because private charities make up for their failures. When people come to depend on charity for basic foodstuffs, it is a signal that their right to food has not been sufficiently respected, protected and fulfilled. Developed and developing countries alike have a responsibility not merely to plug these gaps, but to dedicate the 'maximum available resources' to fighting poverty to fulfil the human rights they have promised their citizens by signing up to treaties. For developed countries these resources are evidently more plentiful – and the failure to eradicate extreme poverty is that much less excusable.

The contributions in this volume will add to this essential debate. They will help to illuminate the current deficits in the way we discuss and address hunger in the rich world. And they demonstrate the power of rights-based approaches to offer solutions commensurate to the problem.

Olivier De Schutter
UN Special Rapporteur on the Right to Food

Preface and Acknowledgements

It is befitting if not a little ironic that the idea to update and expand the first edition of *First World Hunger: Food Security and Welfare Politics* (1997) should stem from two seminars, one held at the National Research and Development Centre for Welfare and Health (STAKES/THL), Finland, in 2006 and the second at the annual conference of the European Society for Rural Sociology (ESRS) in 2011, which included a paper on charity food aid in Finland. Fitting because the idea of the right to food is deeply embedded in the social and economic rights which inform the Nordic welfare state, and ironic in that the establishment of charitable food banking in Finland in the 1990s had led to the first Helsinki seminar organized on this topic.

We both participated in the Helsinki seminar where the suggestion of an updated edition of *First World Hunger* was initially mooted and one of us, Tiina, presented the paper on Finnish food banking at the ESRS conference five years later. Professor Tim Lang of City University, London, a leading international researcher on food policy, was a keynote speaker at the conference and by good fortune also attended the workshop. His comments were inspiring and encouraging but most importantly he referenced *First World Hunger* and in the same breath, recommended that the book should definitely be updated. An email was quickly sent to Vancouver, British Columbia, as a result of which we both find ourselves as co-editors of this new book: *First World Hunger Revisited: Food Charity or the Right to Food?*

It is not our intention here to introduce the main themes and analysis informing this updated and expanded cross-national study as they are presented and explored in the book's first chapter. However, we do wish to share the ideas (and commitments) which lay behind our own decisions to collaborate on this edited book on the topic of domestic hunger, food charity, public policy and the right to food in rich societies. For each of us they go back over a number of years: to the early 1980s when food banks appeared on the scene in Canada (though dating from 1967 in the United States) and to the early 1990s in Finland, both amongst the wealthiest countries in the world.

Food Banks and the Welfare Crisis (Ottawa, CCSD), a national study of food charity in Canada, was published in 1986, leading in turn to the edited *First World Hunger* in 1997, a cross-national study of domestic hunger and the politics of food security and welfare reform (1980–1995) in five 'liberal' welfare states – Australia (John Wilson), Canada (Graham Riches), New Zealand (Stephen Uttley), the UK (Elizabeth Dowler and Gary Craig) and the US (Janet Poppendieck). The focus was on the de-politicization of hunger as a human rights issue; the failure of New Right policies; the development of charitable emergency relief to guarantee household food security; and public policy neglect. The analysis pointed to the need for alternative integrated policies and the necessity of public action to solve the problem. The lack of such public policy action has certainly been a key motivator in wishing to re-engage with these long-standing issues; and which, certainly three decades later, continue to invite a right to food perspective.

In Finland, surprisingly, it was not a too different story. At the beginning of the 1990s – in the wake of a deep recession – food banks and breadlines emerged for the first time on the street. Despite the Nordic welfare state model they became established during the next decade, which was a confusing development from the perspective of the Nordic welfare regime. There were no official estimates of the number of people who were dependent on charity food, but the Evangelical Lutheran Church of Finland, the biggest distributor of food aid, calculated that the number was annually in the tens of thousands. Numerically it was a minor problem, but in the framework of the Nordic ethos of welfare it had a huge symbolic value.

Even though the subject got some media attention and the Church, especially, maintained the public debate, the political elite mainly denied the problem. Yet there was a group of researchers working at the National Research and Development Centre for Welfare and Health (Sakari Hänninen, Jouko Karjalainen and Kirsimarja Lehtelä) and the University of Helsinki (Tiina Silvasti), who were interested in this alarming new phenomenon of emergency food delivery partly substituting the right to basic security. At this point in 2006 the researcher group invited Professor Riches to Finland for a seminar on charity food aid. As a result the first edited book on food banks and charity food aid in Finland, *Toisten Pankki*, was published in 2008.

However, even though charity food aid became institutionalized and food banks as well as breadlines proved to be vigorous, the idea of updating *First World Hunger* lay dormant for almost five years. This was until time to reconsider charitable food aid in Finland became available, leading to the ESRS paper presentation (Silvasti) in 2011 and Tim Lang's encouraging words to revisit the topic cross-nationally originally explored in 1997. So, it is certainly Tim we must thank for spurring us into action and the book at hand is *First World Hunger Revisited: Food Charity or the Right to Food?*.

Of course it has taken another three years before publication, which is too long a story to tell. However, despite the benefits of almost instant electronic communication, it has involved the complexities of working with a team of invited authors in twelve countries on five continents thereby increasing the scope of the cross-national case studies from the original five high income 'Liberal' welfare states to include seven new states from the Eurozone and fast rising emerging economies.

Despite their heavy teaching and research commitments all our invited authors (from agricultural science, economics, food policy, health and nutrition, international development, political science, sociology, social policy and social work) stayed the course indicative of a very strong commitment to, and understanding of, the importance of the topic. Without them the book would not have been possible and we wish to thank them all, appreciate their patience and acknowledge their contributions in the strongest possible terms.

As the book was in the production process, we received the sad news that Kwong-leung Tang, the lead author of the Hong Kong SAR/China chapter, had passed away. Tang, as he liked to be known, had been ill for some time but remained committed, with the assistance of Yu-hong Zhu and Yan-yan Chen, to completing the chapter. His research was on the leading edge of new theories of social welfare in post-colonial states particularly in Hong Kong, China and East Asia; the role of comparative social policy; the reduction of poverty and inequality with particular interest in social security and pension reform; the rights of workers, the unemployed and those on social assistance; and, with Jacqueline Tak-york Cheung, his wife, among other topics the rights of women in the context of the *International Convention of All Forms of Discrimination against Women*. Kwong-leung Tang believed in, and always sought a common humanity.

The different disciplinary and professional expertise of the authors is of particular interest in the context of exploring the obligations under international law of states to progressively realize the human right to adequate food. It makes the point that the right to food is not simply a legal concept but one imbued with moral and political significance. It emphasizes the significance of food, or, in the case of this book, its absence, not only as a matter of lawful entitlement but as an important metaphor for analysing social change. At the same time access to food is central to debate and analysis in the development of informed and integrated public policy in addressing not only hunger but poverty and income inequality and, as such, a key issue of distributive justice in wealthy (and indeed poor) societies.

The book would not have been possible without the endorsement and support of Palgrave Macmillan and the immediate and always professional, encouraging and kindly advice from our publisher, Christina Brian, and her two Editorial Assistants Amanda McGrath and Ambra Finotello; and also Vidhya Jayaprakash and her production and editing team at Newgen Knowledge Works. Their ability and willingness to provide the right advice at exactly the right moment has been outstanding and most welcome. We would like to acknowledge Professor Gary Craig for recommending Palgrave Macmillan. We are, too, especially grateful to Eija Syrjämäki who has done uncompromising and detailed work in compiling the references.

Several authors would like to acknowledge others who have contributed to the writing of their respective chapters. Sue Booth wishes to thank John Gray, Mark Henley, Greg Ogle, Sarah Pennell, John Lang and Richard Pagliario for informative discussions and to express her gratitude to colleagues John Gray and John Coveney for reviewing an early draft. Kwong-leung Tang, Yu-hong Zhu and Yan-yan Chen wish to thank the Beijing Philosophy and Social Science project (grant number 13SHC030) which supported their research and the Beijing Federation of Social Science project (grant number: 2012SKL008). They would also like to acknowledge and thank Kwun Tong Methodist Social Service, Yan Oi Tong, St. Barnabas Church, Christian Action, Feeding Hong Kong and Mariana Chan of the Hong Kong Council of Social Service, for their participation in their interviews regarding food bank services. Jan Poppendieck would like to thank her husband, Edward (Woody) Goldberg for his patience, support, and sense of humour. Karlos Pérez de Armiño appreciated the contributions of the numerous people interviewed, both academics and technical personnel and managers of social organizations and food banks, and thank them for their kind collaboration. Some of the interviews cited in the text were held with Jordi Peix, founder and vice-president of the Barcelona food bank, and José Antonio Busto, president of the FESBAL. Tiina Silvasti and Jouko Karjalainen would like to thank Mikko Malkavaara and Sakari Hänninen for reviewing an early version of their chapter; Leena Saarela and an anonymous language consultant for revising; and Senior Officer Riikka-Maria Turkia from the Ministry of Employment and the Economy and Senior Officer Outi Nieminen of the Agency for Rural Affairs for informative interviews. In addition, Silvasti is grateful for the research friendly environment and encouraging atmosphere at the Department of Social xvi *Preface and Acknowledgements*

Sciences and Philosophy, in the University of Jyväskylä. The research was supported by the Academy of Finland, project number 21000015231.

Research for the Canadian chapter was facilitated by the Dean of Arts Fund at the University of British Columbia with the ongoing support of Tim Stainton and the UBC School of Social Work. The impetus for its progress and indeed that of the book as a whole was enriched along the way by the ideas, insights and support of many including Valerie Tarasuk, Ken Battle, Ernie Lightman, Susan Draper, Elaine Power, Paul Taylor, Brent Mansfield, Jean Swanson, Joanne Houghton, Judy Graves, Elizabeth Jones, Brian O'Neill, Margo Young, Margo Matwychuk, Martha McMahon, Rod MacRae, Diana Bronson, LeiLani Farha and, especially, of my friend and former colleague, Gordon Ternowetsky, now sadly passed away, who as long ago as the early 1980s encouraged me to pursue the question of food charity and the right to food. In light of the 2012 visit to Canada of Dr Olivier De Schutter, UN Special Rapporteur on the Right to Food, this was clearly the right advice and a clear signal that this new edition is timely. Lastly I wish to thank Mary Riches for her endurance, support and advice as the project unfolded.

Graham Riches
Tiina Silvasti

Notes on Contributors

Editors

Graham Riches is Emeritus Professor and former Director of the School of Social Work, University of British Columbia, Canada. His research has focused on food and social policy and the intersection of unemployment, poverty and hunger with social welfare and the right to food. He has published widely in these fields and contributed to the preparation of the UN Food and Agricultural Organization's *Voluntary Guidelines on the Right to Food* (2005). He has practiced community development in Sarawak (Malaysia), Tanzania and in London and Liverpool in the UK. He is currently a Research Associate with the Canadian Centre for Policy Alternatives-BC.

Tiina Silvasti is Professor of Public and Social Policy in the Department Social Sciences and Philosophy at the University of Jyväskylä in Finland. She has studied the social consequences of structural change in agriculture and cultural models that organize farmers' ways of life, covering also gender and environmental issues. Her recent research interests lie in food system studies, particularly in First World hunger and food aid delivery in wealthy Western countries. Besides publishing articles in scientific journals, both in Finnish and in English, she has written two books (in Finnish) and co-edited a number of books on these topics.

Contributors

Sue Booth is Needs Assessment Fellow for the Collaboration of community-based obesity prevention sites (The CO-OPS Collaboration), Department of Public Health, Flinders University, South Australia where she teaches in the Master of Public Health programme. Her teaching and research interests include food and social policy, food poverty, alternative food systems and qualitative research methods. She has written and co-authored a range of materials including nutrition education materials, policy papers, book chapters, articles, reports and peer-reviewed papers. She has worked in community nutrition, public health, health promotion, research and academic settings for over twenty years.

Yan-yan Chen is a lecturer in the Department of Social Work at Fudan University, China. She was formerly a postdoctoral fellow at the Sau Po Centre on Aging, University of Hong Kong. Her PhD thesis was on the multiple dimensions of elderly poverty and the resilience of the aged poor in China. During her postdoctoral study she participated in research projects that included low-income elders, learning about elderly poverty from the perspective of household resource distribution and the mental health of Chinese elders. Her gerontological research interests mainly include inequality, poverty and gerontological social work. She has published a paper on qualitative research methods in the *International Journal of Adolescent Medicine and Health.*

Elizabeth Dowler, a public health nutritionist, is Professor of Food and Social Policy in the Sociology Department, University of Warwick, Coventry, UK. She draws on science and social science to work on food security, rights and justice, local food initiatives, policy evaluation and 'reconnection' to sustainable food systems. She is a member of the Food Ethics Council, a small charity working for a fairer food system. She does brief international consultancies and previously worked in the global South, based at London School of Hygiene and Tropical Medicine LSHTM. With O'Connor she published (2012) 'Rights-based approaches to addressing food poverty and food insecurity in Ireland and UK' *Social Science and Medicine*, 74, 44–51.

Sheryl L. Hendriks is Professor and Director of the Institute for Food, Nutrition and Well-being, University of Pretoria. She is an expert in global, African and South African food security and food policy. She is a member of the Committee on World Food Security High Level Panel of Experts on Food Security and Nutrition. Between 2006 and 2010 she led drafting of the Comprehensive African Agricultural Development Programme's Framework for African Food Security and the design of the technical review of national agriculture and food security investment plans. She is committed to capacity development and has supervised postgraduates from 18 African countries.

Jouko Karjalainen is a social worker and researcher at the National Institute of Welfare and Health, Minimum Income Unit, Helsinki, Finland. He is a member of many associations and networks working to prevent social exclusion. Publications on poverty, homelessness, ex-prisoner services and voluntary work include *Leaks in the Safety Net: The Role of Civil Dialogue in the Finnish Inclusion Policy* (1999, with Matti Heikkilä); *Local Impact of Church Food Banks* (2000); 'From Hunger Humble to the Hunger

Group' in Hänninen, S. et al., *The Others Bank – Food Aid in the Welfare State* (2008).

Mustafa Koc is a Professor of Sociology at Ryerson University, Toronto. He was amongst the founders of the Ryerson Centre for Studies in Food Security, the Canadian Association for Food Studies and the national coalition, Food Secure Canada. His research and teaching interests include food studies, food security, food policy, sociology of migration and diasporic communities. He has various publications on the sociology of agriculture and food, social change and development, and immigration, including *For Hunger-proof Cities* (1999), *Working Together* (2001), *Interdisciplinary Perspectives in Food Studies* (2008) and *Critical Perspectives in Food Studies* (2012).

Jüri Kõre is Assistant Professor of Social Policy, Institute of Sociology and Social Policy, University of Tartu, Estonia. His main interests are comparative social policy, housing policy, social welfare, social services and local government. He is a member of several international and national social welfare and housing research projects. Formerly an adviser to the Estonian Ministry of the Interior, he has been deputy mayor of the City of Tartu most recently from 2011 to 2013, and a consultant to the Estonian Parliament, the Ministry of Social Affairs, the Statistics Office of Estonia, and the Association of Estonian Cities. He is the author or co-author of six books.

Angela McIntyre is a research associate of the Institute for Food, Nutrition and Well-being and a PhD candidate in Rural Development Planning at the University of Pretoria. Her recent work includes research, advocacy and programme evaluation for United Nations agencies and various international development partners, as well as non-governmental and community-based organizations. Her academic background includes anthropology and social history, environmental management and public health. Her current research focuses on food security and food sovereignty in South Africa.

Michael O'Brien is Associate Professor in the School of Counselling, Social Work and Human Services at the University of Auckland where he teaches social policy. He has published widely in New Zealand and internationally on inequality, welfare reform, social security, child poverty and the reshaping of social services. He is the author of *Poverty, Policy and the State,* and joint author of the social policy text *Social Policy in Aotearoa New Zealand* and of *New Zealand: New Welfare*. He is active in a range of social justice and social service groups and a life member of the Aotearoa New Zealand Association of Social Workers.

Karlos Pérez de Armiño is Associate Professor of International Relations at the University of the Basque Country (Bilbao) and research fellow with HEGOA – Institute of Studies on Development and International Cooperation. He is Head Researcher of the *Research Group on Human Security, Local Human Development and International Cooperation* of the Basque research system (IT816–13).

Janet Poppendieck is Professor Emerita of Sociology at Hunter College, City University of New York, and Policy Director at the New York City Food Policy Center, CUNY School of Public Health. She is the author of *Breadlines Knee Deep in Wheat: Food Assistance in the Great Depression* (1986), (republished, Spring 2014); *Sweet Charity? Emergency Food and the End of Entitlement* (1998) and *Free For All: Fixing School Food in America* (2010), which received the 2010 Book of the Year award from the Association for the Study of Food and Society.

Cecilia Rocha is Director of the School of Nutrition and an associate researcher at the Centre for Studies in Food Security at Ryerson University, Toronto, Canada. Her research interests are on assessing the efficiency of food security initiatives, the role of market failures in food insecurity, and the effectiveness of markets as policy tools. She has authored a number of papers on innovative food policies in Brazil, and has conducted research on food security conditions amongst immigrant populations in Toronto, urban food insecurity in South Africa, and the manifestation of food sovereignty in an indigenous settlement in Brazil.

Kwong-leung Tang passed away as this book was being completed. He was a Professor and former Director of the School of Social Work, University of British Columbia, Canada. Between 2003 and 2008, he served as Chair of the Department of Social Work, Chinese University of Hong Kong; and earlier of the Department of Social Work, University of Northern British Columbia. His research interests included poverty and inequality, comparative social policy and social welfare in East Asia, and law and social work. His publications included: *Colonial State and Social Policy: Social Welfare Development of Hong Kong 1842–1997* (1998); *Social Welfare Development in East Asia* (2000); and *Social Policy and Poverty in East Asia: The Role of Social Security* (2010, with James Midgley).

Valerie Tarasuk is a Professor in the Department of Nutritional Sciences and the Dalla Lana School of Public Health at the University of Toronto. Much of her research is focused on food insecurity, elucidating the scope and nature of household food insecurity in Canada and examining policy and programmatic responses. Her work has included studies of food banks and charitable meal programmes, research into the experiences of food insecurity amongst low-income families and homeless youth in Toronto, and analyses of national population survey data to explore the social policy underpinnings of household food insecurity in Canada.

Yu-hong Zhu is an Assistant Professor of Social Work at the School of Sociology and Population Studies, Renmin University of China, Beijing, China. She received her PhD from the Department of Social Work and Social Administration, University of Hong Kong. Her main research fields include child protection, social welfare and social policy. She has published papers in journals such as *International Social Work;* the Hong Kong Institute of Asia-Pacific Studies *Occasional Paper Series; Collection of Women's Studies* and *China Youth Studies*.

List of Acronyms and Abbreviations

AAFC	Agriculture and Agri-Food Canada, Ottawa
ABS	Australian Bureau of Statistics
ACOSS	Australian Council of Social Service
ACT	Australian Capital Territory
AFDC	Aid to Families with Dependent Children programme, USA
AHRC	Australian Human Rights Commission
AIHW	Australian Institute of Health and Welfare
AKP	Justice and Development Party, Turkey
ANAP	Motherland Party, Turkey
ANU	Australian National University
ARIB	Agricultural Registers and Information Board, Estonia
ARRA	American Recovery and Reinvestment Act, USA
BDA	The BDA Group, Melbourne
BI	The Broadbent Institute, Ottawa
BWI	Bread for the World Institute, Washington, DC
CAFB	Canadian Association of Food Banks
CACFP	Child and Adult Care Feeding Programme, USA
CAP	European Union Common Agricultural Policy
CBC	Canadian Broadcasting Corporation
CBO	Community Based Organisation
CESCR	UN Committee on Economic, Social and Cultural Rights
CFPA	Council of Food Policy Advisors, UK
CFHS	Community Food and Health Scotland
CIS	Centro de Investigaciones Sociológicas, Spain
CONSEA	National Council for Food and Nutrition Security, Brazil
CPI	Consumer Price Index
CSI	Corporate Social Investment
CSR	Corporate Social Responsibility
CSSA	Comprehensive Social Security Assistance Programme, Hong Kong
DoHA	Department of Health and Aging, Canberra
Defra	Department for Environment, Food and Rural Affairs, UK
DWP	Department for Work and Pensions, UK

EAG	Expert Advisory Group on Solutions to Child Poverty, New Zealand
EAPN – Spain	European Anti-poverty Network – Spain
EBT	Electronic Benefits Transfer swipe cards, USA
EITC	Earned Income Tax Credit programme, USA
EEC	European Economic Community
EFFB/FEBA	European Federation of Food Banks
ELCF	Evangelical Lutheran Church of Finland
EMPRAPA	Brazilian Agricultural Research Organisation
ES	Eesti Statistika
ESRS	European Society for Rural Sociology
EU	European Union
FAO	United Nations Food and Agricultural Organisation
FBA	Foodbank Australia
FBC	Food Banks Canada
FBSA	FoodBank South Africa
FEBA	European Federation of Food Banks
FEC	Food Ethics Council, UK
FHK	Feeding Hong Kong
FESBAL	Federacion Española de Bancos Alimentos, Spain
FIAN	FoodFirst International Action Network
FINA	Standing Committee on Finance, Parliament of Canada
FOESSA	Fomento de Estudios Sociales y Sociologica Aplicardo, Spain
GA	General Assistance programme, USA
FSC	Food Secure Canada
GDP	Gross Domestic Product
GFN	Global Foodbanking Network
GLA	Greater London Authority
GMI	Guaranteed Minimum Income
HHS	Department of Health and Human Services, USA
HKCSS	Hong Kong Council of Social Service
HKSAR	Hong Kong Special Administrative Region
HLPE	High Level Panel of Experts on Food Security and Nutrition, Committee on World Food Security, FAO, Rome
HMT	Her Majesty's Treasury, UK
HRC	Human Rights Council, Geneva
HSRC	Human Sciences Research Council, South Africa

ICESCR	International Covenant on Economic, Social and Cultural Rights
ICP	Individual Complaints Procedure, United Nations Human Rights Council
IFPRI	International Food Policy Research Institute, New York
IFS	Institute for Fiscal Studies, UK
IMF	International Monetary Fund
INE	Instituto Nacional de Estadistica, Spain
ISMMMO	Istanbul Chamber of Public Accountants and Financial Advisors
JSA	Job Seeker's Allowance, UK
JCHR	Joint Committee on Human Rights, UK
KFC	Kentucky Fried Chicken
MAF	Ministry of Agriculture and Forestry, Finland
Mavi	Agency of Rural Affairs, Finland
MDP	European Union's Food Distribution Programme for the Most Deprived Persons of the Community
MDS	Ministério do Desenvolvimento Social e Combate à Fome (Ministry of Social Development), Brazil
MEE	Ministry of Employment and the Economy, Finland
MIS	Minimum Income Standards, UK
MSA	Ministry of Social Affairs, Estonia
MSAH	Ministry of Social Affairs and Health, Finland
MSD	Ministry of Social Development, New Zealand
NACLC	National Association of Community Legal Centres, Australia
NDP	New Democratic Party, Canada
NGO	Non Government Organisation
NHRCC	National Human Rights Consultation Committee, Australia
NHS	National Health Survey, Australia
NMW	National Minimum Wage, UK
NSLP	National School Lunch Programme, USA
NTSARS	National Treasury and South African Revenue Service
NZCCSS	New Zealand Council of Christian Social Services
OECD	Organisation for Economic Co-operation and Development
OHCHR	Office of the High Commissioner for Human Rights, United Nations
LOSAN	National Law on Food and Nutrition Security, Brazil
PAA	Food Acquisition Programme, Government of Brazil
PRWORA	Personal Responsibility and Work Opportunities Reconciliation Act, 1996, USA

REDES	Rede Desenvolvimento, Ensino e Sociedade (Network for Development, Learning and Society), Brazil
RPI	Retail Price Index
RSA	Republic of South Africa
RTF	Right to Food
SACOSS	South Australian Council of Social Service
SBP	School Breakfast Programme, USA
SESC	Serviço Social do Comércio (Social Service of Commerce Association), Brazil
SFFA	The Sydney Food Fairness Alliance
SNAP	Supplemental Nutrition and Assistance Programme, USA
StatsSA	Statistics South Africa
SUC	Service Unit of the Evangelical Lutheran Church, Finland
SUT	Statistiline üleuaade Tartu
TANF	Temporary Assistance to Needy Families, USA
TBMM	Türkiye Büyük Millet Meclis
TCU	Tribunal de Contas da União, Auditor General Office, Brazil
TFA	Turkish Foodbanking Association
THL	National Research and Development Centre for Welfare and Health, Finland
TSU	The Strategy Unit, Cabinet Office, UK
TURDEP	Turkish Diabetes Epidemiology Study
UK	United Kingdom
UN	United Nations
UNICEF	United Nations International Children's Fund, New York
UNCESCR	United Nations Committee on Economic, Social and Cultural Rights
USDA	United States Department of Agriculture
VGs	Voluntary Guidelines on the Right to Food, FAO, 2005
WACOSS	Western Australian Council of Social Service Inc.
WADH	Western Australia Department of Housing
WHO	World Health Organization
WIC	Special Supplemental Nutrition Programme for Women, Infants and Children, USA
WWG	Welfare Working Group, Wellington, New Zealand

1
Hunger in the Rich World: Food Aid and Right to Food Perspectives
Graham Riches and Tiina Silvasti

Introduction

The relationship between food poverty and food charity in developed countries was initially explored in the book *First World Hunger: Food Security and Welfare Politics* (1997), the first cross-national study of the development of food aid and the charitable food bank movement from the early 1980s to the mid 1990s. It examined the rise of food banks as community and philanthropic responses to the growing issue of food insecurity in five residual welfare states: Australia, Canada, New Zealand, the UK and the USA. It revealed a growing reliance on the collection and redistribution of surplus and wasted food to feed hungry people. During this period of neo-liberal welfare reform publicly funded social safety nets were being dismantled and government obligations to ensure the adequacy of social benefits sufficient to both pay the rent and feed oneself and one's family, even during times of strong economic growth, were increasingly neglected. These residual approaches to hunger and poverty turned out to be highly problematic particularly in the short term and pointed to food banks as symptoms and symbols of welfare states in decline if not in crisis. The book anticipated the international growth of charitable food banking in the North as a system comparable to emergency food aid in the South. It argued for right to food approaches and strategies for public action including the importance of inter-sectoral collaboration and a stronger advocacy role for civil society.

A decade and a half later this initial cross-national study of the early period of charitable food banking has been updated and expanded so as to explore newly emerging issues and right to food perspectives to provide a more informed and enriched understanding of increasing hunger and food poverty in high and upper income states; and what to do about it. The period since 1997 has been one of ever stronger and more and more 'uni-dimensional' global neo-liberal economic and welfare policy, as well as more extensive international debate about global hunger including domestic food insecurity in rich societies and right to food discourses, strategies and analyses. Not unexpectedly it has also witnessed the national and global expansion of charitable food banking in First World states, increasingly supported by transnational food corporations, in the absence of public policy, inviting questions why, and who is actually benefitting from such food charity.

Against this background *First World Hunger Revisited* explores and analyses the rise and development of charitable food banks and emergency food aid since the mid 1990s as a continuing response to growing domestic hunger in basically food secure, rich 'First World' countries. While recognizing the strength of human compassion and the moral imperative to feed hungry people it challenges food charity as a practical, effective and ethical response to hunger and poverty. It examines the origins and development of food banking and asks whether this increasingly influential form of global food charity – collecting, sorting and distributing surplus or wasted food to feed the hungry poor in wealthy nations, is part of the solution to, or part of the problem of entrenched food poverty (Dowler, 2003, p. 151).

The book offers a cross-national study of the intended and unintended consequences of global and increasingly corporate food charity and its implications for the role of nation states and public policy informed by the right to food in addressing domestic hunger and food poverty. The focal questions posed are to what extent does charitable food banking, now more often institutionalized and corporatized in many countries, undermine food justice and the human right to adequate food and nutrition; and, in what ways, does it extend and exacerbate food poverty and inequality? It has been suggested that food charity acts as a moral safety valve (Poppendieck, 1998, p. 298) and that it de-politicizes First World hunger as an issue requiring the full attention of states and their governments. The book also considers the possibility that the human right to adequate food (Eide, 2005; Kent, 2008; Ziegler et al., 2011) and 'joined-up' food, health, income and social policy (Lang et al., 2009) might offer alternative approaches to achieving universal food security inclusive of disadvantaged and vulnerable populations, people whose lives are surplus to the requirements of global and local labour markets.

The text includes 12 national case studies invited from a mix of high and upper income states of which the majority are members of the

Paris based Organisation for Economic Co-operation and Development (OECD) and non-OECD states and of emerging upper income states which, in aggregate terms, are food secure by internal production or import, and where food aid and charitable food banking are either established or being introduced. They comprise the original five residual 'Anglo-Saxon' welfare states and seven additional countries selected in Africa, Europe, South America, the Middle East and Asia, thereby expanding the study to include cases from the five continents.

The additional cases are from Estonia, Finland, Spain, South Africa, Brazil, Turkey and Hong Kong SAR/China. Spain is a eurozone state experiencing a deep financial crisis and a catholic country with a very different cultural background for delivering food aid compared for example to the Lutheran Nordic welfare state of Finland. Estonia, the neighbouring country of Finland, is a post-socialist hard line capitalist country and an emerging economy with high income disparities and growing food poverty.

The rapidly expanding economies comprise Turkey which has been used as a model within the Middle East and combines Islamic approaches to welfare within its philanthropic model; South Africa where the right to food is entrenched in its constitution as it is also in Brazil, which has a specific 'zero hunger' policy for food relief; and Hong Kong SAR/China which is now experiencing the introduction of food banks, and offers an example from the rich rising Asia. In 2004 national case studies regarding the right to food in Brazil, South Africa and Canada as well as India and Uganda were the subject of an FAO Intergovernmental Working Group seminar held in Rome, which were to inform the development of the UN FAO *Voluntary Guidelines on the Right to Food*, approved later that year (CFS, 2004).

Food aid perspectives

Three different but interrelated perspectives of food aid inform the book's analysis dating back to the mid-1990s. The first considers the steady rise, institutionalization, corporatization and globalization of charitable food banking in selected rich food secure countries attested to by the growth of national food banks organizations in which, with the exception of Finland, the Global Foodbanking Network (GFN) and the European Federation of Food Banks (EFFB) are now active. This invites the question why domestic hunger and food insecurity continue to remain obscure issues for public policy in relation to food, income security, public health and social policy. One possibility is that the social construction of First World hunger as a matter for charity and privatized welfare has resulted in domestic hunger being largely de-politicized

and neglected by national governments despite its increasing prevalence. Also, from an ethical and right to food (RTF) perspective there
is a pressing need to explore the benefits, failures, latent functions
and unintended consequences of the moral imperative to feed hungry
people with surplus and wasted food in hitherto neglected areas of food,
nutrition, public health and social policy.

Second, we are interested in the relationship, if not tension between
food charity, now increasingly corporatized by the global food industry,
and the legal and political obligations of First World states to advance
public policy informed by the human right to adequate food and nutrition in the context of national food security. In evaluating corporatized
food charity the case studies give voice to new conversations and public
debate about food justice in relation to the hungry poor. In so doing the
book considers the de-politicization of food poverty and hunger as matters
requiring priority attention by governments, particularly so in light of
the large majority of UN member states' having today ratified the 1966
International Covenant on Economic, Social and Cultural Rights (ICESCR)
including the right to food, with the USA being a notable exception.

Third, the case studies consider possibilities for public policy informed
both by the right to food and 'joined-up' food, health, income and social
policy in First World countries. In this context domestic hunger and
food poverty are understood as ideological and political questions of
distributional justice, asking what can be learned from the experiences
of different countries. In particular there is a need, emphasized by the
UN Special Rapporteur on the Right to Food, for states to prioritize social
protection policies in their national agricultural, food policy, income
security, public health and social welfare debates.

Changing global context of First World hunger

Several factors invite this re-examination of charitable food aid as a solution to food poverty in high and upper income states. The 2008 economic
meltdown; the Eurozone crisis; deep cuts in many countries to social
spending and widening income inequalities in the rich world combined
with continuing economic uncertainty; the aftermath of the 2007–2008
world food crisis and the ongoing instability of global food markets; and
the seemingly permanent crisis of precarious living and economic livelihoods for surplus and marginalized individuals, families and populations.
Due to increasing social inequality and growing income differentials, an
ever-growing number of people living in wealthy countries are coming
to depend on food aid. Populations at risk include women and children,

especially single parent families, unemployed and underemployed individuals, and the working poor, as well as refugees and Aboriginal peoples for whom the further dismantling of publicly funded social safety nets can only lead to increased poverty and social deprivation.

In the context of global hunger, the stubborn prevalence and recent growth of food poverty and undernourishment in high and upper income states requires attention. First and foremost, food insecurity is a problem of developing countries. Hence, it is important to distinguish First World hunger from undernourishment in developing regions, currently estimated by the FAO's most recent study, *The State of Food Insecurity in the World 2013*, at 842 million people, continuing its two decade decline since the early 1990s. It reports that over that same period undernourishment has also declined in the world's developed regions, yet indicating that between 2005–2007 and 2011–2013 it rose from 13.6 to 15.7 million people, a 15.5 per cent increase (FAO, 2013a).

These FAO-developed region numbers are, however, likely underestimates when compared with the numbers given by the US Department of Agriculture (USDA) of the people in need of food aid in the USA. On this account alone in 2012, 14.5 per cent of households (17.6 million households) were food insecure (Coleman-Jensen et al., 2013). To be food insecure does not necessarily mean to be undernourished, but it means that these households had difficulty at some time during the year in providing enough food for all their members due to a lack of resources (Nord et al., 2010). During 2008–2009 the prevalence of food insecurity was the highest observed since nationally representative food security surveys in the USA were initiated in 1995 (Nord et al., 2010) and it has stayed essentially unchanged since then. Thus, more and more people who are living in advanced industrial societies simply cannot afford to buy their food normally in the marketplace. The fact that not even the richest countries in the world can guarantee food security for all their citizens indicates that food policy as well as social and public policy is badly failing.

Clarifying the meaning of food poverty

Food poverty is primarily a matter of access to healthy food and its affordability, and in the context of this book is informed by two basic concepts, hunger and food security/insecurity, which require clarification. Given that hunger is politically as well as emotionally a polysemic and contestable concept and, thus, sometimes difficult to apply in First World societies, many researchers prefer nowadays the concept of food security. There is no single definition of food security, but in the context of global hunger different multilateral organizations, such as the FAO, the International Fund for Agriculture and Development (IFAD) and the World Bank, continuously tend to redefine the term according to their topical needs or interests. Critics of this concept sharply point out, that the food security model is basically a derivative of the model of globalization that reduces human relationships to their economic value and understands human beings as *homo economicus*. Accordingly, the driving force behind food security rests on the idea that economic growth, mediated via market mechanisms, will offer the best solution to reduce poverty and to achieve food security. The means to economic growth, again, are familiar in terms of neo-liberal economic policy: deregulation, free competition, privatization and trade liberalization (Schanbacher, 2010, p. viii–xi).

Food security/insecurity

The World Food Summit of 1996 defined food security as existing 'when all people, at all times, have physical, social and economic access to sufficient, safe and nutritious food which meets their dietary needs and food preferences for an active and healthy life' (FAO, 1996), reasserted in the *Declaration of the 2009 World Summit on Food Security* (FAO, 2009). Food insecurity, consequently, means 'limited or uncertain availability of nutritionally adequate and safe foods or limited or uncertain ability to acquire acceptable foods in socially acceptable ways' (Andersson, 1990). Food banks, soup kitchens and breadlines are not socially accepted ways to acquire food for oneself or for the family in the developed world, nor is begging, shoplifting or dumpster diving, that is searching for thrown away food in skips.

According to definitions of food security/insecurity, people who receive food aid are not inevitably hungry, but they are food poor: they either lack the financial ability to put food on the table and/or do not always necessarily know how they will manage to provide for their families and themselves the next sufficient, nourishing and culturally acceptable meal for an active healthy life. This does not, though, exclude the possibility of hunger as a sign of absolute poverty also in First World countries. As Riches (1997a) indicated in the introductory chapter of *First World Hunger*, food expenditure is the most flexible part of the budgets of vulnerable people. When the food budget gives way, individuals and families easily become and remain hungry and are in need of immediate help.

Critics of the concept of food security underline this fact. From their perspective, food security embraces charitable food aid as a solution to

food poverty rather than empowering sovereign actors to democratically manage their own food production and distribution systems. This
has been taken seriously within the food sovereignty movement, which
promotes the 'right of peoples to healthy and culturally appropriate
food produced through sustainable methods and their right to define
their own food and agriculture systems' (Via Campesina, 2012). Both as
a concept and a movement food sovereignty challenges the prevailing
global food system and offers a powerful response to the current global
food, poverty and environmental crises.

Hunger

Hunger is a difficult term to conceptualize, but three dimensions are
typically distinguished: biological, social and economic. According to
Poppendieck (1998, p. 79) defining hunger as food insecurity neglects
human sensations, the fact of 'hunger as the uneasy and painful
personal sensation caused by a lack of food' (Andersson, 1990, p. 1560).
Consequently, this definition is not just semantic but conceals moral
sentiments and political motives. An answer given to the question
whether people receiving food aid are really hungry at all is thoroughly
political. The response depends on the ideological standpoint and
is thereby dependent on moral values. In the research literature and
practical discourses both concepts, hunger and food security/insecurity,
as aspects of food poverty, are often used in parallel fashion without
paying careful attention to their politically distinctive differences. Both
of these concepts are also widely used in this book but an informed
effort is made to keep in mind their differences in orienting and coordi-
nating human action.

The new food policy: A more equitable, ecological and healthy global food system

The previously emphasized need for a public policy informed by the right
to food inclusive of 'joined-up' food and social policy in developed countries focuses attention on the concept of food policy. According to Lang
et al. (2009, p. 6–8) it is necessary to re-think the interface between health,
environment and society, the core issues of food policy in the 21st century.
The point of departure is that the environment is the infrastructure and
context for humans to live and eat. How humans eat has a deep impact on
environment, affecting simultaneously the health and welfare of populations. The value of researching food policy is, thus, to expose the complex
and often hidden relations between food, health, environment and society
and to make those relations more explicit and democratically accountable.

Instead of an ever more productionist food system, the new food policy searches for a socially equitable, low-carbon alternative which would actively promote public health and welfare (MacRae, 1999; Lang et al., 2009). This is called the 'food first' principle in contrast to the 'profits first' principle. The primary aim is to guarantee for all people economic, physical and social prerequisites to acquire safe and nutritious food and, in this way, promote health and welfare (Lezberg, 1999). In this reasoning the new food policy connects health, welfare, society and environment with each other, seeking to find an alternative – more equitable, ecological and healthy – way of organizing the global food system.

Global food waste

In this book we approach First World food poverty from the combined societal perspectives of integrated income, health, nutrition and social policy informed by the right to food, focusing primarily on matters of income and food distribution. At the same time the question of feeding poor people, surplus to labour market demands, with wasted food in the institutionalizing and corporatizing global charity food system links our exploration closely with the environmental dimension of food policy.

There is a growing public awareness of the abundance of global food waste in rich and poor countries alike. The prevailing global food system, based on globalized markets, wastes huge amounts of edible food (Stuart, 2009). The contradiction between unrestrained waste, ecological unsustainability and growing food poverty is ethically intolerable. As a social problem hunger could be easily solved. There is no shortage of food in wealthy industrialized countries. Vice versa, agricultural policies in many of these countries constantly struggle against over-production and the message that 'food banking is the link between food waste and hunger' (GFN, 2013b) is, thereby, gaining strength: when there is so much food waste, there has to be a 'politically correct' way to recycle it. Delivering wasted food for surplus people is one way of doing it (Poppendieck, 2000b; Tarasuk and Eakin, 2003). A global, corporately sponsored food bank model using wasted food to feed hungry people raises significant questions for 'joined-up' food policy directed at advancing just and environmentally sustainable food systems.

Corporatization and government denial

There is a strong and steady tendency of institutionalization and corporatization of charitable food banking within an expanding number of high and upper income states on all continents although it is likely these developments vary between countries. For example, the entrenchment of food aid delivery and the linkages between donating, collecting and delivering emergency food by corporate actors mostly in the finance, food and transportation sectors have specific national features. In order to obtain a clearer picture and understanding of these phenomena, cross-national comparisons will shed light on these developments.

At the same time the public legitimacy of charitable food delivery presents an interesting contradiction. While governments often simply deny or at least actively belittle and de-politicize food poverty and hunger as major social problems, there takes place, simultaneously, the strengthening corporatization and global outreaching of food banks led by the *European Federation of Food Banks* (1984) and *The Global Foodbanking Network* (2006) in the majority of wealthy OECD states and rapidly developing economies. Most surprisingly, perhaps, this includes the introduction and institutionalization of food banking in one Nordic welfare state – in Finland since the mid 1990s and its recent introduction in Denmark (EFFB, 2014). The re-emergence of hunger and food insecurity in wealthy societies stands in contrast not only to increasing general prosperity but also to common standards of human decency. Governments of these countries still refuse to acknowledge food poverty and, consequently, hunger is not understood as a political issue (Silvasti, 2014). The steady drip of welfare residualism is returning the collective and public responsibility for food poverty from the state to the vagaries of ad hoc and under-resourced private charity.

Food charity and right to food perspectives

In consumer society freedom of choice and consumer sovereignty are important principles. People dependent on food aid necessarily lose part of their freedom of choice and inherent human dignity, because they have to accept charity food in spite of their actual needs and preferences. Such food is not always sufficient, nutritionally balanced or otherwise adequate (Popendieck, 1998; Tarasuk and Eakin, 2003; Tarasuk, 2005). When people lose their entitlement to food they actually lose the possibility to choose their own food. In the prevailing food system the right to food is provided by money in the market place. If the consumer, for one reason or another, lacks money, she or he loses the right to food. Food aid is not an entitlement, it is a gift. Even though food bank clients may be well treated, they do not have the legal right to food aid. At present the right to food is displaced by a private business relationship created through the purchasing power of money in the food market. When citizens are made to be consumers, rights are easily made to be business transactions or contractual agreements (Silvasti, 2008). The right to choose and human dignity is lost.

A further remarkable problem in emergency food delivery as poor relief is the well documented failure of philanthropic food banks to meet the demand for food aid and to satisfy healthy nutritional standards. Many food banks run out of food and turn clients away, many of whom have special dietary needs as a result of diabetes, cardiovascular diseases and so on. At the same time the increasing use of emergency foods to provide long-term food provision for destitute individuals and families is clearly acknowledged and expressed by food banks themselves.

The human right to adequate food

In the meantime governments continue to turn a blind eye despite the fact that 160 states have ratified the right to food. This crude non-compliance of the majority of wealthy states to 'respect, protect and fulfill' the right to food for vulnerable populations is unacceptable, and raises the question of the role of public policy in addressing domestic hunger and food poverty. Nevertheless, at the international level right to food discourses and advocacy seeking to address hunger and food poverty have been gaining ground. These include an assemblage of international instruments which clarify and amplify the meaning of the right to food including, for example:

- *General Comment 12* (CESCR, 1999) which clarified the core elements of the right to food as set out in the ICESCR;
- the creation by the UN Commission on Human Rights of the post of *Special Rapporteur on the Right to Food* (2000) whose task it is to ensure that all governments are meeting their obligations 'to respect, protect and promote' the human right to food;
- the establishment by the UN Food and Agricultural Organisation (FAO) of its *Right to Food Unit*, and the adoption by the FAO Council and member states of the *Voluntary Guidelines on the Right to Food* (VGs, 2005);
- the 2008 adoption by the UN General Assembly of the *Optional Protocol on Economic, Social and Cultural Rights* (OPESCR) making it possible to create a complaints and inquiry mechanism at the inter-national level to strengthen the justiciability of the right to food for individuals for whom this right has been violated.

These global right to food initiatives, fora and activities including those of international NGOs such as FoodFirst International Action Network

(FIAN), Bread for the World (BWI) and Oxfam, are, of course, principally aimed at food insecure countries of the South, yet they hold important policy implications for established wealthy societies and newly emerging economies. In this respect it is of interest to note that the UN Special Rapporteur undertook an official visit to Canada in 2012, his first visit to a high-income OECD country.

Ziegler et al. (2011) provide an extensive discussion of the content and contribution of *General Comment 12* (CESCR) and the *Voluntary Guidelines* (VGs) regarding the progressive realization of the right to food as an important framework for action. Inter alia they require all states, rich and poor alike to fulfil their relevant human rights obligations under international law. These include guaranteeing: the availability of food in quantity and quality sufficient to satisfy the dietary needs of individuals; physical and economic access for everyone, including vulnerable groups, to adequate food, free from adverse substances and acceptable within a given culture or the means to its procurement (CESCR, 1999). The VGs (2005) inform States Parties to the ICESCR of their obligations to '*respect, promote and protect*' the right to food, more particularly the human right to adequate food and nutrition. Recognizing the primary responsibility of States they 'are encouraged to apply a multistakeholder approach to national food security ... encompassing civil society and the private sector.'

Specifically, Ziegler et al. (2011, p. 19) remind States Parties of their obligations to:

- *Respect* the right to food meaning 'that Government should not arbitrarily take away the people's right to food or make it difficult for them to gain access to food'. In the context of rich societies this would mean, for example, not denying access to adequate welfare benefits nor to maintain or cut benefit levels that are insufficient for the purchase of food, clothing and shelter.
- *Protect* the right to food requiring that 'Government must pass and enforce laws to prevent powerful people or organizations from violating the right to food'. This would include regulating 'non-State actors, including corporations or individuals who may threaten other people's right to food'. It would also include ensuring that nutritional and food safety standards are met.
- *Fulfil* the right to food meaning that 'Government must take positive actions to identify vulnerable groups and to implement policies to ensure their access to adequate food by facilitating their ability to feed themselves'. This would include not only stimulating employment

but also ensuring a living wage, adequate benefits, social housing, universal child care and so on, including progressive taxation and acting as the provider of last resort in terms of social protection.

The point is that all governments, rich and poor alike, which have ratified the ICESCR are required to act in domestic compliance with their obligations under international law to ensure food security in their own countries. As Ziegler et al. (2011, p. 20) further comment, 'this support should be provided as a matter of right, rather than charity, in order to ensure human dignity'. In other words RTF approaches imply a framework of national law which moves beyond benevolence and policy guidelines to legislative action. The RTF requires the adoption of coordinated national plans, strategies and tools to advance and ensure the development of 'joined-up' food policy including the setting of targets, benchmarks and indicators, monitoring, justiciable remedies and all actions necessary to secure a just and sustainable food systems.

What role therefore, if any, is there for charitable food banks in advancing the human right to adequate food and nutrition? Whilst acknowledging that the goal of philanthropic food banking is the amelioration of hunger for impoverished and surplus populations, awkward questions continue to arise concerning the hidden functions of food charity. This suggests there is strong justification to think and act outside the charitable food aid box in the development of policies designed to achieve food security for all inclusive of the most vulnerable: in other words, not to accept charity food as a component of food security, but to recognize it as part of the problem in addressing domestic hunger and food poverty.

Cross-national research and analytic framework

Cross-national research and comparative analysis which aims to describe and understand societal and charitable responses to entrenched hunger and food poverty in developed nations informs and enriches knowledge of the social consequences of widening income inequality and failing public policies. In particular it makes apparent the impact of weakened publicly funded social safety nets, the disappearance of universal social welfare and the ascendancy of global neo-liberal economic and social policies and practices on the lives of vulnerable peoples and their families.

Importantly the study of food poverty, food charity and the right to food in the rich developed world is increasingly a subject of inter-disciplinary and inter-professional interest and, as such, lends itself to internationally comparative approaches. However as Alcock and Craig (2009, p. 7) point out in relation to the comparative study of social policy there are 'inevitable limitations to the scope and explanatory power of overarching theoretical accounts of international social policy development or classification.' The same will hold true in the field of food policy. Indeed, the attempt to explain the rise of food charity and the issues it poses for addressing domestic hunger from a right to food framework in different national contexts will need to recognize, as Alcock and Craig (2009, p. 7) also succinctly note, 'what are in practice complex and varied social processes across differing social and political contexts'. In other words the dangers of theoretical over-generalization are great as well as the problem of empirical comparability in light of the fact that data collection is unlikely to have been obtained in a similar manner.

At the same time they make a strong case for more detailed analyses of individual countries, arguing that they provide an important supplement to the generic trends identified by comparative scholars using international databases such as those of the OECD and the Luxembourg Income Study. Cross-national case studies of food poverty in rich societies with differing welfare regimes and cultures throw important light on convergent or divergent public and social policy responses and consequently the degree to which the internationally ratified right to food has, or does not have, a strategic role to play in the struggle against domestic First World hunger. Such comparative study will build knowledge regarding the advances that have, or have not been made since the late 1990s and will make clear whether the right to food has 'legs' or is more a case of empty rhetoric and limited possibility. In this sense there will be lessons to be learned though not necessarily those which might suggest direct policy transfers.

A further strength of the national case study approach adopted in this book springs from the fact that the authors come from different disciplinary and professional backgrounds but all with a post-disciplinary interest in working across these boundaries: agricultural science, economics, food policy, health and nutrition, international development, political science, sociology, social policy and social work. In order for the text to find coherent cross-cutting themes each chapter author was invited to contribute to a common analytic framework considering five key issues of interest in their respective countries:

- the prevalence and causes of food poverty and charting the rise, institutionalization and corporatization of charitable food banking and emergency food aid, and their effectiveness, as front line responses;

- the role played by food philanthropy and its corporate sponsorship in the social construction of hunger as a matter for charity and the decline of public health and welfare, and specifically underfunded social safety nets;
- the extent to which such food charity has permitted governments to ignore their obligations under international law to *'protect, promote and fulfill'* the human right to adequate food and nutrition;
- the possibility of right to food approaches providing an alternative agenda for moral, legal and political action informing 'joined-up' food, health, income and social policy as key strategies directed at resolving the issue of food poverty in wealthy 'food secure' societies;
- alternative roles for key stakeholders: governments, civil society and the corporate sector in terms of achieving just and sustainable food systems.

Even though the writers were asked to construct their contributions around the key issues introduced in this chapter, each author provides his or her own analysis and conclusions. In this way the national case studies can be read as independent narratives which are intended to offer a diversity of viewpoints and analyses. All the chapter authors were invited to interpret the given perspectives in their own personal way bearing in mind the special features of their own countries and divergent developments in the growth of corporate food philanthropy and the responses or non-responses of public policy.

The final chapter will draw together the findings of the national case studies. It will discuss the prevailing grounds as well as preconditions for an agenda for future public policy informed by the right to food and 'joined-up' food policy, strongly emphasizing the binding nature of international law. All governments, which have ratified the ICESCR are required to act in domestic compliance with their obligations under international law to ensure food security in their own countries. Accordingly the right to food should be understood as a legal obligation, not a preference based on benevolence.

2
Food Banks in Australia: Discouraging the Right to Food

Sue Booth

Introduction

Food banks have been a fact of life in Australia for 20 years and Wilson's prediction that, 'Food banks are here to stay' (1997) has come to fruition. The first food bank was officially opened in Melbourne by Hazel Hawke, wife of the former Labour Prime Minister Bob Hawke in 1994. Today food banks operate nationally and have an overarching body, Foodbank Australia (FBA).

Despite the existence of food banks, according to official interpretation Australia is a food secure nation (Australian Government, 2012), albeit with glaring food inequalities. Concerning levels of food insecurity are experienced by a range of vulnerable people (Gallegos et al., 2008; Ramsey et al., 2011). Efforts to address food insecurity have tended to focus on downstream approaches including charitable emergency food relief, community gardens and subsidized cafés with food banks now occupying a dominant part of the response to food poverty in Australia. This chapter will start by exploring levels of food insecurity and contributing factors and how this has helped to foster the rise and proliferation of food banks.

From a moral perspective, food banks meet intrinsic human desires of compassion and caring for those in need. From a technical standpoint, some may view food banks as an efficient and logical way of distributing food to charitable agencies that provide sustenance to food insecure people. Yet whose interests are being served by the business of food banks? From a cost–benefit perspective, food banks feed hungry people, but there are significant 'costs'. We 'pay' in terms of loss of individual dignity and food justice for the marginalized, limited public discourse on hunger and perpetual demand for food relief. There is also a deflection of government responsibilities with respect to addressing the structural factors underlying poverty and stalled progress on the realization of the human right to food.

These costs outweigh the short-term benefits for hungry people. Are food banks about hungry people or something else? Have government and other policy actors deliberately represented the problem of population level hunger in particular ways? Inspired by a 'What's the problem' approachto problem representation of social policy and issues (Bacchi, 2009). This chapter will examine these questions, as well as the underlying assumptions and policy silences.

There is a role for charitable food responses in dealing with the immediate need of hunger, but they should not dominate the food poverty response. Seeking fundamental solutions requires a shifting from the provision of food relief and hunger alleviation to more structural efforts which overcome the poverty and inequality that underpins food insecurity. In short, breaking the cycle of food charity necessitates moving from food provision to food politics and rights-based approaches; from alms to entitlements and realization of rights. Australia ratified the *International Covenant on Economic Social and Cultural Rights* (ICESCR) in 1975. However, the ICESCR does not form part of Australia's federal domestic law and is not scheduled to, or declared under the Australian Human Rights Commission Act. In terms of the right to food, this means that complaints are not able to be lodged with the Commission, leaving the option of raising hunger as a general systemic issue with government. Until the ICESCR becomes part of domestic law legal remedies will not be available. This notwithstanding, some aspects of the ICESCR have been incorporated into other structures such as the Aboriginal and Torres Strait Islanders Social Justice Commission. Overlap with related instruments such as the Rights of the Child, offers limited traction for action on the right to food. The latter part of this chapter explores the possibility of operationalizing rights-based approaches to food poverty in this context.

Who is food insecure in Australia?

According to the *National Food Plan Green Paper*, Australia is a food secure nation with only 5 per cent of people in the National Health Survey (NHS) 2004–2005 reporting that they had experienced 'at least one occasion when they had run out of food and could not afford to buy more' (Australian Government, 2012). Five per cent prevalence is the most recent available data and equates to approximately 1 million people. However this is probably an underestimate. Population level surveys measuring food insecurity are intermittent and limited to a single question which infers financial causation; this neither captures the temporal nature of the experience nor the degree of severity. The lack of a comprehensive food insecurity measure and regular monitoring means it is difficult to acknowledge the size of the problem.

Temple's analysis of the NHS 2004/2005 data constructed a new variable to measure severity and found that of this 5 per cent that had run out of food at least once, 40 per cent were considered to be 'severely' food insecure, meaning they ran out of money to buy food and went hungry. The remaining 60 per cent were 'moderately food insecure' that is, they ran out of money for food but did not go without. Severely food insecure persons were more likely to be public housing tenants and in the bottom 20 per cent of the household income distribution (Temple, 2008).

Although sample sizes and methods are not strictly comparable, two studies suggest household food insecurity levels may be rising. According to a Public Opinion Poll (n = 1200) on food security 8 per cent of households reported they were food insecure. This suggests an increase over the 5 per cent reported in the 2004/2005 *Australian National Health Survey* (Lockie and Pietsch, 2012).

Not all Australians have benefitted from increased economic prosperity in recent years; disturbing levels of food insecurity are experienced by groups including children from socioeconomically disadvantaged households (34 per cent) (Ramsey et al., 2011), refugees (71 per cent) (Gallegos et al., 2008) and single parents (23 per cent) (Burns, 2004). Aboriginality and remoteness are significant risk factors for food insecurity. According to the Aboriginal and Torres Strait Islander Health Performance Framework 2008 report (AIHW, 2009) five times as many indigenous Australians reported running out of food in the previous twelve months compared with the general population (24 per cent compared to 5 per cent). The Northern Territory had the highest proportion of people aged fifteen years and over who reported running out of food (45 per cent), compared to other jurisdictions (18 to 29 per cent). Approximately 8 per cent of indigenous people reported they went without food when they could not afford to buy more compared with 2 per cent of non-indigenous people. A higher prevalence was found in remote areas (36 per cent) compared to non-remote areas (20 per cent) (AIHW, 2009).

How is food insecurity influenced by other cost pressures?

Numerous complex factors contribute to food insecurity and full exploration is beyond the scope of this chapter. However, salient drivers include poverty, food affordability, access and increasing household utility costs.

In 2010, the Australian Council of Social Service (ACOSS) reported that after taking account of housing costs, an estimated 2.2 million people (13 per cent of all people), including 575,000 children (17 per cent of all children), lived in households below the most austere poverty line widely used in international research. This is set at 50 per cent of the median disposable income for all Australian households. In the case of a single adult this poverty line was $358 per week and for a couple with two children it was $752 (ACOSS, 2012a).

Poverty is a salient feature for people on social security payments. A 2012 report found that 'households where the unemployment benefit is the main source of income are more than five times likely to be in poverty' and that a 'very high proportion of these unemployed households persist in poverty for at least two years (47 per cent) compared to the national average of 8 per cent' (Phillips and Nepal, 2012). *The Poverty in Australia* report also found this to be the case, for example, amongst recipients of Newstart, the government income tested job support programme for employment seekers. The Newstart Allowance for single adults was $74 per week (21 per cent) below the 50 per cent of median income poverty line (ACOSS, 2012a).

Food affordability and access are key determinants, making 'food stress' both a financial and a health issue for low-income households (Ward et al., 2013). South Australian data shows the price of healthy food has increased faster than both the price of food generally and the rate of inflation since 1990 (SACOSS, 2011). Not surprisingly, a healthy diet is unaffordable for welfare dependent families; hence they may turn to cheap food of low nutritional quality (Kettings et al., 2009) or seek food charity.

Australians living in regional and remote areas fare worse than those in metropolitan centres in terms of food access. For example, research in Western Australia compared the proportion of income needed by a welfare recipient household, versus an average income household to purchase a healthy food basket each week. Taking into consideration differences in food prices between major cities and remoteness, people in regional and remote areas faced higher food prices. Consultations with Aboriginal communities find exorbitant food prices in outback community stores are a common complaint and it has been suggested that the government should subsidize the cost of healthy food (Nicholson et al., 2009). In major cities, the average fortnightly cost of a healthy food basket was $542.19 compared to $627.11 in very remote areas of Western Australia (WADH, 2010).

Spiralling utility costs put pressure on households resulting in a greater proportion being spent on bills, with less money available for food. Between June 2007 and June 2012, the consumer price index for utilities (including electricity and gas) in Perth, Western Australia increased by 64 per cent. Many low-income families rent homes that are not energy efficient and are unable to afford to make any significant energy saving changes to the property such as solar panels or rainwater tanks (WACOSS, 2012). Another marker of utility stress is the number of households disconnected for non-payment of energy bills. A jurisdictional comparison of residential electricity disconnection rates (per 100 customers) shows South Australia had the highest rate in 2010/2011 (WACOSS, 2012).

The growth of charitable food banks

The first food bank made an appearance 20 years ago in New South Wales and they have now expanded to a network of seven food banks and associated distribution centres. Food banks do not serve individuals directly; rather, donations of manufactured food are diverted to the food bank system for re-distribution to charitable and non-government agencies who in turn use it to support hungry people. Nationally, 2600 charitable agencies have become registered members of food banks and pay a 'handling fee' per kilogram of food, which can range from zero (for fruit and vegetables) to $1.16 per kilogram depending on the types of products (Ms S. Pennell, personal communication, 7 February 2013).

Food banks source food in three main ways: by donation from food manufacturers; by buying food directly from manufacturers at cost price; and through the Collaborative Supply Program (CSP). In the CSP, manufacturers are approached by food banks to produce staples such as milk, pasta and breakfast cereal for donation. Estimated to constitute 15 per cent of operations, the CSP is government funded for $4.3 million over 4 years (SNS, 2012) begging the question, is this not just a cheap food manufacturing programme subsidized by government in an attempt to distance themselves from food poverty? In 2011/2012, 24 million kilograms of food and grocery items were donated, up from five million kilograms in 2003/2004. Total revenue was approximately $22.5 million in 2011/2012 and of this only 15 per cent was government funding (SNS, 2012).

From a purely technical viewpoint, food banks seemingly offer a nationwide solution – indeed an internationally used model – to feeding hungry people, with minimal cost to government. However the food bank model is not working. Data from the FBA report, *End Hunger*, reveals nearly 90 per cent of charitable agencies reported insufficient food to meet demand. Six in ten agencies require at least 25 per cent more food with almost three in ten agencies requiring double the amount of food (FBA, 2012). Technicalities aside, there are compelling moral arguments or 'costs' as to why the rationale behind food banks is flawed. Not the least of which is why as a society Australians are prepared to accept the fact that vulnerable people continue to experience hunger and be reliant on food charity. As a society Australia 'pays' for the food bank model in other ways such as perpetual demand, limited public discourse on hunger, and public policy silences from government. Despite 'Good Samaritan' intentions, donor food corporations representing global multinational brands such as Kraft and Heinz are unable to solve the problems of food inequalities and hunger.

Who benefits and why from charitable food banking?

In Australia a range of players benefit from the existence of food banks. Firstly, food manufacturers and retailers gain considerable advantages including reduced costs for storage, transport and landfill charges. Food waste is a significant problem with uneaten food worth $5.2 billion dollars annually. The average Australian household throws out $616 per year of food or $239 per person (Baker et al., 2009). Waste management charges to dump surplus food in landfill have been increasing and are likely to continue (Mr J. Lang, personal communication, 24 October 2012) as sites for landfill become scarcer and more remote (BDA Group, 2009). In South Australia levies for dumping waste have increased from a flat rate of $1 per tonne in the late 1990s to a current rate of $90–100 per tonne (Mr J. Lang, personal communication, 24 October 2012) and these increasing costs provide impetus for product diversion through the food bank system. Other benefits for the food industry include the tax deductibility of donations, brand strengthening and potential cause-related marketing, namely fostering a public recognition as a brand that cares about 'Aussie battlers'.

Secondly, governments gain political advantages from the food bank operations. There is no public outrage or riots about the extent of food poverty; the activities of food banks operate as a way for government to 'outsource' the political risk of food poverty and soothe any public disquiet. The popularity and profile of the food bank serves to deflect queries on effectiveness or national debate on the underlying structural causes of food poverty. Food banks support the default policy response within neo-liberal governments which is to push responsibilities for problems such as food insecurity back onto individual citizens, invoking freedom of choice and food skills arguments (Dowler and O'Connor, 2012). Additionally, it allows government to neglect its right to food obligations to respect, protect, facilitate and fulfil.

Thirdly, corporate bodies benefit by aligning themselves with the food bank brand, offering corporate volunteering opportunities and building a public perception of trust and 'good corporate citizenship'. Finally, charities can continue to provide food assistance without the inconvenience of sourcing product themselves. For example, in an attempt to streamline food provision for charitable agencies, Food Bank South Australia is planning to introduce 'Everyday' hampers to charities. Available in three sizes, these boxes contain sufficient non-perishable food for 2–3 days and can be easily stored (Mr R. Pagliaro, personal communication, 25 February 2013). Food banks give charities a legitimizing role in society as well as a ready-made 'community' to serve and draw thanks from.

The construction of hunger as a matter for charity – The role of food philanthropy

Bacchi's work investigates the nature and framing of social problems which underpin public policy development. In particular, her interest is in how governments and other policy actors give a particular shape to these problems in the ways we speak about them and in the solutions offered. Bacchi argues that understanding how social issues (that is hungry people) are represented as 'problems' is crucial to identify competing problem representations because they constitute a form of political intervention with a range of effects (Bacchi, 2009). Inspired by Bacchi, the question here is, what is the problem of food insecurity and hunger represented to be?

Hunger in Australia has been represented as a problem which is being effectively solved by food charity. Historically, not much has changed; hunger has been a matter for churches and charities since the 19th century and this continues (Hickey, 1980; Ayton et al., 2012). Food charity started with emergency responses and churches giving 'alms for the poor'. This stems from a moral Christian imperative to feed the hungry and less fortunate. Despite a comprehensive social security system, rising costs of living mean welfare recipients are finding it increasingly difficult to provide for themselves. Now in the 21st century, charitable agencies funded to provide emergency food services are unable to meet demand. Additionally, the arrival of food banks as a relatively 'new player' has offered little more than an entrenched industrialized version of the 19th century emergency response, with the food manufacturers and government indirectly giving 'alms for the poor'.

Food philanthropy and food banking are salient ways of de-politicizing hunger nationally. There is no significant public debate, no moral outrage about hungry people in a wealthy country, no public protests and no attempts to probe deeper into the underlying causes of hunger. Locating hunger within the realm of charity suggests the issue is being solved by experts and the corporate and volunteer community and effectively outsources the political risk of hunger for government. The provision of humanitarian food relief and quasi measures of effectiveness such as 'tonnes of food waste diverted from landfill' lulls the general public into complacency. In its policy silence, government is active in the creation of this problem representation. Olivier De Schutter, the UN Special Rapporteur on the right to food has warned against allowing charity food aid (including food banks) to become a permanent feature of the welfare landscape as they have in wealthy western countries such as the United States and Canada. He notes 'Food banks are the safety net of the safety net. It is only when government fails that food banks have to step in' (Butler, 2013), prompting the question as to how the government has failed?

Mismatch between welfare payments and rising costs of living

An examination of the tensions which exist between welfare payments and increased living costs offers insight. Between 2000 and 2010, the rates of two common federal social security payments (Newstart and the Youth Allowance) have increased by 40 per cent (Centrelink, 2011). In the corresponding period the consumer price index (CPI) increased overall by 34 per cent. However, the CPI is a composite measure and disguises significantly larger increases for water and sewerage (90 per cent), electricity (87 per cent) and food (46 per cent) (ABS, 2011). Further evidence of the inadequacy of social security payments is highlighted by the fact that two thirds of those living below the poverty line were reliant on benefits. Hardest hit are the unemployed, single parents and disabled people with, respectively, 52 per cent, 45 per cent and 42 per cent of people receiving government benefits living below the poverty line (ACOSS, 2012a). A report investigating indications of food stress by conducting analysis modelling on various welfare benefits found a single parent family with two children aged seven and eight years, needed an additional $1028.39 annually for a healthy diet (WACOSS, 2012).

Successive federal governments, both Labor and Liberal have pursued fiscal savings and welfare re-structuring, tightening requirements and eligibility criteria in an effort to shift people from welfare into work. The latest change targeting single parents is estimated to save the government approximately $725 million by shifting 25,000 sole parents from the Parenting Payment to the more meagre Newstart Allowance when their youngest child turns eight. Critics argue this is not about encouraging employment as these parents are already required to seek part time jobs and many already have such jobs (Karvelas, 2012). The move prompted community welfare groups and human rights lawyers to send an urgent appeal to the United Nations Special Rapporteur on Extreme Poverty and Human Rights (ACOSS, 2012b). Neoliberal approaches designed to keep welfare benefits low in an effort to push people off welfare and into employment are driving vulnerable people deeper into poverty. Welfare recipients turn to food charity, not so much for emergency provisions but rather to meet regular shortfalls in their ability to feed their families. Charitable agencies are in turn underpinned by the nationwide food bank system, making the expansion of food banks hardly surprising.

The impact of these tensions has also spread to middle Australia, albeit it to a lesser degree. For example, *The Victorian Lifestyle and Neighbourhood Environment Study* (Kavanagh et al., 2007) found socioeconomic differences in the percentage of people who reported running out of food and not being able to afford more. This situation occurred three times more often in low socioeconomic areas (12 per cent) compared to mid (9 per cent) and high socioeconomic areas (4 per cent). Consequently it is likely more working Australians may be forced to seek charitable food assistance.

Food charity or the right to food

To what extent has food charity allowed the federal and state governments in Australia to ignore their Right to Food obligations under international law? There are three tiers of government in Australia: federal, state and local, and responsibility for human rights and the right to food (RTF) falls within federal jurisdiction. However as mentioned earlier, the ICESCR does not form part of Australia's federal domestic law. Addressing food insecurity and hunger occurs at all levels albeit unsystematically. For example funding to support food banks, charitable agencies and NGO's may come from both federal and state government sources. Also at the local government level, there has been some interest investigating how to support ratepayers experiencing food insecurity.

Food charity in Australia has not proved to be a solution to domestic hunger and is a legitimized feeding system that is deeply flawed in several ways. Firstly, food assistance can be disempowering for recipients, and provided in ways that reflect arrogance and an inadequate understanding of recipients' needs on the part of the provider (Kent, 2005). Independence, in this case the ability to take control and provide one's own and one's family's sustenance leads to greater empowerment and dignity (Freire, 1996).

Secondly, human rights uphold dignity and encompass entitlements. According to Kent (2005) dignity does not come from being fed, but rather in one's ability to provide for one's self. With entitlement come standards and mechanisms of accountability to ensure that the standards are achieved. Substituting excessive charity for human rights entitlements may inadvertently and deliberately advance a neo-liberal agenda where disadvantaged people are left to feed themselves (Kent, 2005). In other words, the approach of food charity runs counter to the Government's right to food legal obligations, namely to *respect, protect, facilitate* and *fulfil* that right (UNCESCR, 1999). Kent argues voluntary provision of food supplies to the poor by private parties or business may lead to the decline of public assistance and shift the cost of caring for the poor to the private sector (2005, pp. 124–125). There is no hard evidence of this trend in Australia, but it warrants monitoring.

Further evidence of the degree to which the Government has neglected its international right to food obligations can be found in Australia's obligatory five-yearly reports to the United Nation's Committee on Economic, Social and Cultural Rights (CESCR) outlining progress towards the realization of the right to food. The review of the 4th Report on the implementation of the *International Covenant on Economic, Social and Cultural Rights* (ICESCR) noted an incomplete and unaddressed assessment with the RTF (AHRC, 2009). The subsequent Common Core Document incorporating the 4th report (Commonwealth of Australia, 2006) submitted in 2007 was limited to general information (#485 on p. 136) describing *Eat Well Australia*, a ten-year public health nutrition agenda. Shadow reports by peak human rights law NGOs provide more accurate insight into food insecurity, clearly documenting the extent to which Australia is falling short of its right to food obligations (NACLC et al., 2009).

The limits and possibilities of right to food approaches in Australia

Human rights approaches strengthen and bring additional dimensions to anti-poverty work including: an acknowledgement of poverty's multiple dimensions; enshrining socially and legally guaranteed entitlements; providing a framework to pursue accountability for poverty and a mechanism for promoting the dignity and autonomy of people (Donald and Mottershaw, 2009). The use of rights-based approaches to address public policy issues (including food poverty) is a rarity in Australia. As suggested by Donald and Mottershaw, they may be perceived as jarring with cultural norms, remote, legalistic or overly adversarial.

However, the recent release of the new *National Aboriginal and Torres Strait Islander Health Plan 2013–2023* (DoHA, 2013) offers potential, although details of the implementation have not been released. A key principle informing this Plan is health equality and a human rights approach, the latter being described as '…about providing equal opportunities for health by ensuring availability, accessibility, acceptability and quality health services…a rights-aware approach is not necessarily about more services, but about better services through better informed policy, practice and service delivery decisions, and the processes that enable Aboriginal and Torres Strait Islander people to participate in all levels of health care decision-making.' The Plan, which sits under The *National Partnership Agreement on Indigenous Health*, was supposed to be signed by all jurisdictions by 30 June 2013 but the deadline has passed without one state or territory signing on. At the release of the Plan the federal government has again called on jurisdictions to sign up to the Plan and proposed funding arrangements.

Rights-based approaches to food poverty lack traction

Rights-based approaches provide a new framework for answering 'what the problem' of food banks is represented to be, namely one which offers legal entitlements and allows duty bearers to call the state to account. Yet, despite human rights approaches representing 'a powerful antidote to punitive public discourses which stereotype people in poverty as lazy, fraudulent or agents of their own downfall' (Donald and Mottershaw, 2009), they are not being embraced by key players such as politicians, practitioners, policy makers or public servants. Indeed, there are no clear drivers of human rights-based approaches to food poverty with a suggestion that 'rights' are perceived as politically left wing, marginal and inefficient (M. Henley, personal communication, 20 February 2013).

A rights-based critique of food charity and food banks provides an entry point for dialogue, however barriers exist which may prevent such appraisal occurring. For example, NGOs and government funded welfare agencies focus on health, housing and employment, rather than food policy (G. Ogle, personal communication, 21 February 2013). Additionally, the not-for-profit sector is also used as a service delivery vehicle for government programmes which have stringent accountability measures and contractual obligations. This role allows no scope for food policy advocacy work, nor does the Government want to be the focus of criticism. Work contracts that require Ministerial approval to make public comment mean NGO workers are effectively gagged from any debate (M. Henley, personal communication, 20 February 2013). Despite a history of charitable food provision, religious institutions have recently retreated from progressive debates as they struggle to maintain the integrity of the church in the midst of recent child sex abuse allegations (Zwartz, 2010). Whilst some international academics are vocal about food poverty, there is little Australian academic research and critique on this issue.

A tipping point: alternative roles for right to food stakeholders

Action on rights-based approaches to food poverty will materialize when Australia reaches a critical tipping point where it is no longer possible to maintain the status quo. It has been said that human rights become a mobilizing force when they are connected to people's everyday existence (Donald and Mottershaw, 2009). Hence the impetus for change may come when food poverty starts to bite deeper into the middle and upper-middle classes on a daily basis, when the spread of food banks becomes more localized and rampant or as a result of public action. Rights-based approaches go beyond the use of perfunctory 'rights' language in documents and must represent integrated and tangible action that holds the nation state accountable for its human rights obligations. Several long-term opportunities for advancing food insecurity and the right to food in Australia are discussed below.

Human rights act

Despite being a modern democracy, Australia does not have a federal human rights act or bill of rights and the idea continues to be strongly debated (Williams, 2007; NHRCC, 2009). Indeed, it was a central recommendation of the National Human Rights Consultation Committee report (NHRCC, 2009). The Committee was established by the federal government in 2008 to consult the Australian community on three key questions: (i) Which human rights and responsibilities should be protected and promoted? (ii) Are these human rights currently sufficiently protected and promoted? and (iii) How could Australia better protect and promote human rights?

The federal government's response to the NHRCC report (Australian Government, 2010) cherry picked from the NHRCC recommendations but failed to provide for any form of Human Rights Act. The development of state and territory human rights acts such as those by the Australian Capital Territory (ACT) in 2004 and Victoria in 2006 offered promise. A review (ANU, 2009) of the Acts' operation in the ACT suggested it had created a 'fledgling human rights culture'.

National right to food policy

A Charter of Rights would provide a suitable platform for the subsequent development of a National Right to Food Policy as recommended by De Schutter, the UN Special Rapporteur on the Right to Food after his recent Canadian mission (De Schutter, 2012b). The Right to Food Voluntary Guidelines provide member states with a roadmap towards this realization (FAO, 2005). The Guidelines encourage states to establish a specific institution responsible for the coordination, implementation and evaluation of a national strategy to address food insecurity and poverty. Ideally, an Australian right to food policy would be overseen by such an independent body external to Government, but such a policy is unlikely at this time.

Mobilizing alliances and communities

New social movements such as The Sydney Food Fairness Alliance (SFFA, 2013) have emerged out of concern for Australia's food future, as well as the impact of the current food system on people and the environment. The Alliance which represents a range of stakeholders, operates independently of government structures and aims to influence and effect social change. Its structure and activities support collective action on issues including food security as a human right and sustainable food policies.

Structures such as Get Up! – Action for Australia (Get Up!, 2013) which mobilize the general public to engage in advocacy work may offer capacity to shift into rights-based approaches. Get Up! is an independent, grass-roots community advocacy organization which aims to build a more progressive Australia by giving people the opportunity to get involved and hold politicians accountable on important issues. Members take targeted, coordinated and strategic action to effect real change on topical policy issues.

In some cases mobilizing poor people into action may be curtailed by the disparateness of their experiences, for example mental health or housing issues. The establishment of Poverty Truth Commissions such as those in Scotland and the United States (Donald and Mottershaw, 2009) acting as a platform for 'a movement to end poverty led by the poor' show promise (The Poverty Initiative, 2013). However, in the Australian context, capacity building in terms of rights-based education for participants would be essential.

Rights-based education

The NHRCC recommended that education be the highest priority for improving and promoting human rights in Australia (NHRCC, 2009). A key strategy included the development of a national plan to implement human rights education programmes in schools, universities, the public sector and the community generally. However, the federal government indicated it will support human rights education across the community including schools (Australian Government, 2010). Building rights-based intelligence is fundamental to supporting collaborative and integrated approaches which underpin progressive efforts to realize the right to food, for example: supporting practitioners and policy makers by promoting best practice in rights-based approaches; disseminating case studies; and assisting in knowledge translation and exchange.

Conclusion

Despite taking into account the principle of progressive realization of rights, obvious gaps still remain in domestic human rights protections in Australia, with respect to the right to food. The expansion and entrenchment of charitable food banks should serve as an early warning system of inadequate social policies and the failure of government to meet its right to food obligations. Despite inherent inequities in the design of their approach, food banks are likely to grow and expand due to the escalating cost of living pressures. Limited support for rights-based approaches to addressing food poverty currently exist. However, an emerging national human rights agenda, combined with a critical tipping point or food crisis, may provide sufficient impetus for manoeuvring Australia towards building rights-based approaches and stemming any further expansion of food banks. Critical to success is the political will to adopt the ICESCR into domestic law and embrace a Federal Charter of Rights in conjunction with efforts to build strategic alliances, mobilize communities and strengthen rights-based education.

3

A Right to Food Approach: Public Food Banks in Brazil

Cecilia Rocha

Introduction

Brazil presents a fascinating case for studying the role of food banks in food and nutrition security. The success of the country in the social policy arena in the past two decades is well documented (Rocha, 2009; HLPE, 2012, pp. 53–55; Kiggundu, 2012). By the end of 2012, Brazil had met four of the eight United Nations Millennium Development Goals, and was well on its way to meeting the other four by their 2015 target date. In fact, the country had reduced extreme poverty and malnutrition by half by the end of 2009, six years ahead of the UN deadline (CAISAN, 2009). Between 1999 and 2009, close to 14 million Brazilians moved out of poverty (Del Grossi, 2010). The incidence of extreme poverty fell from 17.4 per cent of the population in 2001 to less than 9 per cent in 2008, an extraordinary 8.7 per cent reduction (Barros, 2009). The prevalence of undernourishment declined from 11 to 6 per cent of the population from 1990 to 2008 (IFPRI, 2012).

National Household Surveys showed a decline in the percentage of households reporting any degree (mild, moderate or severe) of food insecurity, from 34.8 per cent in 2004 to 30.5 per cent in 2009, with the more pronounced decrease being in the number of households reporting severe food insecurity (Burlandy et al., 2013). Growth in family incomes, along with improvements in basic sanitation, mothers' education, breast-feeding rates and vaccination coverage, complemented increased food and nutrition security to put Brazil above the world average in the reduction of child (less than five years old) mortality rates. Between 1990 and 2011 the child mortality rate in the country declined 73 per cent, from 58 to 16 per thousand live births, while worldwide the average decline in the same period was by 40 per cent (UNICEF, 2012b).

It is important to note that income disparities have also been decreasing, as policies in the past ten years have benefitted mostly lower income households (Barros, 2009; Santos et al., 2009). Still, the reduction of poverty and inequality has brought with it new challenges for the government. As middle-class strata increase in this process, higher expectations for better public services in health, education and transportation emerge. In the past twenty years, investments in reducing poverty were not matched by the necessary investments to meet the needs and demands of the higher number of people joining the middle class. Street protests throughout the country in 2013 can then be seen as expressions of frustrated expectations, as an enlarged middle class witnessed the deterioration of their public services.

The integrated policy to combat food and nutrition insecurity through the various programmes under the *Zero Hunger* strategy (Graziano da Silva et al., 2010), along with rising minimum wages and higher formal employment rates, have all contributed to the significant improvements in the country's social indicators. Of notice, *Zero Hunger* included expanding cash transfers to the poorest families under the *Bolsa Família* (Family Grant) programme, which is now the largest conditional cash transfer programme in the world. In 2013, *Bolsa Família* was reaching over 13.5 million of the poorest families, covering about 50 million people, a quarter of the country's population (MDS, 2013a).

However, beyond *Bolsa Família*, when one looks at the list of programmes composing the *Zero Hunger* strategy (Table 3.1), there is little doubt about the food-system approach its designers had in mind. Increasing access to food was the main concern, but the strategy also aimed at supporting smallholder food producers, increasing income generating opportunities for low-income groups, promoting healthy eating, providing food and nutrition education, and engaging civil society in the fight against hunger (Aranha, 2010). It is also clear that *Zero Hunger* designers, rather than relying on only one initiative, thought of a set of programmes to increase the access to adequate food for the population.

What might be surprising to some people, particularly social justice activists in countries of the North, is that food banks have been part of the *Zero Hunger* strategy. That is, food banks in Brazil have been part of a 'joined-up' food policy, a component of a set of built structures, which include subsidized popular restaurants and community kitchens, put in place to combat hunger and food insecurity. Given that one of the major criticisms of food banks in countries of the North is that they 'allow governments to look the other way and avoid their roles and

Table 3.1   Zero Hunger strategy (*c.* 2004)

I – Food Access
- *Bolsa Família* – Family Grant (BF)
- National School Meals Programme (PNAE)
- Food for Specific Groups
- Rainwater Cisterns
- Popular Restaurants and Community Kitchens
- Food Banks
- Urban Agriculture
- Food and Nutrition Surveillance System
- Distribution of Vitamin A
- Distribution of Iron
- Food and Nutrition for Indigenous People
- Food and Nutrition Education for Consumption
- Promotion of Healthy Habits/Healthy Diets
- Workers Food Programme (PAT)
- Basic Food Basket Tax Reduction

II – Strengthening Family Agriculture
- National Programme for Family Agriculture (PRONAF)
- Harvest Insurance
- Family Farming Agriculture Insurance
- Food Procurement Programme (PAA)

III – Income Generation
- Social and Professional Training
- Solidarity Economy and Productive Inclusion
- Food Security and Local Development Consortium
- Food and Nutrition Security Organization
- Cooperatives of Recyclable Material Collectors
- Guided Productive Micro-credit

IV – Partnership and Civil Society Mobilization
- Social Assistance Reference Centre
- Social Mobilization and Citizenship Education
- Social and Public Agents Capacity Building
- Volunteer Work and Donations
- Partnership with Private Sector and NGOs
- Social Development Councils

Source: MDS website <http://www.fomezero.gov.br/>, cited in Rocha (2009), p. 54.

responsibilities' (see Chapter 1), what do we make of food banks as part of a government policy? Can food banks be part of a right to food approach to policy?

In an attempt to answer these questions, this chapter focuses on public food banks, run by municipalities as public institutions, and supported by a federal government programme. The next section first examines the different types of food banks in Brazil (private and public), and the roles played by corporate sponsorship, civil society and food charity in their operation. Then the evolution of public food banking, the focus of this inquiry, is analysed, followed by an exploration of the right to food (RTF) approach in Brazil, and how public food banks may fit into it. Finally, some conclusions are drawn in the last section.

Corporate sponsorship, civil society and food charity

There are three types of food banks in Brazil: those run and supported by the public sector, those run and supported by business associations as part of their social responsibility agenda, and those run by non-governmental organizations (NGOs). All food banks, public or private, are governed by the same legislation concerning food safety and consumers' protection. Under prevailing consumers' protection legislation, donors can be deemed criminally responsible in cases of negative health effects resulting from the consumption of inadequate or unsafe food. Food bank operators have long complained that this significantly inhibits corporate and private donations, and a 'Good Samaritan' legislation, which exempts from liability corporations and individuals who donate food, has been under debate in Congress for over ten years (TCU, 2005; ONG Banco de Alimentos, 2011).

A proposal for tax exemptions on donated food is also being debated. Since 2003, donations destined for government programmes have received tax exemptions, but this initiative has not been extended to donations to private food banks. Nor has it been passed as legislation, in which case it can be revoked at any time. Nevertheless, donations to both public and private food banks have been increasing in the past ten years, and there seems to be some agreement that tax exemptions would have a significant positive impact on donations, even without a 'Good Samaritan' law.

Unlike many food bank operations in other countries, food banks in Brazil rarely distribute food directly to individuals. They operate as centres for receiving and processing food donations, which are then distributed to philanthropic organizations, or to other government programmes as in the case of public food banks. Recipient organizations mostly include homeless shelters, charitable children day-care centres and old-age homes, community kitchens and restaurants, and even hospitals and schools in low-income areas. Recipient organizations are encouraged to prepare meals from the food donated before distribution. In the case of philanthropic organizations that distribute food directly to individuals or families, such distribution must occur on the same day the food is picked up from the food bank.

The growth of public food banking in Brazil in the past ten years is paralleled by the growth of food banks from business initiatives and by NGOs. The first food banks in the country emerged from the work of the Social Service of Commerce Association (SESC) in 1996, a private initiative. Today, SESC's *Mesa Brasil* programme has a large network of food banks, with 82 units. It distributes food donated by over 3,000 corporate partners to over 5,500 philanthropic organizations serving low-income populations (SESC, 2013). Still, SESC's food banks are in operation in only 408 of the more than 5,570 municipalities in the country.

NGO-run food banks have also appeared in various cities of Brazil. Many do not have the facilities to store foodstuffs, so they are run more as 'urban harvest' operations, picking up surplus perishable food items in the mornings to be distributed to philanthropic organizations in the afternoons. Typically, over 60 per cent of food from NGO food banks are fruits and vegetables, and 15 per cent are eggs and dairy products. Industrialized food items account for less than 20 per cent of the food donated (ONG Banco de Alimentos, 2011). As it happens with most NGOs, civil society food banks depend on fundraising and volunteers for their operations, making their year-to-year activities quite variable.

The government's *Zero Hunger* strategy had originally sought partnerships with the private sector and civil society to develop food banks, on the premise that in a country such as Brazil 'eradicating hunger is a project that requires the involvement of society at large' (Belik, 2010, p. 113). Indeed, despite significant advances, close to 30 per cent of the country's households still report some degree of food insecurity, and over 16 million Brazilians are extremely poor, according to the 2010 Census (IBGE, 2011). Hence, rather than substituting government policy, the work of the private sector and civil society through food banks is seen as complementary to the role of government in increasing food security. 'There is a widespread perception in Brazil that the state is not able to provide the necessary conditions to secure an adequate quality of life for all its citizens' (Griesse, 2007, p. 22). While this perception continues and portions of the population suffer from food insecurity, we can expect the co-existence of private and public food banks.

Food charity sustains some of the donations to NGO-based food banks, particularly faith-based ones. There is, however, a much stronger notion which has emerged in the past two decades and which seems to drive the desire for participation in initiatives such as food banks. That is the idea of *cidadania*, roughly translated as 'participatory citizenship' – the idea that to be part of Brazil, people have rights and responsibilities (Valente, 2003; Oxhorn, 2010). Brazilians increasingly expect the government to protect their rights, but they are also aware of a duty to participate. *Cidadania* inspires action, both by NGOs moved by civic duty rather than by religion or faith, and by individual and corporate donors.

Charting the evolution of public food banking in Brazil

While food charity and *cidadania* sustain private (corporate and NGO) food bank initiatives, the right to food and the state's responsibility to uphold it are behind the development of public food banks in Brazil. Food insecurity is also often identified with market failures, and food security is seen as a public good (Rocha, 2007). As such, there seems to be among Brazilians little reluctance to accept the need for government intervention in the food system, particularly in areas to address social inequities. Hence, eradicating hunger and promoting food and nutrition security are seen primarily as government responsibility. In this context, government-run food banks have become just one more instrument to reduce hunger and food insecurity.

Private food banks were already in existence in the country when public food banks emerged in 2000 as initiatives of local municipal governments in Santo André (São Paulo state) and Salvador (Bahia). Federal participation in food banking started only with the Zero Hunger strategy in 2003, with the Federal Government granting funds for the installation, modernization or expansion of food banks by municipal governments (TCU, 2005). By 2012 there were 67 food bank units supported by the Ministry of Social Development and Fight Against Hunger (MDS), distributing close to 39 thousand tons of food around the country (MDS, 2013b). Given the number of units under construction, it is estimated that there will be over 120 public food banks in the country by the end of 2013, surpassing, then, the number of private food banks.

The introduction of public food banks was not without controversy. Food banks in the United States, Canada and Europe were often cited as models, and many people in Brazil were aware of the criticisms of food banks in the North (Riches, 1997a, 2002; Tarasuk and Eakin, 2003). They were concerned that food banks would provide an opportunity for governments to abdicate their responsibility to uphold the right to food; that food banks would be a source for low-quality food given to people without a choice and through undignified ways. An early evaluation of the federal food bank programme, conducted by the country's Auditor-General office (*Tribunal de Contas da União* – TCU) in 2004, pointed out a number of concerns (TCU, 2005). Some of the most significant concerns included: lack of established norms for installation and operation of public food banks; lack of technical capacity in some municipalities for the effective installation and operation of food banks; existing legislation which makes food donors liable for possible negative health effects from the consumption of donated food, discouraging food donations; lack of monitoring the proper handling of food in the recipient organizations; early favouring of municipalities in the relatively richer South and Southeast parts of the country rather than in the poorest regions of the North and Northeast; and operations based on donations not connected to food waste, moving food banks away from one of their expressed goals.

Since then, a number of guidelines and manuals have been created by MDS to govern the installation and operations of public food banks. These guidelines apply only to food banks receiving federal funding and have not been extended to private food banks, although given their availability on the MDS website, there is nothing to prevent private food banks from also adopting them.

In partnership with EMBRAPA (the Brazilian Agricultural Research Corporation), MDS has prepared documents on good practices for food handling, processing fruits and vegetables, vegetable dehydration and canning, to be implemented in food banks (EMBRAPA/MDS, 2006a, 2006b, 2006c, 2006d). The preoccupation with the proper handling and preparation of fruits and vegetables reflects the high proportion of fresh produce donated to food banks in Brazil. These come mostly from food terminals, supermarkets and the numerous farmers markets that are common in most cities in the country. The products received are cleaned, selected and separated, eventually processed (freeze-dried or canned), and packaged before being distributed to organizations, which will then prepare meals for the people they serve.

The amounts of fruits and vegetables available at public food banks have recently increased through the connection with the federal government's Food Acquisition Programme (PAA). PAA has been developed to support small family farmers in the commercialization of their production, increasing their incomes and providing an incentive for more people to stay in rural areas rather than migrating to the cities. Also included in the *Zero Hunger* strategy, PAA promotes direct crop and milk purchases by the government for building food stocks, regulating food prices, and to be used in government food programmes such as school meals, popular restaurants, community kitchens and food banks (Rocha et al., 2012). Public food banks are now major recipients of food purchased by the Federal Government from small family farmers.

In 2007, MDS published guidelines on the construction and installation of public food banks, detailing ten physical standards that should be met (MDS, 2007):

- food reception/pre-cleaning;
- selection/triage/hygiene;
- waste/composting;
- food processing (optional);
- packaging and identification (including weight and date of validation);
- storage;
- containers' hygiene and storage;
- loading area;
- administrative area; and
- area for training/capacity building/experimental kitchen.

The training area is important. It is to be used to train both the food bank's personnel, as well as personnel from the philanthropic organizations, who will be receiving the food and preparing the meals. It can also be used for community educational activities, reflecting additional goals of public food banks. Promotion of healthy eating joined reduction of food waste, including full utilization of foods and eliminating hunger as goals. In 2009, MDS published two other guides compromising a list of suggested equipment and furniture (MDS, 2009a), and a list of suggested utensils and personal protection equipment (MDS, 2009b) for public food banks.

MDS has also developed a *Model Guideline for Internal Operations of Food Banks* (MDS, 2013c). The document details: the objectives of public food banks, including promoting food and nutrition education; procedures for receiving, manipulating and storing food; how food will leave the banks; operation; and the responsibility of the municipal government in the maintenance and administration of the food bank. The Model Guideline also specifies the duties of the municipal public workers who are to compose the multi-professional personnel team in each food bank. All public food banks must have at least one nutritionist and one social worker as part of its staff. Social workers usually make the selection and evaluate the needs of the client organizations, and also monitor the proper use of the food donated. Nutritionists are usually responsible for overseeing the proper handling and processing of the food in the food bank, as well as developing and providing the training on food handling and nutrition education for food bank staff and clients.

The guidelines produced by MDS were in response to an evaluation study conducted by the ONG REDES (*Rede Desenvolvimento, Ensino e Sociedade* – Network for Development, Learning, and Society), funded by the Brazilian government (REDES, 2006). The study pointed out significant diversity in the implementation of public food banks until 2005. Municipalities throughout the country showed wide variation in infrastructure, physical and managerial capacity, and access to potential food donors. The main demands by the organizations which received food from the food banks were for more food and nutrition education and greater donations of fruits and vegetables. At the time (2005), only three of the 53 food banks studied operated under some municipal legislation/regulation. This, the study pointed out, created significant uncertainty concerning how future municipal administrations would relate to food banks, threatening their long-term political sustainability.

In a recent call for proposals from the federal government for the installation of new food banks (MDS, 2011), one can detect further attempts to create a minimum standard for public food banks as part of a set of integrated programmes to meet food and nutrition security as a right. The three sets of criteria governing minimum standards for public food banks considered for evaluation of proposals are quite revealing.

The first set of standards, Socio-economic and Food Security Conditions (worth 30 per cent), asked for the number of households in a situation of food insecurity and the percentage of families below the poverty line in the municipality. This indicates a concern with proper targeting of this programme, a concern with reaching populations at higher risk of food and nutrition insecurity.

The second set of minimum standards, Management and Integration of Policies for Social Development and Fight Against Hunger (40 per cent), asked if the municipality had

- coordinated food security and other social policies;
- established procedures for food purchases through the PAA;
- a functioning Municipal Council for School Meals (with participation of civil society);
- a functioning Municipal Council for Food and Nutrition Security (with participation of civil society);
- a Municipal Food and Nutrition Security Law (LOSAN);
- an inter-departmental council;
- a budget item specific to food and nutrition security.

What is interesting about this set of standards is that it reflects the whole philosophy of public food banks as part of social development. Through this, MDS is requiring municipalities, which want to install a food bank, to think of it as part of an overall strategy for food and nutrition security. Municipalities must have integrated policies, legislation and budgets specific to food and nutrition security. As a condition for receiving federal government support for food banks, municipalities must demonstrate their responses to other federal programmes such as PAA and School Meals.

The third set of standards, Quality of the Proposal (30 per cent), asked about:

- the proposed site for the food bank;
- the strategy for integration with the PAA;
- planning of activities for training and professional qualification;
- partnerships and strategies for integration with the local School Meals programme;
- forms of social participation and monitoring;
- a plan for management and maintenance of the food bank.

These are related to the quality of the day-to-day operations of food banks.

In light of this public policy intent, what emerges is a picture of food banks very different from the ones we see in North America. For the past ten years, in Brazil, public food banks have been an integral part of 'joined-up' government policy rather than its replacement. They are also part of the many ways in which the government attempts to fulfil its obligations to uphold the right to adequate food.

A right to food (RTF) approach

The period witnessing the growth of food banking in Brazil has also seen the rise of social policy making based on human rights, including the right to adequate food. This may be what makes the difference between the food bank experiences in Brazil in the past decade and the experiences of other countries featured in this volume.

In 2010, Brazil's constitution was amended to include the Right to Food. This was the culmination of an organized civil society campaign, which has been behind many of the accomplishments in the area of food and nutrition security (Valente et al., 2001; Menezes, 2010). Having ratified the United Nations' *International Covenant on Economic, Social and Cultural Rights* (ICESCR) in 1992, Brazil was one of six countries contributing a case study, which led to the development of the Food and Agriculture Organization's *Voluntary Guidelines to Support the Progressive Realization of the Right to Adequate Food in the Context of National Food Security* (FAO, 2005).

While it is ultimately the role of the state to *respect, protect,* and *fulfil* the right to food, civil society organizations in Brazil have carved spaces for effective participation in the discussion, development, implementation, and monitoring of policy and programmes in food and nutrition security (Rocha, 2009; Maluf, 2010). At the national level, the National Council for Food and Nutrition Security (CONSEA), an advisory body to the President of Brazil, has served as an important forum for highlighting the right to food as the basis for policy, 'both as a goal and a tool for achieving food and nutrition security' (FAO, 2013b, v). Two-thirds of the CONSEA's members are representatives from civil society and the private sector, and one-third are representatives from government. CONSEA's Standing Commission on the Human Right to Adequate Food provides continuous analysis and advice on food and nutrition security policy and programming from a human rights perspective.

In 2006 CONSEA was instrumental in the elaboration and passing of the *National Law on Food and Nutrition Security* (LOSAN). Article 1 of LOSAN establishes definitions, principles, guidelines, objectives and composition of the National System for Food and Nutrition Security – SISAN – through which the state, with the participation of organized civil society, will formulate and implement policies, plans, programmes and actions towards ensuring the human right to adequate food (Burity et al., 2011). LOSAN and the national system being developed from it have institutionalized the right to food as a matter of public policy and an obligation of the state, ensuring the political sustainability of food and nutrition security programmes.

Public food banks are being increasingly consolidated as part of the country's National System for Food and Nutrition Security – along with school meals programmes, popular restaurants, and community kitchens – to increase access to adequate food by marginalized populations. However, as food banks become more like social service programmes to fulfil the rights of the population, they become less effective in meeting the goal with which they were first associated: reduction of food waste. Each consecutive evaluation of the programme (TCU, 2005; REDES, 2006; FEC/DATAUFF, 2011) has pointed out how public food banks are increasingly moving away from that original intent. While they still list reduction of food waste as a goal, in reality, only those food banks located in close proximity to food terminals and large supermarkets (i.e., those in relatively large cities) can afford to rely on donations of surplus food. In smaller municipalities, not enough food is wasted given the lower circulation of products in the local markets (REDES, 2006). Food banks, thus, increasingly rely on donations not related to food waste (motivated by charity, *cidadania*, or tax exemptions), or food donated through the Food Acquisition Programme.

Conclusion

This chapter has explored the rise of public food banking in Brazil as part of a 'joined-up' public food policy to increase food and nutrition security. Private (corporate- and NGO-led) food banks have existed in the country since the late 1990s, supported by donations motivated by charity and civic duty (*cidadania*), and with the double goal of reducing food waste and alleviating hunger. The introduction of food banks as part of the *Zero Hunger* strategy in 2003 brought with it the challenge of shaping the programme from an RTF perspective.

In the past ten years, the Federal Government has responded to concerns, expressed in successive evaluation studies, by developing a set of criteria determining minimum standards for the establishment and operation of public food banks. These standards have created a network of public food banks designed to function as public social service agencies, covered by specific legislation, regulation and guidelines, and staffed by multi-professional personnel. While this has improved the quality of the food and of the services provided, the standards have also increased the complexity of public food banking in Brazil. Meeting the criteria established by calls for proposals from the federal government can be a problem for some of the very municipalities most in need of instruments to combat hunger and food insecurity. Poor areas of the country lack the physical, technical, financial, and political capacity to respond to the calls. The complexity of implementing good food banking practices, which follows an RTF approach and is integrated into a broader food and nutrition security policy, requires some minimum local capacity, which many poorer regions do not have. This complexity limits the expansion of the programme. At the moment (2014) there seems to be no government plans on how to tackle this problem.

Another consequence of the RTF approach to food banking has been a steady decline of food banks in Brazil as mechanisms for reducing food waste. Only in large cities can food banks rely on donations of food that would otherwise be wasted. Instead, public food banks are now major recipients of food produced by small family farmers who are compensated through another federal initiative, the Food Acquisition Programme (PAA). This integrated policy has the aim of reducing hunger and supporting small family farms. Reducing food waste, it seems, is not a goal always compatible with an RTF approach. It is less and less cited as a goal of public food banks.

Public food banks are one example of a set of government programmes which have focused on reducing poverty and increasing food and nutrition security. Others include the conditional cash transfer programme *Bolsa Família*, the School Meals programme, Popular Restaurants, Community Kitchens, and the Food Acquisition Programme (PAA). The increased presence of the state in social services can be surprising in an era perceived as dominated by neo-liberal ideology, which dictates less state-provided and greater privatization of social services. While economically Brazil is very much integrated into the global market (it is, after all, one of the largest food exporters in the world), it has been able to develop its rights-based social policies relatively independently from international neo-liberal influences (Leubolt, 2013). The middle class in Brazil has indeed seen greater privatization of health services and education in the last 30 years, but the past decade has brought both an increase in state-run social services for the poor and an increase in the middle class, as more people rise from poverty. Public food banks are part of this overall policy approach.

The bottom line, however, is that the existence of food banks in Brazil, as in anywhere else, is a sign of precarious food security for given segments of the population. Private or public, food banks signal and reflect the extent of social and economic vulnerability in our societies. They are indicators of how much is still to be done to bring everyone to a basic level of food security. Thus, a truly food secure Brazil will be one without food banks, public or private. As the country's social indicators improve, as poverty levels continue to decrease, one can expect (or hope for) the need for food banks to decline in the future.

In the meantime, the increase of public food banks in Brazil is also a sign of greater food and nutrition security. This apparent paradox is explained by the fact that public food banks are part of an integrated social policy system developed to combat food and nutrition insecurity. They indicate both the presence of food insecure groups and the actions of a state committed to the progressive realization of the right to adequate food. The case of Brazil suggests that food banks do not have to be a sign of government abdication of its responsibility to uphold the right to food. On the contrary, food banks can be instruments for reaching some of the most vulnerable in society.

4
Canada: Thirty Years of Food Charity and Public Policy Neglect

Graham Riches and Valerie Tarasuk

Introduction

In May 2012, Olivier De Schutter, the UN Special Rapporteur on the Right to Food, undertook an official visit to Canada, the first to an OECD country. His report, informed by national statistics, indicated widespread and increasing food insecurity; a deplorable incidence of hunger and poverty amongst First Nations communities and Aboriginal peoples living in Northern Canada; and the lack of a national food policy. He drew attention to the nearly 900,000 people per month dependent on charity-based food aid, noting this 'reliance on food banks was symptomatic of a broken social protection system' which served as 'a moral safety valve for the State'. Observing that Canada had escaped the worst of the 2007–2008 global financial crisis, De Schutter questioned the Government's lack of compliance with its obligations under international law (ICESCR, 1976) to implement the human right to adequate food (OHCHR, 2012; HRC, 2013a).

Federal Government ministers abruptly dismissed his findings. His central recommendation to introduce a national right to food strategy received no acknowledgement. The Minister of Health complained the recommendations were ill-informed and 'made from afar' (CBC, 2013); and he was condemned for focusing on constitutional issues outside his mandate regarding matters of federal/provincial jurisdiction and accountability (HRC, 2013b).

After thirty years of charitable food banking (Riches, 1986), these observations raise significant and provocative questions regarding the lack of evidence-based and accountable public policy for addressing food insecurity. What is the relationship between food charity and food insecurity? What explains the public acceptability of both corporate food charity at national and provincial levels and the expansion of local charitable food provisioning as the primary response to food insecurity? Furthermore to what degree has entrenched food charity undermined the publicly funded social wage and acted as a serious obstacle to public policy and the progressive realization of the right to food (RTF)?

In exploring this tension between food charity and the RTF this chapter reviews the scale of the continuing crisis of hunger and food security within Canada since the late 1990s (Tarasuk and Davis, 1996; Riches, 1997a) including its determinants, prevalence and scope; the expansion and diversification of food banking and charitable meal programmes; and, in light of evidence-based research, the effectiveness of the food charity model. It examines the social construction of hunger as a matter for charity and the consequent de-politicization of food insecurity as the responsibility of the state; and how the vacuum of public policy neglect has been filled by increasingly corporatized food banking and the proliferation of community-based food provisioning. The chapter finally considers the critical issue of public accountability informed by a national right to food strategy and the challenges and possibilities of such an approach.

Determinants and prevalence of food insecurity

It is not coincidental that the growth of food charity in Canada has paralleled its thirty-year experiment with global neo-liberalism. This ideological commitment to economic growth, deregulated markets, minimal government and reduced taxation has come at the expense of assured and adequately recompensed employment (good jobs) and of the welfare state addressing the income, health and social needs of the precariously employed and those without work.

During this period the Canadian state has retreated from its redistributive roles and responsibilities. Battle, referencing a study by the Centre for the Study of Living Standards (Sharpe and Capeluck, 2012), noted that at their peak in 1994, 'taxes and transfers reduced market income inequality by 28.7 per cent, but that share has fallen to 23.7 per cent in 2010. The redistributive power of Canadian governments has, overall, weakened since the mid-1990s, due in large measure to cuts to two of Canada's most important income security programmes – Employment Insurance and welfare. Canada is below the OECD average and ranks 23rd out of 34 countries in terms of after-tax inequality' (Battle, 2012, p. 5).

At the same time, the Federal Government has been downloading social programme expenditures and responsibilities to the provinces.

With the abolition of the Canada Assistance Plan in 1996, it also absolved itself of its obligation to monitor national welfare standards. Poverty amelioration was thereby left to provincial governments and their restrictive policies of welfare reform and workfare (Goldberg and Green, 2009, p. 16), resulting in the rise of charitable food provisioning. In these political and economic circumstances, it is little wonder that food insecurity has not only flourished amongst the welfare poor but also, strikingly, within families in working households.

Scope and nature of food insecurity

The social epidemiology of food insecurity in Canada has been well documented with indicators of this problem included on national population health surveys since 1994. In 2011 3.9 million Canadians, 11.6 per cent of the population, were estimated to be food insecure, an increase of almost 450,000 people since 2008 (Tarasuk et al., 2013). First and foremost, food insecurity is a problem of income inadequacy. Vulnerability is tightly intertwined with labour conditions. In 2011, 60 per cent of food-insecure households were reliant on employment for their incomes. Their vulnerability reflects problems of low wages, short-term and part-time employment, and the reliance of multi-person households on the wages of a single earner.

Those unable to compete in the labour market are also at high risk for food insecurity. Two-thirds of social assistance recipients were food insecure in 2011 (Tarasuk et al., 2013), a finding that reflects the very low benefit levels and the asset restrictions that have come to define these programmes (NCW, 2010). In contrast, policy interventions have reduced poverty rates among seniors in recent years, and the benefits available to those over 65 years of age appear protective against food insecurity (Tarasuk et al., 2013).

Other 'risk factors' for food insecurity consistently identified on population surveys include Aboriginal status, renting rather than owning one's dwelling, and being a lone-parent female-led family. Although problems of food insecurity are sometimes conflated with geographic barriers to food retail access ('food deserts') or insufficient knowledge of nutrition and food preparation ('de-skilling'), there is little empirical support for these contentions.

Aboriginal hunger and the North

Although recent data on food insecurity among First Nations peoples living on reserves are lacking, earlier studies indicated extreme levels of deprivation. Additionally, one in five of those off-reserve were food insecure in 2011 (Tarasuk et al., 2013), reflecting the greater depth of poverty experienced by this group (Willows et al., 2009). Food insecurity is also highly prevalent in Canada's North, with 36 per cent of households in Nunavut food insecure in 2011 (Tarasuk et al., 2013). Even higher levels of deprivation have been documented in Inuit communities in Nunavut. Almost 70 per cent of Inuit preschool children were living in food insecure households in 2007–2008, and almost half of these were severely food insecure (Egeland et al., 2010). This problem is in part attributed to the nutrition transition affecting Arctic communities, the loss of access to traditional foods, and the extraordinarily high costs of 'market' foods, but it has also been linked to changing livelihoods and climate change (Ford and Beaumier, 2011).

A public health crisis

Individuals' health and wellbeing in Canada is tightly linked to their household food security. Integral to the experience of food insecurity are compromises in food selection, which heighten nutritional vulnerability. Adults in food-insecure households have poorer physical and mental health and higher rates of numerous chronic conditions, including depression, diabetes and heart disease. Once chronic diseases are established, their management is also compromised in the context of food insecurity. The experience of severe food insecurity ('hunger') leaves an indelible mark on children's physical and mental health, manifesting in greater likelihood of such conditions as depression and asthma in adolescence and early adulthood (Kirkpatrick et al., 2010; McIntyre et al., 2012b).

Food charity: our primary response

Despite an abundance of evidence that food insecurity is a serious population health problem, with clear social policy roots, there has been no targeted public policy response. Instead, the primary response has been food charity. At the core of these efforts are 'food banks', a label that in Canada denotes voluntary, extra-governmental community organizations that collect surplus/wasted and donated foodstuffs and redistribute them to the 'needy', working largely with volunteer labour and donated facilities.

Food bank expansion and diversification

The arrival of food banking from the United States was a consequence of the deep recession of 1980–1982 and Canada's failing social safety net. Food banks rapidly expanded, and in 1987, the Canadian Association of Food Banks (CAFB) was founded, later renamed Food Banks Canada (FBC). A decade later over 900 food banks, the majority in Quebec and Ontario, were providing emergency food relief to nearly 690,000 people per month (CAFB, 1997). By 2012 those assisted rose by 23 per cent to an all-time high of 882,000 monthly recipients, supported by 4,558 organizations (FBC, 2012, p. 31).

The expansion and institutionalization of food banking charted by growth in the national association has been paralleled by a steady growth in 'independent' operations. These food banks, established by faith groups, community organizations and agencies, are similar to FBC's 450 affiliated member agencies in that they too enlist volunteers to collect donations, fundraise, and distribute food to 'those in need'. A 2010 inventory of charitable food provisioning in five Canadian cities indicated that 37 per cent of the 340 agencies and organizations running food banks in those cities were not linked to FBC, accounting for 20 per cent of the total food assistance delivered through food banks in these cities (Tarasuk, unpublished).

Related to the rapid growth of food banking has been the proliferation of charitable meal programmes, including initiatives for children, but also a myriad of meal and snack programmes for homeless and impoverished youth and adults. This work has been taken on by a wide variety of community organizations including multi-service agencies, faith groups and even health centres. Many receive food supplies via the FBC network, and in 2012, FBC reported that their member agencies supplied almost 4 million meals in one month (FBC, 2012, p. 4).

As food banking has become entrenched, the lines between the charitable food provisioning and the delivery of other community services for low-income and marginalized groups have become increasingly blurred. Food charity has been inserted into many mainstream services (e.g., free snacks in the waiting room of a health centre, a school breakfast programme, a lunch programme in a drop-in centre for homeless and socially isolated adults), often in response to the recognition by staff that problems of hunger among their clients are thwarting the effective delivery of other services and supports. At the same time, many food banks have added other programmes to their repertoire including personal counselling and advocacy for clients, community kitchens, nutrition education, employment training, referrals to other services and supports in the community, and even health promotion programming (FBC, 2012; Saul and Curtis, 2013). However, the provision of food assistance remains an act of charity in these settings, supported through corporate and private philanthropy.

The limits of charity

Although some of the initiatives described here have been supported at least in part by provincial and municipal funding, Canada has no federal programme to augment the food supplies of charitable distributors. Instead, food assistance programmes of all sorts rely on food and cash donations from the general public, philanthropic organizations, the local business community, and the food retail, production and manufacturing sectors.

Industry donations of food that cannot be retailed have been encouraged through the passage of 'Good Samaritan' laws that absolve donors of responsibility for the health and safety of the food they donate, but the donation of food that would otherwise be discarded in landfills also has strong environmental appeal. Food banks are uniquely positioned to handle this 'surplus' food. They have a surfeit of volunteers available to sort and cull a wide variety of food products, including fresh (or once-fresh) produce, but also a lot of processed foods, and the charitable model of food distribution encourages clients to 'take what they get' (Tarasuk and Eakin, 2005). Nonetheless, food safety is an ongoing concern because quality control lies in the hands of food bank workers. When interviewed, food-insecure Canadians routinely comment on the poor quality and questionable safety of the food obtained from local charities (Miewald et al., 2010; Runnels et al., 2011; Loopstra and Tarasuk, 2012).

While statistics on food bank usage and meal provisioning give the illusion of standardized services, the charitable, voluntary underpinnings of these programmes set the stage for restrictions on the frequency, amount and selection of food assistance available to clients. Most agencies included in FBC's 2012 report only aspired to provide 3–7 days' worth of food once per month to those who seek and are deemed eligible for their assistance, but most were not even able to consistently fulfil these goals.

The voluntary nature of charitable food provisioning in Canada also means that individual food providers set their own schedules of operation, establish criteria for whom they will serve, and determine the frequency with which those seeking their assistance can receive help. Many charitable food programmes are 'add-ons' to other services; rather than being designed to achieve specific levels of nutritional support, they are constructed to fit within the existing operations, resources and mandate of the host agency (Dachner et al., 2009). There appears to be little coordination of service delivery in many areas, and food is anything but a right for those who seek assistance.

Food charity: an ineffective response

Disconnect between food insecurity and food bank usage

The high public profile of food banks gives the impression that these programmes are a mainstay for those in need, but only 20–30 per cent of people experiencing food insecurity report seeking food assistance (McIntyre et al., 2000; Rainville and Brink, 2001; Vozoris and Tarasuk, 2003; Loopstra and Tarasuk, 2012). Food charity is most likely to be accessed by people facing severe food insecurity, but even among this group, food bank usage is very low. Even when children are at risk of food deprivation, only about one-third of families seek food bank assistance and this proportion has remained remarkably consistent over the past decade (McIntyre et al., 2012a). Interviews with food-insecure families in Toronto who did not use food banks revealed some barriers to access (e.g., limited operating hours, long line-ups, ineligibility for assistance, lack of information about available services), but most were not using food banks because they did not perceive them to be a way to address their needs (Loopstra and Tarasuk, 2012). They spoke of food banks as degrading programmes, to be used only as a last resort, and many explained that whatever assistance they could get from a food bank would be unlikely to meet their family's needs anyway (Loopstra and Tarasuk, 2012).

One tangible illustration of the incongruence between food banks and food insecurity comes from the contrast between the demographic profile of food bank users and the picture of food insecurity that emerges from national surveys. Social assistance recipients comprised 52 per cent of food bank users in 2012 (FBC, 2012), but only about one-quarter of the food-insecure population. The 'working poor', in contrast, comprise the majority of food-insecure Canadians, but only 12 per cent of FBC's clientele. Whether this reflects a deliberate decision to prioritize the needs of social assistance recipients or unintentional barriers to access for working people, it suggests that FBC's annual *HungerCount* reports offer a skewed picture of the problem of food insecurity in this country and thus limited public policy guidance.

Food charity does not prevent hunger

The public messaging around food banks gives the impression that they are effective in dealing with problems of hunger among those who seek their services, but there is little to support this claim. Research with people who use food banks or eat in charitable meal programmes indicates that many still go hungry, despite receiving food assistance (Hamelin et al., 2002; Hamelin et al., 2007; Tarasuk et al., 2009; Loopstra and Tarasuk,

2012). Part of the explanation for this lies in the extraordinary levels of vulnerability of those who seek food charity (i.e., it is a last resort), but the finding also reflects the limited food assistance provided by this 'system'. Food charities, by design, do not aspire to fully meet food needs of their clients, but rather to provide short-term or 'emergency' relief. Although public appeals for donations often convey the impression that giving to a food bank will 'help end hunger', FBC publications routinely acknowledge that food banks cannot solve food insecurity.

Food charity: the de-politicization of hunger

The ineffectiveness of charitable food banks is masked by their high degree of public legitimacy. Increasingly they have become embedded within popular and now corporate culture as practical compassion and a common sense response to household food insecurity and the country's broken social safety net. Despite research to the contrary the food charity model, and not public policy, has become the accepted norm for meeting the food and nutritional needs of income poor Canadians. This de-politicization of hunger as an issue of fundamental human rights has been promoted by the corporatization of the national food bank network and the proliferation of local community food provisioning. Hunger has successfully been socially constructed as a matter for charity and not an issue requiring the priority attention of the state and public policy.

The corporatization of charitable food banks has been a work in progress for a number of years. In 2006, the CAFB in partnership with food bank associations in Argentina, Mexico and the United States was a founding member of the Global Foodbanking Network (GFN) whose founding partners include transnational corporate giants Cargill Incorporated and the Kellogg Company. GFN positioned itself globally as 'the link between food waste and hunger' (GFN, 2013b). In 2008, the CAFB re-branded itself as Food Banks Canada creating a new managerial image of efficiency and effectiveness. Interestingly, Food Banks Quebec itself acknowledged that it took a major shift when its own board restructuring was undertaken to 'better meet the requirements of the food industry for the 21st century' (FBC, 2010, p. 3).

A key function of FBC is the organization and administration of the National Food Sharing System whereby major transportation companies (e.g., Canadian Pacific, Canadian National Rail, Purolator Inc.) and national food corporations and global retail giants (e.g., Conagra, Kellogg, Kraft, Loblaws, McCains, Pepsico, Wal-mart) partner to assist in the distribution of donations across Canada to affiliated member food banks. In 2012, 87 per cent of the 13.5 million lbs of food provided was from the corporate sector (FBC Annual Report, 2012, p. 10)

Corporate food bank sponsors include professional sports, the music entertainment industry as well as the national TV and broadcast media including the CBC, Canada's public broadcaster. Annually since 1985 the CBC holds day-long on-air Christmas provincial food bank drives. Leaving aside the question of crossing ethical journalistic boundaries one might ask whether such action constitutes a misuse of public funds to support private philanthropy of which the long-term effect is to undermine the role of public policy in addressing food insecurity.

At the same time the actions of numerous church and community-based and volunteer-run food banks and meal programmes uncon-nected to the national FBC network are also de-politicizing hunger. Largely dependent on voluntary donations, this extensive *ad hoc* local food charity gives further credence to the idea that food insecurity is being addressed, enabling governments to look the other way.

Recent developments suggest, however, it is not policy neglect alone which is bringing corporations and private citizens to the food charity table but rather deliberate public policy. In 2013, the House of Commons Standing Committee on Finance brought forward a number of tax related recommendations 'to enhance charitable giving' so as to accommodate the Government's 'stated intention to balance the budget in the medium term' (FINA, 2013, pp. 1, 26) through projected spending cutbacks. While such tax recommendations are not yet enacted such declarations of intent are expressions of a government increasingly unwilling to accept public accountability for its poorest citizens.

Public accountability and the right to food

As a State party to the ICESCR the Federal Government is the primary stakeholder and duty bearer publicly accountable for the progressive realization of the right to food. In practice this requires integrated public policies, what some have termed 'joined-up' food policy (Barling et al., 2002; MacRae, 2011), focused on national food security inclusive of the food needs of income poor Canadians. It includes connecting the dots between food policy, income redistribution, public health and social policy; the adoption of coordinated planning and the setting of targets, timelines, benchmarks, indicators, monitoring mechanisms, justiciable remedies; and 'a multi-stakeholder approach' with the participation of civil society and the private sector (FAO, 2005, pp. 11–15). Such a public agenda with federal leadership remains missing.

Justiciability: a remote possibility

A right is a right when it can be claimed. However this is not the case in Canada where the justiciability of the right to food lacks constitutional entrenchment and is not explicitly recognized in the *Charter of Rights and Freedoms* (1982). Yet a recent study, *Towards a More Equal Canada*, from the Broadbent Institute (BI), a national economic and social policy think tank, states that 'the Supreme Court of Canada has increasingly pointed to international law ratified by Canada (e.g., *ICSCER*) as a touchstone for interpreting the constitutionality of Canadian legislation'. It comments that 'distinguished legal experts have argued that the security of the person provision in the *Charter of Rights and Freedoms* entails recognition of economic and social rights' and 'that these rights should be added to the Charter to ensure that economic and social rights have the same full constitutional recognition and respect as political and civil rights' (BI, 2012).

These points are not new and have been forcefully argued by former Supreme Court Justice and UN High Commissioner for Human Rights, Louise Arbour (Arbour, 2005, pp. 5–8). However the likelihood of constitutional entrenchment is remote even though both the federal NDP and Liberal opposition parties are seemingly committed to national food strategies.

Federal government: continuing neglect

In 1998, the Liberal Government of the day responded to the 1996 World Food Summit by releasing *Canada's Action Plan for Food Security*. It cited the RTF as an important element in advancing domestic food security and the importance of all sector participation in 'its full and progressive realization' to reduce poverty and ensure access to safe and nutritious food (AAFC, 1998, p. 6). Yet fifteen years later a national food policy and action plan remains unrealized.

Certainly, one very important step taken by the Federal Government has been the implementation of a national monitoring system. A standardized, multi-item measure of food insecurity, developed for monitoring in the United States, has been included in the *Canadian Community Health Survey* since 2004 (Health Canada, 2007, 2010). Although this module has been 'optional content' for some years, most provinces have so far not opted out of the measurement. The data provide an invaluable tool for policy development and evaluation at both the provincial/territorial and federal levels.

Despite this the signs are not encouraging that the Federal Government will act. Canada's five-year Periodic Reviews to the UN Committee on Economic, Social and Cultural Rights (CESCR) reveal a disturbing history of non-compliance regarding the right to food. The UN's 2006 response to Canada's 4th and 5th reports regretted 'that most of the 1993 and 1998 recommendations (regarding the right to an adequate standard of living) had 'not been implemented'. Of the twenty-three principal subjects of concern many adversely affected individual Canadians' rights to adequate food (UNCESCR, 2006, pp. 2–5). Canada's 6th Periodic Review (2005–2009) awaits consideration by the Committee (Canada, n.d.).

Given that food insecurity is primarily a matter of income inadequacy it is Ottawa with its broad taxing powers and major control of the country's key income transfer programmes which has the fiscal capacity and ability to act. To address poverty reduction Battle suggests social policy restructuring and reforms including boosting the Canada Child Tax Benefit, increasing the Working Income Tax Benefit, strengthening and broadening EI and addressing the income needs of those with disabilities (Battle, 2012). Such measures would increase the disposable incomes of the working poor and those in and out of the labour market, with a long-term goal of realizing a living wage. A national affordable housing policy; publicly funded child care outside Quebec where it is already established; as well as increasing social transfer payments to the provinces to ensure the adequacy of social assistance benefits would increase the ability of the poorest Canadians to purchase the food of their choice. However the more likely scenario is continuing federal neglect.

Provincial and municipal governments: lacking resources and political will

Responding to civil society advocacy, the majority of Canadian provinces and territories have now introduced poverty reduction legislation or strategies with five provinces and the Yukon and Northwest Territories (NWT) including small scale food security projects as examples of RTF approaches (Canada, n.d.). It is however highly questionable whether these actions coupled with modest increases in provincially set minimum wage rates or welfare benefits can lessen the prevalence or severity of food insecurity. In 2002, the Government of Quebec unanimously passed an *Act to Combat Poverty and Social Exclusion* including an Action Plan. While this has been praised by anti-poverty activists, food insecurity in Quebec sits at the national average (Tarasuk et al., 2013).

Many provinces have also provided support to community-based initiatives designed in part to alleviate problems of food insecurity. Chief among these is the support of provincial governments for school-based nutrition programmes. Although initially focused on child hunger, many current initiatives are intended to be universally accessible, designed to address the broader goals of healthy eating and obesity prevention. While such initiatives might mitigate children's experiences of food insecurity, they are unlikely to alter household circumstances. Some provincial governments are also working to foster community food security through investments in community kitchens, farmers' markets, gardens and other community-based food initiatives. The link between these interventions and problems of hunger and food insecurity is also tenuous. Provincial governments lack the political will to implement the RTF and have yet to pledge to reduce the prevalence or severity of food insecurity.

Food policy councils, creatures of municipal governments and their public health or social planning departments, actively promote food security. In 2001, the *Toronto Food Charter*, proclaimed by the Toronto Food Policy Council, supported national commitments to food security, highlighting the ICESCR and 'the fundamental right of everyone to be free from hunger'. Food policy councils across the country (e.g., Toronto, Saskatoon, Vancouver) have initiated public debate about the need for economically viable, ecologically sustainable and socially just food systems and building the national food policy movement. They have generated support for locally sustainable agriculture, urban gardening, and various neighbourhood-level interventions to improve food retail access, but municipal groups have little capacity to tackle problems of income inadequacy that underpin household food insecurity because the key policy reforms fall outside their jurisdiction.

Civil society – Public education and advocacy

Recent Federal Government cutbacks including the elimination in 2012 of the fifty-year-old National Council of Welfare, an advisory anti-poverty federal agency, have cast a long shadow over public education and advocacy regarding poverty and human rights. Despite this, national NGOs such as Canada Without Poverty, the Canadian Foodgrains Bank, Food Secure Canada and Citizens for Public Justice have kept alive the idea of public accountability, poverty reduction and the right to food. The enactment of Quebec's anti-poverty legislation was a direct response to public pressure from the Collective for a Poverty Free Quebec, but in the rest of Canada social policy advocacy whilst generating public debate has yet to achieve federal legislative success.

In 2006, the loosely knit Canadian Food Security Network restructured itself as Food Secure Canada (FSC), today's lead national food policy organization. Its activities and advocacy are based on three interlocking principles: zero hunger; healthy and safe food; and a sustainable food system. FSC is informed by a strong human rights framework and played a central role in convening civil society organizations to brief the UN Right to Food Rapporteur in advance of his visit and meet with him during his visit to Canada. Its 2011 national report, *Resetting the Table: A People's Food Policy for Canada*, is a leading voice calling for a publicly accountable national food policy rather than one shaped by the Conference Board of Canada and the Canadian food industry.

Health NGOs and professional organizations are also proving to be staunch advocates on this issue. In many provinces, public health nutritionists and community groups routinely monitor the cost of food in relation to social assistance benefit levels and minimum wages, with their reports providing a potent reminder of the policy underpinnings of food insecurity. Recognition of the need for more concerted policy action has prompted organizations like the Dietitians of Canada and the Heart and Stroke Foundation to issue position papers on food insecurity.

It cannot however be assumed that all national food policy organizations speak with a collective voice on the RTF. Whilst FBC has active representation within Food Secure Canada, FBC is itself heavily subsidized by the corporate food industry with 73 per cent of its operating revenues from corporate donations (FBC, 2013). Certainly FBC presents a credible set of on-line policy recommendations to address domestic hunger, yet these are rarely the topic of public advocacy. Indeed, FBC's 2012 lobbying of the Federal Government to approve corporate tax breaks for food businesses donating surplus food to food banks (Power et al., 2012) aims to further entrench the corporate food charity model at the expense of public policy.

Corporate sponsorship: furthering food bank entrenchment

Corporate sponsorship of the national food bank network has been a win-win for the food industry. Not only is it perceived as 'solving the hunger problem' but also as addressing environmental issues of food waste. Certainly it does no harm to the branding and promotion of its food products and profit margins. From an RTF perspective the hidden functions of corporate food charity are profoundly problematic, obscuring an informed analysis of the causes of domestic food insecurity and obviating the need for public policy.

The food industry's image of corporate efficiency allows the public and politicians to believe that its support of charitable food banks is effectively meeting the immediate food needs of the welfare poor and thereby resolving the issue of food insecurity. Yet such sponsorship distracts attention from the fact that the majority of food insecure

Canadians are the working poor, unable to meet the everyday costs of putting food on the table. As evidence-based research has shown, most food insecure people do not even use food banks, and those who do, still go hungry. The indignity of having to use food banks is only one of the problems with this 'system'. The highly restrictive nature of the food access offered by food banks means that few are ever truly 'fed' by them which is not surprising given that they are continually running out of food themselves.

In these ways corporate food charity both masks the ineffectiveness of food banking and obstructs the development of public policies directed at the achievement of food security for all. These hidden functions further entrench an unaccountable charitable food banking system. At a time when government is being lobbied for corporate tax breaks to sustain a failing system of food aid and poor relief, the private sector should be asking itself to what extent, in tackling the root causes of food insecurity, it would review its own employment policies and practices to ensure that its workers and their families can be food secure. Furthermore how willing would it be to support increases in corporate taxes to assist the rebuilding of Canada's social safety net, a strategic component of a national right to food policy?

Conclusion

In summary, household food insecurity is a serious, pervasive problem in Canada. The social epidemiology is well documented, as are the deleterious health consequences, but to date it has been a case of public policy neglect. Instead, a massive web of food charity has been established, fuelled by donations from the public and corporate sectors and largely staffed by volunteers. Yet, only one in four food-insecure Canadians even seek charitable food assistance, and many of those who receive help still report going hungry. While models of operations continue to evolve, with food charity becoming increasingly integrated into mainstream community services and public institutions, the provision of food assistance remains an act of charity, with no accountability for the adequacy or accessibility of the food or nutrition supports provided.

In a wealthy and food secure country such as Canada, hunger is not a problem of food supply but of people's financial inability to acquire adequate, nutritious food in normal and customary ways. It is primarily a matter of federal and provincial economic and social policy, income distribution and public health. The recommendations of the UN Special Rapporteur reminded Canada of its obligations under international law to develop a national food policy informed by the right to food. In terms of addressing the food needs of income poor Canadians his recommendations included: setting the minimum wage as a living wage; raising social assistance levels to meet basic adequacy with federal market basket guidelines and a legally enforceable right to adequate assistance for all persons in need; increasing the value of housing benefits; introducing a nationally funded children and food strategy; ensuring access to land and water rights for all Aboriginal peoples and re-establishing national standards for social assistance and social services. He also stressed the importance of launching a process for adopting a framework law on the right to food to inform Canadian food strategy.

The evidence is clear. Canada's entrenched system of food charity has proven itself to be an ineffective response to household food insecurity and should be understood as part of the problem not the solution to domestic food insecurity. Accountable federal and provincial public policy informed by the right to food is urgently required. As Louise Arbour has stated 'there will always be a place for charity, but charitable responses are not an effective, principled or sustainable substitute for enforceable human rights guarantees' (2005, p. 8).

5
Hunger and Food Aid in Estonia: A Local Authority and Family Obligation

Jüri Kõre

Introduction

Estonia is a post-socialist country which regained its independence in 1991 following the collapse of the Soviet Union. In light of this recent history and its rapid transition to a market economy Estonia provides an intriguing case study regarding domestic hunger, social protection and poverty reduction policies and the provision of food aid. Today, Estonia, with a population of 1.3 million, has full membership within the European Union, the Eurozone and the OECD, and enjoys an advanced, high-income economy.

Yet it is important to reflect that Estonia's current approach to food insecurity and anti-poverty policies as well as its broader social policy have been shaped by its specific history and not simply the events of the past two decades. Before World War II Estonia lacked a social security system that covered the entire population. Benefits (allowances and services) were only granted to state workers and officials and their family members, and to employees of industrial and transport companies covered by mandatory insurance and their family members. In 1940 the health insurance system extended to 20 per cent of the population. The fight against poverty was primarily the duty of local authorities and charity though during the periods of recession (1924–1925 and 1929–1934) the state offered its citizens more assistance. People were either helped to find work (the state and local authorities organizing public or emergency work) or given food aid (Kõre, 1998). Estonia's early social security system is often connected to the corporate social policy of Bismarck, due to the country's strong Baltic German community.

However, the fundamentals of social protection changed dramatically after World War II. During the Soviet regime (1944–1991) social security and welfare became national systems and organized charity such as faith-based care was prohibited by law. Nevertheless, individual people donated food, clothing and money and provided assistance to the poorer members of society. Officially, national social protection was a universal system that was inclusive of everyone. Interestingly, Soviet social protection had *de facto* some things in common with Bismarckian social policy organization. Social rights were tied to social status immediately after the war, which explains why access to childcare, housing, health and welfare services was easier for some people than others. For example the proletariat (workers on salaries) had the right to receive free medical care and a state pension while craftsmen, farmers and sole traders had to pay for health services, neither did they have the right to a state pension. The extent of social protection nevertheless increased during the Soviet regime, but it is noteworthy that obtaining any statistical data about the incidence of poverty after 1944 is very difficult as the subject was taboo in the framework of socialist ideology.

Ration stamps were used in Estonian cities to distribute food to the population from 1940–1947 (during the first Soviet and German occupation and at the beginning of the second Soviet occupation). The food situation in cities started improving again in the early 1950s. However, life in rural areas became complicated in both the social and economic sense as a result of the destruction of traditional farm-based agricultural production and the establishment of collective households (collective agricultural enterprises). The so-called personal auxiliary household (0.16 ha of land rented from the state on which food and/or animal feed was grown) was the main source of food and livelihood for collective agricultural enterprise workers. The food balance (manufacturing and consumption) remained tense until the end of Soviet rule in 1991.

At present the social policy regimes of Estonia and other eastern European countries are not well understood. It can certainly be said that during the 1990s the resources that could be allocated for social protection were limited as a result of the transition period towards the capitalist economy. Generally, social insurance benefits (e.g., family allowances and unemployment benefits) were equal for everyone or were dependent on a person's income, as in the case of old age pensions. In that sense the social protection system reflected Beveridgean values and policies (Cerami, 2007). Today, most benefits are tied to income (e.g., unemployment insurance and sickness, parental and health insurance benefits) and pensions are more differentiated than previously.

In other words, Estonia's current social protection system parallels the Bismarckian system, which is also described as dual social protection offering a level of welfare that is very high for some and relatively low for others (MSA, 2008).

Within this historical social policy context this chapter explores who is at risk of food poverty or food insecurity and why in present-day Estonia. The obligations, and the different roles and expectations of the family, third sector, local authorities and the state in addressing the issues are then considered. The chapter concludes by outlining some future prospects: is the need for food aid increasing or decreasing, and why; how is Estonia going to answer its critics in terms of its performance in respect of its ICESCR obligations, including the right to food; and is charitable food aid in Estonia here to stay or is there the political or moral will to tackle the hunger problem through public policy within the framework of the right to food?

Understanding poverty in Estonia

Poverty in today's Estonia, including the short- or long-term lack of food, is often associated with an inability to cope with daily life, and is generally understood in the context of four types of circumstances: low income or lack of income caused by a person's way of life (e.g., alcoholism, drug abuse or homelessness) often resulting in eating problems including hunger; exclusion, whereby individuals or groups do not know how to apply for financial assistance or food aid; refusing to seek help for fear of stigmatization or dependency on others; and the lack of formal or public assistance and the absence or unreliability of informal helping networks (ES, 2010).

Monitoring poverty, exclusion and material deprivation

Understanding poverty in Estonia is also influenced by the state's preference for measuring it in absolute rather than relative terms, which is the practice of the European Union (EU). In the EU, 18 common statistical indicators are applied to monitor the progress of member states in the fight against poverty, including food insecurity, and social exclusion (Laeken Indicators). The main indicator of poverty is the 'at-risk-of-poverty threshold', which is fixed at 60 per cent of a household member's median equivalized income (applying the OECD-modified equivalence scale of 1:0.5:0.3) in the given country.

However, while the focus of EU monitoring is therefore on the relative risk of poverty, this is not considered the preferred approach to poverty research for post-socialist countries (MSA, 1999; Laes, 2013). It understates the general severity of the problem. In 2012 the at-risk-of-poverty rate in Estonia was 17.5 per cent and in the EU generally 17.1 per cent (data from 28 countries). According to these figures, by European comparison the material situation and subsistence of Estonian people is not bad or critical, but rather ordinary (EUROSTAT, 2013b). The real problem is the prevalence of absolute poverty and low average income.

Absolute poverty and want of food

While measuring absolute and relative poverty are both established approaches and methodologies, absolute poverty is the preferred indicator in Estonia due to the low average income in the country. It defines the resources that are necessary to meet fundamental basic needs such as food, housing and clothing. The national method of calculating the absolute poverty rate was created in 1999 when the rate was set at 1250 EEK (79.90 EUR) per month. At this time 37.6 per cent of the population lived below the absolute poverty line (MSA, 1999). Absolute poverty decreased rather rapidly in subsequent years and reached its lowest level in 2008 (4.7 per cent). However, as a result of the global recession, poverty in Estonia again increased, nearly doubling to 8.1 per cent in 2011. Meanwhile the relative poverty rate remained constant in Estonia in the 2000s, increasing from 18.3 per cent in 2000 to 19.7 per cent in 2008, then dropping to 17.5 per cent by 2011 (Statistics Estonia, 2013).

Interestingly, politicians seek to avoid talking in straight terms about 'poverty', preferring instead to use the concept of the 'minimum means of subsistence'. While this measure is largely similar to the absolute poverty line, it calculates the minimum subsistence level income necessary to maintain and reproduce an individual's capacity for work. The minimum food basket and its cost including types of food and their nutritional content is designed to guarantee an individual balanced protein, carbohydrate and fat consumption as well as 2,400 kcal of energy per day.

In 2012, the cost of the minimum food basket per capita was 88.34 euros, but 61 per cent of Estonian residents had an even smaller amount of money to spend, which is a truly painful fact affecting large numbers of people (Sotsiaaltrendid 6, 2013). Simply selectively targeting single individuals or population groups such as single-parent families and those with disabilities cannot therefore reduce poverty, or want of food, in Estonia. Instead, raising the general standard of living (wage income) is very important in the fight against poverty and food insecurity.

Population groups at risk of poverty and food insecurity

Prevalence

In Estonia there is no tradition or methodology for the official assessment of food insecurity. However, poverty relief does include issues of food insecurity and the shortage of food. Given that income poverty is the main reason for food poverty, mapping the population groups living at risk of poverty also offers some indirect data about people living at risk of food insecurity. After all, 129,000 people using EU food aid prove that there is food poverty in Estonia.

Poverty risk varies between population groups. The absolute poverty rate for women in 2011 was lower than that of men (7.6 per cent and 8.7 per cent, respectively). In terms of age groups, the absolute poverty indicator is highest (13.6 per cent) among young people (16–24) and lowest (1.6 per cent) among the elderly (65+). These findings, however, should not be used as grounds for any broad conclusions about the incidence of absolute poverty in Estonia. People do not generally live alone but in families and households. The poverty rate is highest among single-parent households (18.6 per cent) and families with at least three children (13.6 per cent). The poverty rate is also high (16.5 per cent) among working-age people (younger than 65) who live alone. The poor may be low wage earners and connected to the labour market or receiving benefits or support from the social protection system. In a smaller number of cases they are not connected to such formal systems, but may receive help from private persons. Immigrants are a traditional group at risk of poverty. Estonia is an exception as the share of immigrants at risk of poverty (18 per cent) is lower than the general share of people at risk of poverty (20 per cent) (EUROSTAT, 2011).

It should also be stressed that the labour market does not guarantee economic coping capacity or a life without poverty. In fact, 8.3 per cent of workers were at risk of poverty in 2012. This percentage is somewhat better than the EU average (9.2 per cent), but indicates that it is still necessary to develop labour market policies (EUROSTAT, 2013a).

Social protection and benefit inadequacy

The benefits system in Estonia is graduated. In other words, those without work who are not eligible for unemployment insurance benefits (which are based on wages) because they have not been insured for the required minimum period may receive unemployment benefits, or the subsistence benefit (a uniform benefit – social assistance in nature), if they are not eligible for unemployment benefit. Yet, the low levels of unemployment and subsistence benefits mean that people depending on them can only secure the minimum coping capacity, with implications for their food budgets. The dire economic situation and increased coping problems of the families living on unemployment or subsistence benefits have forced jobless people to apply for benefits more actively in recent years.

Estonia does not have a guaranteed minimum income (GMI) policy, but the state subsistence benefit paid to those on a small or inadequate income is more or less equivalent to the GMI. The *Social Welfare Act* defines the subsistence level (the amount required for minimum daily subsistence for a period of one month), which must be guaranteed to every person legally residing in Estonia (RT I 1995, pp. 21, 323). The subsistence benefit combines a housing benefit with a guaranteed minimum income allowance which includes the cost of food.

Approximately one-fifth of benefit recipients make use solely of the housing component (their income is higher than the subsistence level but is insufficient to meet housing expenses). Four-fifths of recipients make use of both the housing and income components. Some 24,332 households received subsistence benefit in 2011, which is around 4.2 per cent of all Estonian households. Households that receive social benefits are greater than the average household. This means that in terms of the population, the percentage of benefit recipients is higher than the above-mentioned percentage of households. However, the subsistence benefit is not adequate to prevent absolute poverty: in 2009 the average subsistence benefit comprised 71.1 per cent of the absolute poverty line or subsistence level income. The subsistence benefit received by families with many children comprises around two-thirds of the absolute poverty line, and the percentage of this support is approximately the same in households with an unemployed family member. In families with a single parent, subsistence benefit rises to approximately 80 per cent of the poverty line (Trumm and Kasearu, 2011).

Considering this overview, the majority of households on a subsistence benefit are living in deep or absolute poverty. There is no doubt that the benefits received improve their material situation, but they do not necessarily help them acquire adequate food. On the other hand, indirect data allows us to claim that the number of children living with a permanent lack of food is small in Estonia. Despite the fact that 129,000 people are receiving EU food aid, only 0.7 per cent of those interviewed in Estonia admitted that they go to bed hungry every night (2.2 per cent every night or often), because they do not have any food at home (WHO, 2012).

Homelessness and food insecurity

Homelessness is the most visible and extreme form of poverty, and an important indicator of hunger and food insecurity. Following the collapse of the socialist regime, it had become established as a social phenomenon in Estonia by the mid 1990s. Many factors had combined and become more acute in Estonia by this time. The influence of social institutions such as the state, schools and the family on an individual's existence or behaviour had weakened. At the same time, in comparison to the earlier period, the responsibilities of some other social institutions such as local authorities, the church and civic institutions had expanded. However, the latter had been unable to offer sufficient support to vulnerable individuals due to a lack of resources and mandate. The influence of public bureaucracy and the collective organization of life weakened, resulting in the spread of a so-called asocial way of life. Unemployment, which rose to 20 per cent, left people without income and housing at the same time as other reforms (e.g., replacement of state-regulated prices with free market prices) suddenly increased the kind of expenses that used to demand only a small part of the weekly budget. In this context food insecurity emerged as a significant health and social issue.

The first national estimate of homelessness was obtained in 2002, citing 5,000 people, including 2000–3000 in the capital, Tallinn (Kõre et al., 2006). The number of people in shelters and rehabilitation institutions also gives an indirect indication of the number of homeless people. In late 2011 social workers and the police carried out the first homeless census in Tallinn, finding and interviewing 1,225 people without a permanent place of residence (Kodutud Tallinnas, 2012). Interestingly, this survey suggests that the number of homeless people has decreased – as much as halving. From a food insecurity perspective the homeless are a group of people who eat irregularly or eat low-quality food – sometimes due to a lack of food or money and sometimes due to their lifestyle.

Food aid distribution

According to article § 28 of the *Constitution of the Republic of Estonia*, every citizen is guaranteed government assistance in the case of old age, incapacity for work, the loss of a provider or need. Citizens of Estonia and foreigners legally residing in Estonia have equal rights to receive assistance. The *Social Welfare Act* (RT I, 1995, 21, 323) delegates the obligation to provide assistance to local authorities, requiring them to pay benefits and provide or organize services and emergency assistance. The third sector also provides services in the form of public–private partnerships represented by non-governmental organizations (NGOs) and foundations, numbering 31,656 at the beginning of 2013 (SK, 2013). Half of them are housing and apartment associations whose establishment is required by law. The Ministry estimates that, of the remaining NGOs or foundations, 10,000 are currently active in the fields of education, cultural activities, sport, youth work, environmental and heritage protection, social work and health promotion. According to research exploring civil initiatives and civil society, 2.5 per cent of NGOs or nearly 250 agencies in Estonia are involved in health and social welfare, including the distribution of food aid (Kõre, 2010).

EU food aid

The EU Food Distribution Programme for the Most Deprived Persons (MDP) of the Community is the largest food aid scheme in Estonia. The Estonian Agricultural Registers and Information Board (ARIB) is the responsible authority and has been distributing MDP food aid in partnership with NGOs and voluntary organizations since 2008. ARIB had 18 partners in 2012, the largest being the Red Cross. There is no specific personal assessment of need. Food aid recipients can be roughly divided into two groups. The first comprises those who receive social benefits (support or services) from the local government. Their need for aid has already been assessed by a social worker. The second is the clients of (charity) organizations that distribute aid for people who are generally in need of help (single parents, families with at least four children, people with disabilities and pensioners) (ARIB, 2012).

The volume of aid distributed, the types of food and the number of aid recipients have increased year by year. Between 2008 and 2012 the volume of food distributed rose from 279,000 kg to more than three million kg; the variety of food expanded from pasta and cereal to include flour, rice, semolina, cooking oil and sugar; and, as noted earlier, the number of people receiving food aid increased fivefold from 26,020 to 129,498. While the quantity of EU food aid decreased by 2.9 million tons between 2012 and 2013, the forecast number of people needing help from partner organizations requesting food increased to 132,281 (ARIB, 2013). The organizations that distribute EU food aid lack suitable storage space which explains why the distribution of food is a short-term, one-off action for them.

A limiting factor is that organizations which do have storage space distribute food over a longer period of time. The Food Bank is one such organization. However, interest in free pasta, flour and oil does not mean that the people who receive them could not buy these foodstuffs themselves, but they can use the money they save in this manner to buy more expensive food items such as meat, fish, cheese, fruit and sweets.

Local authorities and the third sector

Estonia's *Social Welfare Act* places the obligation to deliver emergency food aid on local authorities. It is mainly put into practice by supporting soup kitchens, which are usually owned and managed by third sector groups such as the Salvation Army, faith-based care and non-religious associations. Local authorities pay the cost of the food of those clients referred from social workers to the soup kitchens, while others finance the food of clients without referrals. In 2013, soup kitchens were primarily operating in larger cities. In Tallinn, soup kitchens were run by three non-profit organizations – the Salvation Army, the Red Cross and the 'Hand of a Friend' Social Work Centre. On average, the municipality bought 450 food packages for distribution to people in need on a daily basis (Martinson, 2013). There are two permanent soup kitchens in Tartu, Estonia's second largest city. One is financed by Tartu City Government and the other is run by the Salvation Army, which self-finances its food aid activities. Tartu City Government funds 45 portions of food (soup and bread or food packages) per day from the soup kitchen run by St Paul's Congregation (SUT, 2012).

In addition to Tallinn and Tartu, the Salvation Army also operates in Narva and Võru. The second largest provider of food aid is the Food Bank. The Salvation Army, the Red Cross and the Food Bank are all NGOs in the legal sense. They all operate simultaneously through established private–public partnerships (under contract with the state and/or local authority for the provision of certain services) and as charities (with activity based on donations made by individuals).

The Food Bank, established in 2010 and a member of the European Federation of Food Banks, has reached its third year of operations. It currently works in eight cities and delivers 1,300 food packages per week. The Food Bank accepts products nearing their expiry date from traders and manufacturers, prepares food packages with the help of volunteers and distributes them to people in need. The Food Bank has set itself the goal of helping all families with children on income support – numbering 7,543 in 2012 (Toidupank, 2012).

Family obligations

The responsibility of local authorities for the ability of individuals to cope is not absolute. In assessing the need for food aid and other forms of assistance, social workers must consider the *Social Welfare Act* as well as the mutual maintenance obligation of family members stipulated in the *Family Act* (RT I, 2009). According to the *Family Act*, children or grandchildren, where necessary, are responsible for their parents' ability to cope, and parents or grandparents, where necessary, must support their children if they run into financial or other problems. Only a court may release an obligated person from the obligation to provide maintenance in certain cases specified by law.

The *Family Act* states that ascending (parents and grandparents) and descending (children and grandchildren) family members are obliged to help their relatives where required. However, the large proportion of co-habiting couples, the high divorce rate and complicated relationships between family members do not favour the performance of this obligation. This means that the ability of individuals in Estonia to cope is based on the result of the cooperation between families and the public sector as well as the combination of social and individual responsibility.

Although family relationships have weakened, the role of the family in ensuring that people cope is large in Estonia. The importance of these family obligations can be understood by analysing the sources of economic support of the unemployed. Welfare benefits were the main source of income for just 14.4 per cent of all unemployed people in 2012. The coping capacity of the majority, (64.4 per cent) was guaranteed by their families, dependent on the income of other family members. Additional sources of income (21.1 per cent) were earned from odd jobs – for example, picking and selling wild berries and mushrooms (MSA, 2012a).

Nursery, school and day centre meal programmes and meals on wheels

Nursery schools and primary and secondary education often include monetary and material support for those with low incomes. The goal is to secure a person's capacity to cope not only economically but also socially. For example, children are supported using indirect methods whereby local authorities pay for the meals of some children who attend nursery schools. This is a selective system with support being granted on the basis of an application submitted by the parents and an assessment of the family's income. However, there are no statistics for nursery school meal support.

Free or partially subsidized meals for primary and secondary school students (classes 1–9), are provided on a universal basis financed from the state budget. A total of 111,455 children attended basic school in 2010/2011. Although some children refuse free meals (instead buying buns and soft drinks from the school kiosk), we may consider this as the number of children receiving school meals. Some 14.5 per cent of all children aged 7–14 stay in 'long day groups' to do their homework and/or to wait for public transport after school. In some cases, children in these groups get a second meal either free or for a fee. There are no official statistics about the number of children who receive the second meal. Children who live in complicated economic and/or social conditions or who live far away from their schools stay in student homes during the week. In 2010/2011 there were 545 general education schools in Estonia, 43 of which had student homes. There were 704 places in the student homes financed by the state, with students served meals four times a day. Food is free for the majority of students.

Day centre services are also an important form of providing food. In 2011 there were 109 day centres for children, young people, working-age (homeless) people, the elderly and people with disabilities, providing services to 51,400 people in total. The most popular services were counselling, health service and senior day centre lunches (MSA, 2012b). The number of people who used the food service increased from 2007–2011, probably as a result of the recession, as 15.7 per cent of all day centre visitors used this service. Since most day centre clients are elderly people, 80 per cent of food recipients were also pensioners. The food offered by day centres is subsidized by the local government. The price of food delivered to the homes of people in need (meals-on-wheels) is also cheaper than market price. Meals-on-wheels is mostly organized in larger cities.

Fighting poverty in Estonia

Estonia has ratified a number of international conventions that cover the fundamental, social, economic, cultural and other rights of people. The *International Covenant on Economic, Social and Cultural Rights* (ICESCR) was ratified on 21 January 1992. Article 11 of the Covenant sets out that the States Parties of the Covenant recognize the right of everyone to an adequate standard of living, including adequate food, clothing and housing. The States Parties recognize that the right to food (to be free from hunger) is a fundamental right of people and will take appropriate steps to ensure the progressive realization of this right.

The UN Committee on Economic, Social and Cultural Rights pointed out in its final conclusions published in the first (October 2001) and second (October 2008) periodical reports on Estonia's performance in respect of its Covenant obligations that a significant number of people receiving social insurance benefits live in poverty. The Committee advised Estonia to review its social policy and to ensure that benefits guarantee their recipients and their families an adequate standard of living in terms of their amounts and duration (ICESCR, 2001).

In its second report, the Committee noted that the efforts made to reduce poverty had not been adequate and that the number of people living below or close to the poverty line remained high. The Committee advised the government to prepare and implement actions and strategies to reduce poverty, which would as a consequence address issues of domestic hunger and food insecurity (ICESCR, 2008).

Article 24 of the *Convention on the Rights of the Child* (RT, 2006)(), which entered into force in Estonia on 20 November 1991, covers the health of children, including access to nutritious food and clean water and the commitment to fight malnutrition. The UN Report on Estonia's performance regarding the rights of the child states that '...in general, there is no mass malnutrition in poor families, but the diet of many children is not diverse enough...The average food expenditure remains below the cost of the minimum food basket in non-working-parent families with children. By the non-working-parent family it is meant a family with a parent who is unemployed (but able to work) or a parent who lives on social insurance (disabled)' (CRC, 2001).

It should also be noted that in terms of the preparation and implementation of poverty reduction policies, plans and strategies, Estonia is primarily bound to achieve the goals agreed in the *EU Memorandum on Poverty Reduction and Social Inclusion*. The relevant Memorandum, (CEC, 2004), comprised three action plans prepared for its implementation (2004–2006, 2006–2008 and 2008–2010). According to the systematic analysis of the action plans and their performance it can be said that the relevant poverty reduction policy has been vague and cooperation between different levels of jurisdiction (transnational, national and local) is weak. Although the policy was designed to assist different population groups struggling with poverty, it has not focused sufficiently on eliminating the causes of poverty (Kõre and Karpuskiene, 2010).

According to the political will and public attitudes prevailing in Estonia, economic policy is thought to be the best social policy. This means policy aimed at the dynamic creation of new jobs and focused on ensuring that existing jobs do not disappear. This approach basically recognizes the expedience of an active labour market policy. Indeed the real intent of this policy is indicated by the proportion of social policy funding in relation to GDP which likewise supports job creation and work as the best social policy. In addition to the funds allocated for labour market policy in the state budget, Estonia has used the funds received from the EU Social Fund for the same purpose. This is why the proportion of this expenditure in GDP increased from 0.16 per cent in 2008 to 0.57 per cent in 2010, with a slight decline to 0.48 per cent in 2011 (MSA, 2012a).

Conclusion

As a post-socialist country, regaining its independence after the collapse of the Soviet Union, Estonia has witnessed a rapid and successful transition to a market economy. However, growing economic prosperity has not benefitted all Estonians equally. Even if there is no official data regarding food insecurity, it can be claimed that domestic hunger and delivery of emergency food aid have become commonplace. During 2012, 129,000 people (around 10 per cent of the population) received EU food aid distributed by charitable NGOs, such as faith-based and non-religious associations. In fact there is an anticipated increase in demand for EU food aid.

The main cause of food poverty is income poverty. The principle reasons for economic distress are unemployment (10.2 per cent in 2012) and low average income. Even though the absolute poverty rate has decreased rapidly from 37.6 per cent in 1999 to 8.1 per cent in 2011, some population groups remain at risk of food insecurity. The absolute poverty rate is highest for single-parent families and large families with many children. The key public policy issue in Estonia is the value placed on economic policy as the best social policy with a prevailing and growing trust in active labour markets. Yet, work does not always guarantee economic security, when 8.3 per cent of all employed live at risk of poverty and, undoubtedly, also at risk of food poverty.

Further, the risk of food poverty increases due to benefit inadequacy, if, for one reason or another, the head of the family is a working-age person, living outside the labour market and dependent on social benefits. In other words, one's incapacity for work, disability or having a large number of dependants may hinder labour market participation. While the *Social Welfare Act* defines the subsistence level which must be guaranteed to all people legally residing in Estonia, its benefit level is so low that the majority of households depending on it are living in deep or absolute poverty; that is to say experiencing, or at risk of, domestic hunger.

Following the collapse of the Soviet regime, the influence of social institutions such as the state, schools and the family on individual lives has weakened. At the same time increased responsibilities for local authorities have expanded as has the growth of civil society through the church and civic organizations. Yet they have been hampered due to the lack of mandate and resources to offer sufficient support for the vulnerable.

While there is, for example, a constitutional right, based on citizenship or legal residence in the country, to assistance in the case of old age, incapacity for work, the loss of a provider or need, the obligation to provide assistance, is, however, delegated to local authorities, requiring them to pay benefits and provide or organize services and emergency assistance. Emergency food aid is mainly put into practice by directing public funding for soup kitchens run by the NGOs. Local authorities pay food for the clients referred to the soup kitchens by social workers, whereas food for those without referrals is financed by the charity organizations or donors. Thus far soup kitchens are primarily operating in larger cities.

However, The Food Bank, established in 2010 and a member of the European Federation of Food Banks, has set itself the future goal of helping all families with children on income support. In light of continuous labour market failures, low average income, benefit inadequacy and ineligibility the public resources allocated to help people in need are not sufficient. Consequently, the need for food aid, food banks, school meal programmes and those carried out by charitable organizations will probably continue, and become further entrenched.

The largest NGOs distributing food aid operate simultaneously through established private–public partnerships (i.e., contracts with the state and/or local authority for the provision of certain services) and as charities (i.e., activity based on donations). The situation is new insofar as, during the Soviet regime, the law prohibited organized charity, whereas nowadays the obligation to deliver emergency food aid is placed on local authorities, which particularly exploit charities. The historical context and the strong pursuit to revive civil society may favour this kind of arrangement.

Another special feature is the *Family Act* which stipulates that family members support one another, meaning that ascending and descending family members are obliged to help their relatives in need. However, this kind of model is fragile in the face of modern ways of life: the high divorce rate, increasing co-habiting and ever more complicated family relationships. Accordingly, individual coping is based on the cooperation between families and the public sector as well as the combination of public and private responsibility. Inevitably, the hungry poor are likely to fall through the cracks.

In January 1992, Estonia ratified the *International Covenant on Economic, Social and Cultural Rights* (ICESCR). Ten years later the UN

Committee on Economic, Social and Cultural Rights pointed out that a significant number of people receiving social benefits continued to live in poverty. The Committee advised Estonia to review its social policy and to ensure that benefits guaranteed the recipients and their families an adequate standard of living in terms of their amounts and duration (ICESCR, 2001).

In its second report, seven years later, the Committee noted that the efforts made to reduce poverty have not been adequate and that the number of people living below or close to the poverty line remained high. The Committee advised the government to prepare and implement actions and strategies to reduce poverty, which would as a consequence address issues of domestic hunger and food insecurity (ICESCR, 2008).

In terms of the preparation and implementation of poverty reduction policies, plans and strategies, Estonia is primarily bound to achieve the goals agreed in the *EU Memorandum on Poverty Reduction and Social Inclusion*. According to the systematic analysis of the action plans and their performance the relevant poverty reduction policy has been vague and cooperation between different levels of jurisdiction (transnational, national and local) is weak. Yet, it is commendable that between 2004 and 2011, benefits in most cases increased more quickly than wages and they also increased in relation to the subsistence level income. The even faster rise in benefits would require increasing the tax burden for both individuals and companies.

While many of the ruling politicians favour 'better targeting of social protection systems', including decreasing universal benefits and emphasizing selective social security, this suggests a limited approach to tackling domestic hunger and food insecurity. Clearly the issue of low wages and inadequate benefits has to be addressed. The question also remains whether there is the political will to advance the achievement of food security for all as a priority for public policy informed by the right to food engaging not only active labour market policies but fully integrated agriculture, food, public health and social policy.

6
Hunger in a Nordic Welfare State: Finland

Tiina Silvasti and Jouko Karjalainen

Introduction

During the 1970s and 1980s people in Finland became used to the idea that the welfare state would satisfy the basic needs of all citizens. Under these circumstances, hunger or food insecurity as a social evil was unthinkable. The deep economic recession at the beginning of the 1990s, however, revealed holes in the social security safety net that affected the most vulnerable. News of the 'hunger problem' was initially made public by activists working in different relief organizations (Hänninen and Karjalainen, 1994, p. 274). Finally, in 1993, a survey published by the Ministry of Social Affairs and Health (MSAH) estimated that approximately 100,000 Finnish people wanted for food – in other words were food insecure – at some point during the period 1992–1993 (Kontula and Koskela, 1993). It was at this time that charitable food aid emerged, and has since become a fixed feature of the poverty policy landscape.

Food, despite being a basic prerequisite for a healthy and active life, does not receive much specific attention in Finnish social policy. This is probably because food is considered to be included as a normal part of income support, which is a constitutional and legal right for everyone living permanently in the country. However, minimum supplementary benefits in Finland have been repeatedly proven to be too low for longer-term adequate living (THL, 2011, p. 82). Consequently, benefits are not always sufficient to satisfy all basic needs like rent, electricity, food and medicines. This means that people living in a vulnerable economic position all too easily face situations where they simply cannot afford to buy enough healthy, good quality food once they have paid for all the other essentials (e.g., Riches, 1997a, p. 10; Poppendieck, 1998, p. 57).

Finland is the only Nordic welfare state that has participated, since 1996, in the European Union's Food Distribution Programme for the Most Deprived Persons of the Community (MDP) and where the basic security of its most vulnerable people is regularly supplemented by food provided by charities. The MDP, in place since 1987, was phased out at the end of 2013. A new replacement fund, the Fund for European Aid to the Most Deprived, as well as a new programme have been established and the statutes regulating the delivery of food aid came into effect at the beginning of July, 2014.

The delivery of emergency food aid and its silent acceptance disconnects Finland from the Nordic ideal of universalism, which has traditionally been an essential principle of the Nordic welfare regime. The ethos of Nordic welfare refers to the public responsibilities of society towards its citizens, based on a strong democracy and a determination to reduce poverty, inequality and vulnerability, in keeping with constitutional pledges for equality and constitutional recognition of basic rights of all the citizens, explicated in the spirit of universalism (Hänninen, 2010).

The resources diverted to food aid are, thus far, minuscule compared to the share of social and health expenditure in the national budget and, hence, in monetary terms food aid is only a minor factor undermining the foundations of the Nordic regime compared, for example, to a declining and increasingly unequal public health care system. The symbolic value, however, of neglecting to satisfy a basic human need such as nutrition is immense and undeniable. This chapter focuses on the emergence and entrenchment of food charity as a means of poor relief in Finland. The reasons for the growing demand for food aid, as well as explanations for the entrenchment or rather normalizing of food aid distribution, are explored. Hunger as a matter of charity and the possibility of the commercialization or corporatization of food aid are then considered. The 'right to food' (RTF) perspective is explored in relation to the complex but disconnected policies relating to food, agriculture, commerce, environment and social welfare. The chapter concludes by summarizing the Finnish case and outlining possible lines for future development.

History of Finnish food aid

The modern need for emergency food aid occurred in Finland in the midst of an exceptionally deep economic recession during the early 1990s. According to a study of the health impacts of the economic recession, 100,000 Finnish people (3.2 per cent of the population over

15 years) experienced an extreme situation where 'the fridge was empty and there was no money to buy food' (Kontula and Koskela, 1993). The first reactions to that information were typically disbelief and passivity. For example, the Finnish media only showed an interest in the issue when the results of a study and some photographs and news reports showing ever-lengthening breadlines outside the Salvation Army in Helsinki were published in Sweden and Austria. Even then, the concern was not the distress of the people in need, but the country's lost reputation abroad, specifically as a result of the reportage but not the policies that had given rise to the food poverty.

Politicians likewise showed no interest in the political circumstances surrounding hunger. The primary reaction was simply to deny the problem. The results of the study and headlines in the media were labelled as exaggerated; the hunger of Finnish people was nullified by comparing it with famines in the developing world or the problem was ignored by claiming that the supply of free food in the breadlines inevitably created demand. Where the hunger problem was recognized, the reason for the situation was eagerly attributed to the hungry people themselves. They were stigmatized as the new helpless, the new poor or as excessively indebted. By using these concepts, it was hinted that the reason for food insecurity or actual hunger was undoubtedly the fault of the individual – some personal qualities or individual behaviour. By contrast, possible defects in the social security system were not put under any serious examination (Karjalainen, 2008).

The first charitable food distributor and still the biggest actor in the field was the Evangelical Lutheran Church of Finland (ELCF) in Myllypuro, Helsinki, which organized food relief with the help of voluntary workers in 1993. The phenomenon is referred to by way of its most practical function – the breadline. The first food bank was initiated two years later by the ELCF in Tampere. At the time that city's unemployment rate was nearly 25 per cent and many ordinary people and families had been driven into serious economic distress.

Originally, food aid was meant to be a temporary emergency relief during a deep recession. Social workers within the ELCF thought that the reaction to the acute emergency by the state and municipalities was too slow and that the Christian voluntary work community would be able to meet the immediate needs of people sooner than the public sector. Nobody, however, thought at the time that public responsibility for the most vulnerable people in society would be permanently delegated to the third sector (Malkavaara, 2002). As the brochure of the food banks said: 'The food bank is a bank that should not exist. It is a cry for help.

The operation will be shut down as soon as hunger ends.' The founding father of the first food bank later described charitable food aid as 'the open wound of social policy'.

After initial hesitation and significant disbelief, the media admitted the existence of the hunger problem in 1994. It was recognized that the level of income support was too low to sustain an adequate living. Yet, in the same breath it was declared that the state could not afford to increase social security funding, even if the state economy was already recovering. In this situation, the media recommended the direct delivery of charitable food aid as the principal solution to the hunger problem. Charity, again, was mainly seen as the task of churches and NGOs.

In other words the overall picture in the media was more or less contradictory, as the breadlines and food banks were also seen as a matter of shame and in conflict with the Finnish welfare model (Karjalainen, 2008). In retrospect, even if the inconsistency between food charity and the Nordic welfare regime was identified, there was no serious public debate or political dispute over the direction of future welfare policy in Finland. In the end, the media saw fit not to call out charitable food aid in the spirit of the Nordic welfare ethos by asking the public sector to take back its responsibility for the most vulnerable. On the contrary, the issue of food aid was little by little relegated to the realm of charity.

The problem, as emphasized by Riches (1997a), is that when food insecurity and hunger are at once seen as part of the mission of the third sector, it is very difficult to reverse. In the Finnish media there was a discrepancy, with charitable food aid presented as an illegitimate form of social security for the Nordic welfare state but, at the same time, legitimate for churches. This inconsistent interpretation has become established among the media, political actors and the ELCF, hardly ever having been challenged. Accepting charitable food provisioning as a solution to hunger, nevertheless, weakens the understanding of food insecurity as a political question. This kind of reconstruction of hunger gives politicians the possibility to avoid acting on their constitutional responsibilities or even having to take a strong political stand on the problem. In other words, it allows the state to 'silently' avoid taking responsibility for guaranteeing the basic security of the most vulnerable.

Food aid hit the headlines again in 1996, when the first shipment of EU food aid (MDP) was received in Finland. The acceptance of MDP was an epochal decision. It was the first decision signed by the Government of the time – the wide-based coalition Government lead by the social democratic Prime Minister – concerning the hunger problem (Karjalainen, 2008). In hindsight, it is easy to conclude that this decision resulted in, or at least precipitated, the entrenchment of food aid delivery as a mission of churches and NGOs. EU food aid became the basic stock for the distributed food of many congregations and associations, who performed the actual delivery. At the time there were no nationwide, regular, large scale corporate food donations from retailers or whole-salers. Thus, it is fair to say that the decision to accept MDP, in fact, solidified and institutionalized third-sector food aid delivery in Finland. In the context of social policy it is interesting that the decision was made by the Minister of Agriculture and Forestry as a part of the EU's Common Agricultural Policy (CAP) (Ohisalo, 2013).

In the public debate, food aid has barely divided opinion. In general, the media had positive attitudes towards the relief work and regarded food banks as necessary. The theme was complemented by discussions regarding whether the distribution had been organized appropriately and whether the recipients were treated with respect. Some doubts were expressed however as to how real the hunger in Finland was and if there was even a misuse of the aid. Churches and NGOs were presented as responsible for recognizing possible misuse and for targeting aid to those who really needed it. Food banks were managed and run somewhat 'neutrally' in respect of public acceptance, though the biggest actor, the reliably viewed ELCF, was seen to meet an urgent need and even to be under some public pressure to do so. The media presented no misgivings whatsoever about the withdrawal of society or the dismantling of the welfare state, although the responsibilities of public authorities were pointed out while not being strongly pursued (Heikkilä and Karjalainen, 1998).

Active role of the ELCF

In 1997 hunger was still being publicly debated. The ELCF appointed a broad-based working group, the Church Hunger Group, which comprised experts from the ELCF, universities, NGOs, municipalities and the National Research and Development Centre for Welfare and Health as well as representatives of the six biggest political parties in Finland. Its aim was to raise poverty permanently back onto the political agenda and to encourage politicians to pursue social policies as a remedy. The message was that eradicating poverty was a matter of public morality (Malkavaara, 2002).

The Hunger Group also aspired to bring about a national consensus in order to solve the poverty problem. The political message was presented in public institutional arenas, increasing the visibility of the hunger problem. Despite the word-for-word incorporation of the Hunger Group's petition in the Government's agenda in 1999, practical policy making took place elsewhere and the Hunger Group could only wait for the outcomes of political processes. When the Hunger Group completed its work in 2002, in spite of petitions and political promises, deep poverty and hunger remained unaddressed through active policies in Finland.

When it comes to questions of poverty and social exclusion, the ELCF has remained constantly active. Previously in 2011, the archbishop Kari Mäkinen established a new broad-based expert group, the Church Poverty Group. The goal of the group was, once again, to demand that the eradication of poverty is taken forward as a key issue of public policy. Poverty and hunger as social evils seem to drop off the political agenda time and again unless there is strong and continuous public pressure.

The economic recession, as deep as it was, was over by the end of the 1990s, while during the first years of the new millennium economic growth in Finland was strong. However, the social policy practiced during the slump had radically weakened the social security of those people living in the most vulnerable positions; and during the period of strong growth which followed, no remarkable improvements were introduced. Consequently, income inequality between socio-economic groups grew substantially. Measured by Gini coefficient, income differentials increased from 22.2% in 1995 to 28.5% in 2011.

With the Finnish welfare state unable or unwilling to take care of the hunger problem, the ELCF, other Christian organizations and associations for the unemployed became the biggest distributors of food charity (Mavi, 2012b). In 2012, half of the congregations or parish unions delivered food aid. Many of the clients are nowadays dependent on charity food – so much so that according to the Church Resource Agency (CRA) they would starve without it (Pajunen, 2012). Thus, there is justification in saying that during the last 15 years, food aid that was originally meant to be temporary emergency relief during a deep recession has become established as a regular way to fix the leaks in the social safety net of the Finnish welfare state. Significantly, a remarkable share of the responsibility for taking care of the most vulnerable in society has been transferred to the ELCF and NGOs. According to oral testimonies of charity workers there have even been some cases of diversion of clients from the public sector to charities.

This development has sparked disagreement within the ELCF. Some parishioners worry that food aid legitimizes the ideology of charitable poor relief and, hence, encourages the transfer of responsibility from the public to the third sector (Kuvaja, 2002, p. 17), thereby alienating Finland from the essential Nordic values of welfare universalism and equality. It leads to a situation that has been dominant for example in North America: more and more disadvantaged people depend on the church and charity organizations when, at the same time, governments refuse to admit the hunger problem or refuse to engage adequately in concrete action to eradicate it (Riches, 1997a; Poppendieck, 1998). Yet, the ELCF emphasizes it cannot give up distributing food aid before the public sector resumes its responsibility for those people in need. Abandoning the most vulnerable is not, after all, an acceptable option.

In 2012, the European Union contributed EUR 500 million to the MDP. Finland's share was 1.1 per cent, equating to EUR 2.9 million. In 2012, MDP aid was accepted by 20 out of the 27 member countries and Finland was, again, the only Nordic welfare state to receive MDP aid (Mavi, 2012a). In the context of the Nordic regime it is notable that the emergence and entrenchment of charitable food aid in Finland seems to follow, in outline, the development in North America, but ten years later.

The growing need for food aid was triggered by the deep economic recession in the early 1990s. Due to austerity measures, basic security and minimum supplementary benefits for the most disadvantaged were cut or frozen during the recession period. When the costs of living began to rise, poor people could no longer afford all the necessities of life. Again, the first to react to this distress were church organizations. Within the ELCF, the primary understanding of the situation was that the need for emergency food was triggered by an exceptionally deep but temporary recession that would soon pass. Food charity was not considered a sustainable solution for the problem. In spite of that, in Finland as well as in Canada, many clients are nowadays dependent on food aid and in the USA more than 10 per cent of the nation's population receive food aid.

Timely official statistics on the numbers of people in Finland who received food aid and the reasons for this are not available. Nevertheless, the ELCF has produced some figures of its own food delivery. However, reliable time series as well as assessment of the Church's capacity to address effectively the hunger problem are missing. In 2012 most of the charity food was distributed to families with several children. Also low-income pensioners as well as people with mental problems or substance abuse problems are in continuous need of help. Students and immigrants make up other growing groups of clients.

The greatest amount of aid was delivered in Eastern and Northern Finland, where access to food is becoming more difficult or even unfeasible for many elderly people as well as for people without a car and driver's licence, due to the closure of village shops and, hence, ever-lengthening distances to fetch groceries. In these cases, church social workers often distribute food bags in conjunction with home visits (CRA, 2013). Unlike in other parts of the world where food charity aid is disproportionately more often distributed to indigenous peoples, Sami-people in Finland are not among the most vulnerable or the most in need of constant food charity.

Food charity and corporatizing of food aid

In Finland there are no central charitable organizations as seen for example in the USA (Feeding America) or Canada (Food Banks Canada) that coordinate food aid nationally. In addition to churches and unemployment associations the Finnish Central Association for Mental Health, the Mannerheim League for Child Welfare (the largest child welfare organization in Finland) as well as some smaller operators deliver MDP aid (Mavi, 2012b).

In general, charitable food aid is organized in three different ways: distributors who deliver only EU-food, usually bags of dry food; those who provide both EU-food and donated food; and those whose aid is made up of completely donated food. The last group of deliverers is small and, obviously, totally dependent on donations, which come from retailers, food processors and wholesalers. Less if any comes directly from farms. In addition, some distributors offer strongly subsidized low-cost meals prepared from EU-food, donations and some complementary foodstuffs bought on the market. The price of the meals that contain EU-food is set by the Ministry of Agriculture and Forestry (MAF) at a maximum of EUR 1.70.

Between 1996–2013 MDP was regulated nationally and coordinated by the Agency of Rural Affairs (Mavi) and controlled by Finnish Customs. Mavi, however, has no jurisdiction over donated food. Thus, concrete practices and contracts between the charities and the donors vary individually. For this reason, there are no statistics or other information on donors or donations concerning who the donors are; how much food or what other goods or commodities they donate; and what kind of attitudes they have towards charity or the motives behind their donations.

Even if charitable food aid is nowadays the final resort for welfare security for many vulnerable people, at least thus far, donating food has not been commercialized or corporatized in Finland as it has in many other countries. In Finnish grocery markets the distribution of food is dominated by a strong oligopoly. There are two retail chains – the S-Group chain and the Kesko Group – who control 80 per cent of grocery trade. The S-Group chain is a co-operative market actor and its attitude towards donating food for food aid deliveries is unclear. The Kesko Group chain, again, is a franchise of retail entrepreneurs and willingness to donate is up to individual storeowners. Nevertheless, some food is donated from both camps, but actions are not systematically coordinated or lead by the central corporations. With a few exceptions, the representatives of agriculture, food processing and retail have not to date wanted to see themselves profiled as donors. According to the food aid distributors, their donors prefer to stay anonymous.

Until recently, charitable food donations have, arguably, not had an unconditionally positive image nor are they seen to promote a reputation for having good standards of corporate social responsibility (CSR). In the state administration, responsibility for promoting CSR rests with the administrative sector of the Ministry of Employment and the Economy (MEE) which has declined to take an authoritative stand on food aid. The Finnish Government's policy on CSR is built upon organizations taking responsibility for their impacts on society. However, food aid is not seen as part of CSR and donating food is not encouraged through tax deductions.

The reasons behind the lack of interest in donating food are probably both cultural and political. As a Lutheran country, there is no strong cultural tradition of charity, voluntary work or, for example, begging or almsgiving in Finland. Instead, people still trust and believe in broad public responsibility, while the Nordic welfare state model has received strong political endorsement. On the other hand, the popularity of a different kind of 'American-style' charity campaign – visibly supported by celebrities – is increasing and in the wake of this positive image, some shop owners have attracted publicity in the media by presenting themselves as 'hero shopkeepers' who donate expired food for hungry people. At the same time, the Finnish Food Safety Authority is loosening the regulations governing expired food stocks donated by grocery stores to charities. In the future, charities will be allowed to freeze donated food on the expiry date or, on the day after offer it as a warm meal. The motive behind the new regulations is food waste prevention with the change receiving a favourable spotlight. With media support these changes suggest a shift in public opinion.

Uncoordinated policies and the right to food

When examining who eventually benefits from food aid, it is necessary to analyse the political and economic activity behind the donating of food and its distribution, since these activities require the availability of surplus or expired food on the one hand and a need for emergency food aid on the other. As Ziegler et al. (2011, p. 4) sharply observe, 'Hunger is not a question of fate, it is man-made'. What is missing in the Finnish context is a coherent national food policy (e.g., Lang et al., 2009) as well as public discussion about the right to food (RTF). However, according to Constitution 19 §, paragraph 1, 'those who cannot obtain the means necessary for a life of dignity have the right to receive indispensable subsistence and care'. Thus, the RTF is recognized in Finnish legislation as is the fact that eradicating hunger and food insecurity is a legal obligation, not a preference based on benevolence.

Food aid in Finland should be understood as a node that connects the typically separate policies of agriculture, commerce, environmental and social welfare. In the quarter century 1987–2012, the EU through the MDP programme bought up agricultural over-production to balance market fluctuations. In practice, this meant managing the entry of agricultural products to the market through buying up products by way of 'intervention stocks' when prices fell below a certain level. This over-production was later delivered as food aid by taking certain products, for example, milk powder, butter or grain out of the intervention stocks and directing them to the MDP. If sometimes there was not a large enough surplus in food stocks, it was also possible to buy some products on the market directly to be distributed as food aid (Mavi, 2010). In this way publicly funded emergency food aid came to be used as a kind of safety valve for the global food marketing system. However, reforms to the CAP together with food price increases on international markets are expected to mean that agricultural commodity markets in the EU will stay balanced without the need for market intervention. Without intervention stocks the MDP as a part of the CAP has lost the rationale underpinning it and, thus, it will be discontinued after 2013.

The MDP was not integral to social or poverty reduction policy, but rather a part of CAP and, therefore, classified as a marketing support. Under these circumstances the MDP aid was directly tied to trade policy. Finland joined the EU in 1995 and accepted MDP aid for the first time in 1996. The EU, however, has no mandate whatsoever to regulate the national social policies of the member states. Hence, during the period 1996–2013, social policy and governance of EU food aid belonged to different domains of administrative responsibility. Poverty relief fell within the remit of the MSAH, whereas MDP – as a part of CAP – was within the remit of the MAF. There was no cooperation or coordination of food aid between the ministries responsible for social affairs and health and for agriculture.

According to Poppendieck (2000b) allocation of significant amounts of surplus food to intervention stocks will in itself generate public programmes for distributing over-production to needy people. Decisions in agriculture and trade, hence, create the foundation for the over-production and intervention stocks. Poor people, again, are needed to get rid of the over-production in legitimate and politically correct ways (Tarasuk and Eakin, 2003). Yet, when food prices are not allowed to fall below politically agreed levels, even in situations of over-production, the price of food stays at a high level which in turn tends to drive people into a vulnerable situation of needing food charity.

It is clear that in Finland decisions regarding food aid are made in the name of agricultural and trade policies, posing particular challenges for social policy. According to the MSAH, as a Nordic welfare state Finland should not accept or even need the MDP aid. Nevertheless, the Minister of Agriculture and Forestry has annually adopted a resolution to accept it. The Agency of Rural Affairs (Mavi), which governs the MDP, operates directly with the ELCH and the NGOs distributing food aid. The MSAH has totally opted out of the activity. This is because the Ministry does not exercise any mandate in agricultural policy. Although a new Fund for European Aid to the Most Deprived is only in the preparation phase, it is anticipated that the situation will not change in this respect. The new Fund will no longer be governed by CAP, but becomes a part of the EU's Cohesion Policy, wherein it will be administered by the MEE. Consequently, as far as EU food aid is concerned the position of the MSAH will probably remain unchanged.

Environmental policy is inevitably connected to food aid, as the prevailing market-based food systems waste huge amounts of edible food. It is usual that charities delivering food aid have two parallel goals: poor relief and environmental protection. The motto of the European Federation of Food Banks (EFFB) is after all, 'Against hunger and food waste', while the Global Food Banking Network claims that 'food banking is the link between food waste and hunger'. In Finland the level of food waste is moderate by international comparison (Koivupuro et al., 2010, p. 27) but, nevertheless, it is recognized as a problem. Yet, environmentalism as a motive for food aid distribution is usually not clearly expressed. Even so, according to common sense, rescuing edible food from dumping grounds for people in need is the right thing to do and albeit there is no explicit ecological motive, it may be a good additional incentive. Whatever the case, wasting food is not culturally acceptable and awareness of the amounts as well as the environmental impacts of waste is growing. This resonates very well with the efforts of food supervision authorities to cut food waste by directing more expired food from retailers to charities.

However, the solution to the problem of food waste should not be organizing another 'secondary food market' distributing surplus food to vulnerable citizens outside the primary market (Tarasuk, 2001). Instead the primary market and prevailing food system need to be reorganized according to socially and ecologically fair distribution. In rich industrialized countries today, hunger is nothing other than an indication of the unfortunate way the capitalist market fails to meet basic human needs (Poppendieck, 2000b).

Finally, food aid is linked to social and labour policy. During the 1990s Finnish basic security moved away from the Nordic welfare regime model in the direction of the Anglo-Saxon model, entailing more means-testing. This change was partly an outcome of cuts in social security costs but especially at the end of the decade there was an increasingly explicit transformation in national social policy. For example, a new kind of means-tested labour market support was created for the newly unemployed and for people outside the labour market. Work was emphasized to be the best social policy. The position of income support also changed. It became the primary source of basic security for a growing number of people – the number of people on the dole doubled – though it was meant to be merely a supplementary form of social benefit. These changes constituted a clear departure from the Nordic model.

The number of people living on welfare was at its highest in 1996, when about 345,000 households and 610,000 individuals (around 12 per cent of the population) were receiving income support. During the period of economic growth and strengthening employment between 1997 and 2008, the number of claimants decreased, but it has permanently stayed at a higher level than before the recession. Consequently income support, which is usually considered to be a marginal form of social welfare in the Nordic context, has become an essential part of basic security in Finland, at least when measured by the number of beneficiaries.

Also during this time, opinions endorsing increased income inequality with a view to supporting economic growth and international competitiveness were strengthened. This indicated that the power-holders had given up the goal of eradicating poverty and taken on another, more modest social aim, of merely managing it. Under these circumstances, income differentials in Finland increased more than in other OECD countries (Ruotsalainen, 2011), until the last financial crisis affected development in 2009. The most important reasons for increasing income differentials were a taxation policy favouring rich people – those living on profits, dividends, options, interests and other market returns; a permanently, relatively high unemployment rate compared to the years before recession; and a freezing of basic security benefits for more than ten years. Such social policy developments have, inevitably, promoted the need for charitable food aid.

As a result, the income level of people relying on benefits lags significantly behind other Finns, while poverty among benefit recipients has increased (Ahola and Hiilamo, 2013, p. 18). At the same time, price increases in residential costs have run well ahead of the level of housing benefits. During 2011, however, the so-called 'guaranteed pension' for the poorest low-income pensioners came into effect and 2012 saw some increases in basic security benefits. As the first improvements for more than ten years they compensated for only a small part of the existing defects. For example, labour market support, standard housing benefit and income support together are currently failing to ensure a minimum subsistence (THL, 2011). In other words, the lack of sufficient or timely changes in social policy will mean that the social security system will fall further behind in fulfilling its constitutional objectives, including the right to food.

Conclusion

In the framework of the Nordic welfare regime nobody should be left on charity. According to the principle of welfare state universalism, the state is accountable for the social protection of those people who cannot take care of themselves or who lack a sufficiently supportive and resourceful social network of their own. The Nordic perception of welfare has historically obligated the state to shoulder responsibility for reducing poverty and inequalities within society, achieving this through democratically established rights for citizens that align to the principles of equality and universalism (Hänninen, 2010). The acceptance of charitable food aid as an eligible policy for dealing with poverty moves Finland away from the Nordic welfare model. It indicates an unwillingness of society to challenge increasing social inequality, including widening income differentials.

The right to food is a fundamental right. It is further derived from the United Nation's Universal Declaration of Human Rights, which proclaims that all human beings are born free and equal in dignity and rights and everyone has the right to life, liberty and security of person. Sufficient food guaranteeing wellbeing, health and activity is a fundamental prerequisite for human dignity. The right to food is laid out precisely in the ICESCR, which came into effect in Finland in 1976. Commitment to the right to food entails obligations on governments to ensure freedom from hunger. It is fundamentally a question of rights and accountability – and not a basic human need to be fulfilled through charity (Ziegler et al., 2011, p. 20) or commercial expedience by, for example, removing the costs of waste management or regulating prices through intervention stocks. Notwithstanding, in Finland, many of the most disadvantaged individuals who have difficulties in providing for themselves and their families with sufficiently healthy and wholesome food and who cannot do it in socially accepted ways have been left to the mercy of charity work and the third sector.

Delivering emergency food is not a sustainable solution for food insecurity. Instead the circumstances and resources of the most vulnerable should be assessed in a realistic fashion and the supplementary benefits of the most disadvantaged should be increased to meet their needs. The foremost reason for the demand for food aid is deepening inequality and poverty. Refurbishing basic income security is the right solution for poverty as it ensures the capacity for people to feed themselves in dignity. If the ability of the individual to provide food is weakened because of substance abuse or mental health problems, access to treatment and services should be available to tackle those problems and hence also improve food security. Recently the Government raised the minimum subsistence level of the most vulnerable through benefit increases. The change was a good start but certainly not enough to displace the food banks, a situation that simply should not exist in a Nordic welfare society.

As Ziegler et al. (2011, p. 20) emphasize, 'the obligation to fulfil the right to food imposes duties to the state, such as the duty to promote redistributive taxation and social security'. As noted before, according to the Finnish Constitution 19 §, paragraph 1, 'those who cannot obtain the means necessary for a life of dignity have the right to receive indispensable subsistence and care'. According to the legally authoritative interpretation, this indispensable subsistence and care to ensure a life of dignity should be understood as a subjective right. Consequently, to allow situations where people, who lack sufficient security of living or whose ultimate income support is insufficient, are required to rely on charitable food aid is a violation of not only the right to food but also the Finnish Constitution.

During the last couple of years there has been a lively discussion about increasing social inequality and widening income differentials in Finland. In the shadow of this discussion, hard-core poverty and long-term unemployment have been allowed to increase. A growing band of Finnish people have had to turn to food aid. At the moment there is some confusion about the future of EU food aid for deprived persons in the community. An ambiguous situation like this could offer the third sector the possibility to withdraw from distributing food aid by seeking to pass the responsibility for the people living in the most vulnerable positions back to the state and municipalities.

So far there are no signs of this kind of strategy. On the contrary, the need for food aid is increasing and along with the relaxation of regulations governing the donation of residual food from grocery stores to charities the supply of donated food will, in all probability, increase. In addition, Finland supported the foundation of the new Fund for European Aid to the Most Deprived and decided also to accept the EU aid in the future. It is our understanding that the ELCF will continue as the key actor in the field. This surely inspires new debate on the meaning of food aid within a Christian community.

The most alarming trend, however, is labour market polarization and growing income inequality. As the share of middle income jobs decreased by 12 percent during 1995–2008, the number of high-and low paid jobs increased (Mitrunen, 2013, p. 2). Politicians seem to be powerless and confused in front of the globalizing economy. Some of them even actively demand the creation of a larger low-wage labour market in Finland. Yet, work can only be the best social policy if people have work and they earn a living wage. More low-paid jobs mean increasing poverty and poverty is a guaranteed recipe for feeding the growing need for food aid.

7
Poverty Amid Growth: Post-1997 Hong Kong Food Banks

Kwong-leung Tang, Yu-hong Zhu and Yan-yan Chen

Introduction

Hong Kong is a special administrative region (HKSAR) in China under the framework of 'one country, two systems'. While still being part of Communist China, it retains its capitalist system and enjoys a high degree of autonomy, except in foreign and defence affairs. Hong Kong is economically advanced, enjoying a high rate of sustained growth, industrialization and exports. It is now one of the world's leading international financial centres, characterized by low taxation and free trade.

Comparative data from the United Nations (UN, 2011) show that Hong Kong scores highly on many socio-economic measures, including the human development index (HDI). Hong Kong's HDI value is now on a par with that of industrial countries and far outpaces other Asian countries. It is classified as a high human development country. In 2011, Hong Kong GDP per capita reached an all-time high of US$37,351 (World Bank, 2012).

Despite its economic success, Hong Kong, South Korea, Taiwan and Singapore have been plagued by poverty, increasing income disparities and environmental degradation (Tang, 1996). Further, the public social expenditures of these countries have been too limited to eliminate or have a significant impact on these problems. Since 1997, when British colonial rule in Hong Kong ended, significant improvements have not been made. In the past decades, the poverty problem has worsened and social inequality has soared. Hong Kong's Gini coefficient, an income inequality measure, rose to 0.537 in 2011 from 0.525 in 2001 (Census and Statistics Department, 2012). This is well above the warning line of 0.40 (UN-Habitat, 2008, p. 17). The wealth gap is wider in Hong Kong than in Canada, the United Kingdom, the US, Australia and Singapore, and is probably the worst in the first world. Hong Kong's Gini coefficient is just below the highly unequal African nations.

A number of empirical studies have shown that income disparity brings about heavy social costs. Thus Wilkinson and Pickett (2009) observe that inequality causes shorter, unhealthier and unhappier lives and it destroys relationships between individuals born into different classes in the same society. They further argue that the removal of economic impediments to feeling valued – such as low wages, low benefits and low public spending on education – will cultivate human potential. Their study indicates that reducing inequality leads to a better society. This chapter will reflect upon Hong Kong's poverty in the midst of its prosperity. The authors believe that the rise of food banks shows the willingness of the public to provide food support. The effectiveness of food banking will be examined, followed by local and global remedies towards reducing the problems of hunger and poverty. A public action framework is then proposed as an action guide to bring the poor back into the public policy limelight.

Poverty: a hydra-headed problem

First, there is a long wait for public housing rentals for the needy. Second, there is the existence of 'multiple have-nots', low-income residents who are wait-listed for multiple reliefs from the government. Additionally, public health care in Hong Kong is fraught with problems such as a shortage of doctors, long waits for consultation and non-urgent surgery, and expensive treatment. Finally, recent analyses by scholars and NGOs indicate that the hunger problem of Hong Kong's poor is a grave cause for concern. The number of people using food banks has been rising (Chan, 2012) with the impoverished including children, immigrants, middle-aged, older people and the working poor.

With regard to the severity of poverty, successive Hong Kong governments post-1997 have yet to provide an official estimate of the number of poor people. Adopting a poverty line of living below a monthly income less than half of the median income of all other households of equal size, it is estimated that Hong Kong's poor population collectively increased from 1.12 million persons (403,800 households) in 2003 to 1.17 million persons (451,000 households) in 2012 (Oxfam HK, 2012a), or a poverty rate of about 17.6 per cent. Over the same period, poverty amongst families of low-income workers (with at least one person employed) has worsened. Larger families suffered most and approximately 10 per cent of all working households were found to be poor. Further, 60 per cent of these households were living below the level of the Comprehensive

Social Security Assistance (CSSA) programme – the Government's social assistance scheme – of whom only 9.8 per cent received the benefit.

A study of children from migrant families has found that they are one of the worst hit groups in poverty. More than one-third of the children of families that move to Hong Kong live in poverty (Chou, 2012). In terms of age distribution, the majority of people living below the poverty line are the middle-aged (aged 45–64) (322,000), followed by one-third (288,000) of Hong Kong's elderly (Chan, 2012). They have few opportunities for escaping chronic poverty and Hong Kong lacks a good retirement programme. Finally, poverty amongst youth (aged from 15–24 years) is estimated to be 150,000 people.

Successive post-1997 Hong Kong SAR governments (Tung Administration, 1998–2004; Tsang Administration, 2005–2012) could have done more to relieve poverty but they delayed immediate measures (Goodstadt, 2012). As the current Leung Administration now admits, it has the resources and capacity to do more than its predecessors within the realm of livelihood issues. Significantly, in terms of fiscal reserves, Hong Kong is cash-rich. Government data for 2011 showed fiscal reserves amounting to HK$591 billion. In March of that year the total asset value of the Exchange Fund stood at approximately HK$2.3 trillion. It follows that the unallocated fiscal reserves and the net surplus of the Exchange Fund are about HK$1.2 trillion in total, representing 68.6 per cent of Hong Kong's GDP.

Typically, relief for the poor in Hong Kong has been the responsibility of families, private charities and local organizations. But as conditions have worsened year by year, their combined efforts increasingly have fallen far short of demand. The CSSA covers only 40 per cent of the 1.17 million who are living in poverty. In 2011, CSSA recipients remained constant at 450,000 to 460,000 per month indicating that some 700,000 poor people are slipping through the government safety net. Apart from the CSSA, only limited public housing and small subsidies for children's schooling are available for the poor. The developmental philosophy of the government, both current and colonial, is one of 'big market, small government'. This ideological foundation engenders very limited social welfare spending and is a glaring example of 'distorted development' where social development is secondary to economic development.

Hong Kong developmental state: the ideology of anti-welfare

Many poor people in Hong Kong face a dire emergency, which is paradoxical in a region whose affluence is unquestionable. The underlying reason for this perplexing question lies in the developmental state of Hong Kong and its governance philosophy. Recently, the thesis of the developmental state has been used to understand the nature of welfare provisions in Hong Kong and other Asian Newly Industrializing Countries (Tang and Midgley, 2002). Essentially, the developmental state thesis argues that these Asian states strive to restrain social spending to modest levels, giving priority to social investment projects that facilitate economic growth (education, health and vocational training) in order to enhance their competitive advantages. When possible, public spending is set below 20 per cent of the GDP.

This thesis reflects cultural dimensions, including the Confucian notions of respect for the elderly and other values that are embedded in Asian societies, which uphold filial piety, self-reliance and familial duty. Additionally, Asian political values and systems are dominated by authoritarianism and conservatism. Likewise, civil society in these societies is more receptive to state patriarchy and state-society coopera- tion championed by elites in power. Social rights are accorded secondary status when compared with political and civil rights. All in all, the inter- play of such forces generates welfare systems whose standards lag behind their level of economic development.

The espousal of a free market, capitalist approach to development has been accompanied by an official disdain for the welfare state (Hodge, 1980; Goodstadt, 2009). This sentiment is widely shared amongst busi- ness people. Along with this school of thought, economic trickle-down was embraced by the government, leaving Hong Kong's social welfare spending at Third World standards. However, in Hong Kong's history, social service spending has mostly been the colonial government's response to crises (Goodstadt, 2012; Wilding, 2007).

Before the onset of the 1997 financial crisis, Tung assumed office as the first Chief Executive of the HKSAR and outlined his 'brave new era'. Essentially, his approach to social policy was paternal. However, his visions were hampered by a wave of crises and he resigned in 2005. The subsequent Tsang Administration strongly believed in neo- liberalism. Since the gradual upturn in the economy after 2005, Tsang belittled and neglected social welfare, showing little appreciation for the concepts of social justice and social integration (Tang, 2011). His raiding of homeless shelters in 2011 showed his contempt for the poor. Without warning, the Tsang Administration raided dwellings under a flyover and threw away the personal belongings of the people living there. It was only after nine months of legal battles that the new Leung Administration accepted an out-of-court settlement, with a small compensatory payment to the victims. It is remarkable that Hong Kong could so flagrantly violate human rights considerations in dealing with the most vulnerable.

Despite its impressive economic achievements, Hong Kong's colonial governments and their successors have never formulated coherent social policies or created comprehensive social welfare programmes. When compared to Japan, Taiwan and South Korea, there is a far lower level of social protection in Hong Kong and Singapore. If a higher standard is used, social protection levels are found to be well below the standards of Western countries (Jacobs, 2000).

Currently, except for education (22.9 per cent), which absorbs the largest share of total government spending, other social services constitute smaller slices: welfare (17.8 per cent); health (15.9 per cent) and housing (0.09 per cent). The percentage of welfare spending has increased slightly while education, health and housing expenditures have remained almost steady. The recent increase in welfare is attributed to the new means-tested, old-age allowance introduced in 2012. Hong Kong's revenues are little threatened by the low base of its public social spending. As of 2009, the proportion of total public spending on health and welfare as a percentage of the GDP has been lower than that in most developed economies. In short, there is an overwhelming case for improving government support for all areas of social services. For instance, Hong Kong needs a social security system that is commensurate with its economic development.

Hunger and food banking

Hunger problems are confirmed in a large-scale study undertaken by Oxfam Hong Kong in 2011 based on interviews conducted with 600 poor households with children aged 15 or younger (Oxfam HK, 2011b). It found that 45.9 per cent of all poor households were food insecure in Hong Kong. It estimated that one in six poor households with children were in a state of high food insecurity as they frequently could not afford to acquire enough food to meet their basic needs.

Given rampant inflation occurring in the past few years, the poor have been affected much more than the rich. Low-income families spent a significant portion of their income on food (40 per cent) compared to Hong Kong's highest income bracket (21 per cent). Eating household leftovers or expired food was a last-ditch strategy that poor people used to cope with surging food prices. In the study, 63 per cent of the respondents chose to 'eat a bowl of soup for 2 days and a dish for several meals', and 25 per cent of respondents even indicated that they were 'eating one less meal a day'.

Such a food crisis threatens people's health, especially children: some 40 per cent of parents reported that their income was insufficient to feed their children a balanced diet; 38 per cent could only buy a few types of low-cost foods for their children; and 26 per cent of the respondents opined that their children did not eat enough. Moreover, 72 per cent of respondents reported that their children ate leftover foods, while 15 per cent ate nearly or already expired foods. The situation was worse in CSSA households, in which 82 per cent of children ate leftovers, on average, nearly four times a week.

Food bank origins

The first food bank in Hong Kong was established in 1998 as a result of the 1997 Asian financial crisis and the widespread poverty which lingered on. South Korea likewise initiated food banks at this time as did Taiwan following the 2008 recession (Wang and Lyu, 2013). In contrast, Singapore introduced food banks more recently, with assistance from the Global Foodbanking Network. Their main issue has been the elimination of food waste. The motto of Food Bank Singapore is illustrative: 'Don't bin it when you can still eat it'.

Similar to Singapore and Taiwan, in 2010 and 2012 China established food banks which are now scattered across the country. They are found in the cities of Shenzhen, Wuhan and Guilin, all run by NGOs with their food supplies coming from individual or local-corporate donations. The Shenzhen food bank (Fangcaodi, 2012) receives funding from the city government, covering only social work services. The Wuhan Agape Foodbank (2010) is probably the first food bank in China collecting and distributing food to the poor. Their key difference lies in the provision of social services (counselling, group work and training) to the food recipients on top of food aid. The rise of private food banks demonstrates the vitality of civil society and its sensitivity to local needs. In contrast, city government is slow to react. Further, international food corporations like Heinz have shown their generosity to China in more recent years. However, their food is normally destined for disaster relief or poor regions, not food banks.

In South Korea, the programme started as a pilot in January 1998. It was originally initiated by private organizations such as the Anglican Church of Korea as a way to share food with the poor. Beginning in 1998, the government helped the programme by providing facilities and equipment and funding operating costs (Kim, 2010). In 2006, the *Act to Promote Food Donations* was passed.

A different development path has been taken in Hong Kong, where the private sector is encouraged to feed the hungry. In sum, as in South Korea, this was very much crisis-driven. Since 2007–2008 the HK government has provided small subsidies to five food banks, under the supervision of the Social Welfare Department (SWD, 2012). Importantly, as Wong (2003) has suggested, the surge in demand for free food 'reflects service gaps and flaws in the welfare network'. Initially food banking was detached from the prevention of food waste (i.e., recycling) though the work of Feeding Hong Kong (FHK) has changed this. It is the first food bank distributing surplus food from local and global corporations and redistributing it to needy people. Its task is to fight hunger and reduce the amount of food waste. FHK is affiliated to the Global Foodbanking Network and its executive director has received training from their Leadership Institute on how to create and run a new food bank system.

Charitable food banks abound in Hong Kong, making it difficult to estimate their total recipients. The Hong Kong Council of Social Service (HKCSS) reports 21 charities and community groups providing direct food banking at 170 service points across the city (cited in Chan, 2012). This excludes organizations that act as middlemen, such as the Foodlink Foundation, which collects surplus food from hotels and food and beverage outlets for delivery to shelters and the needy. Thus the HKCSS estimate is likely too conservative. Unlike South Korea, there has been no legislative attempt to promote the food bank programme.

Charitable and publicly-funded food banks

Many Hong Kong citizens are influenced by the beliefs of Taoism and Buddhism. These religions cherish almsgiving and charity. Almsgiving is not restricted to the rich or those with means; it can come from small acts of charity work – from deeds, words and thoughts. Apart from the five publicly-funded food banks, there are a number of self-financing food banks, community canteens and recycling kitchens run by welfare NGOs or private organizations. The scale and missions of these projects are quite diverse. Some aim to help the poor, whereas others are operated to generate value from surplus food or food waste. Some are run on a Hong Kong-wide basis, while others strive to serve a small population in their local district.

Though many of the food banks have links to big corporations for food or money donations, such as Pret, Kellogg's and Ayam, the degree of corporatization is gradual. According to our estimate of ten food banks, they each average 21 corporate partners. Whilst the Daily Meal Network, run by the five government food banks, is publicly funded, some of these food banks also have corporate partners which support their own food funds that are not backed by the government. For example, there are two food assistance programmes running at the same time in the Kwun Tong Methodist Social Service. One is The Daily Meal Network, with the other having its own food fund.

As expected, the five publicly-funded food banks face more stringent guidelines. Needy applicants are strictly means-tested. Other limiting factors, both private and public, constrain food distribution. Food banks can only distribute dry rather than fresh food such as eggs or fruit, which require storage in fridges. Thus they have begun handing out vouchers for the needy to obtain fresh foods from local markets because of the limitation of dry food. This also addresses the problem of limited storage space. Additionally, canned food is found not to be nutritious, so recipients make their own choices with vouchers. Since 2009, the publicly-funded food banks have been increasing the variety of food available and providing fresh food. Some charitable food banks have partnered with local restaurants and convenience stores to offer hot dishes to those who are unable to cook as well.

Some unreasonable restrictions have been placed on recipients of the public food banks. One has first to apply through the NGOs or social workers in order to receive assistance. Food is normally supplied for up to six continuous weeks with each application. For the publicly-funded food banks, recipients can apply for a one-time extension of an additional six weeks. They are then able to apply again after a waiting period of six months. Those in receipt of government social security are not eligible to apply. Notably the coverage of beneficiaries has been severely limited. From February 2009 to January 2011, only 43,827 people received assistance from food banks, which is less than 4 per cent of the 1.17 million people in Hong Kong living in poverty (Oxfam HK, 2011b).

Effectiveness of food banks

Internationally, controversy surrounds charitable food bank services. As they are being institutionalized, governments have ignored the right to food for all. Corporations, reaping tax advantages, could dispose of their surplus in ways which would not accommodate the needs of the poor. Their operation largely relies on volunteers.

However, in Hong Kong, supporters of food banks are many including charitable agencies and food recipients who positively comment on their role in alleviating hunger with the provision of nutritious food (HKCSS, 2012). Money saved from food expenses is spent on medical and family purposes. Recipients have positive feedback about their experiences (i.e., making friends, breaking exclusion and accessing other social services) at the food banks. The charitable agency running one private food bank (Baptist Oi Kwan Social Service) hopes to widen its scope and target more people in need. Other agencies share this sentiment and would like food banks to be fully funded by the government.

In our research, all local food bank workers expressed the essentiality of food provision services, but they were aware that this was only a short-term solution to poverty. At the same time, all agencies running food banks valued their secondary services such as counselling and social networking, amongst others. Since poverty is related to social exclusion or weakened human capital, factors like enhancing social networking and personal skills are regarded as important indicators of the effectiveness of food bank services.

Solutions to hunger

Given widespread poverty and inequities, no one panacea exists. This discussion of remedies is intellectually stimulated by Drèze and Sen's (1989) consideration of the role of public action in addressing hunger. It is deemed as important to poverty alleviation and it means more than the action of the state. It includes the actions of social movements, NGOs, political parties and the justice work of churches. It embraces two types of activities: 'collaborative' and 'adversarial.' The first involves collaboration with government programmes, while the second emphasizes public demands on the government and alternative policies. They both highlight the importance of public participation. We argue that both types of action have to be adopted by advocates in the case of Hong Kong. Both actions need to be used shrewdly by advocates and NGOs and they must be able to work inside and outside the political system. Importantly, from their research, it is worth noting that the activities of the state could easily deteriorate in the absence of public vigilance and activism.

At the international level, innovative remedies to food insecurity have been advanced by activists and academics, and four ideas for addressing food insecurity in Hong Kong are examined: food sovereignty, engagement with UN monitoring bodies, the individual complaints procedure and re-establishing the right to food for all.

Food sovereignty

Reinventing food policies to counter the globalization of agribusiness, an influential idea is food sovereignty or people's right to decide what they eat and what they produce. The focus is on producing healthy food for local markets, creating jobs and protecting the land and its diversity. The idea is relevant to some countries, but the concept is not applicable to this city state because of its heavy dependence on China for food supplies and in light of dwindling agricultural land and the number of farmers in Hong Kong.

Engagement with human rights monitoring bodies

Immediately prior to 1997, China advised the UN that the *International Covenant on Economic, Social and Cultural Rights* (ICESCR) would continue to be applicable to Hong Kong. At the hand-over of Hong Kong to Chinese sovereignty, China assumed reporting obligations under the ICESCR which it had signed in 1997 and ratified in 2001. By requirement, China's report to the UN was filed in 2003. Lee (2007) notes that the government's emphasis on the realization of economic and social rights as an overriding priority induced China's ratification whilst being aware that the degree of enjoyment of certain rights has not reached the requirements of the ICESCR. There is much to do to combat poverty and environmental damage. But this report shows the confidence that has come from the last 20 years of reforms to the economy.

The Hong Kong Government faces a different reality given its massive social needs and huge reserves. The HKSAR's report under the ICESCR was submitted to the UN as part of China's report. In the 2004 report to the UN, the Monitoring Committee expressed concern about court decisions describing the rights in the Covenant as 'promotional' or 'aspirational' rather than justiciable human rights, noting that 'such opinions are based on a mistaken understanding of the legal obligations arising from the Covenant,' and the Committee urged the government to cease from advancing this argument before courts.

There is potential in using UN treaty monitoring bodies to strengthen domestic social rights practice. This is the platform that allows advocates to articulate the important rights claims and have them considered in the light of international human rights law. The right to food is embodied in Article 11 (the right to an adequate standard of living) and it obligates Hong Kong to implement social rights. This could serve as a benchmark for a rights-based framework for public policy options to achieve food security.

Contrary to official optimism, NGOs and rights activists have submitted their shadow reports to expose the severity of hunger and poverty in Hong Kong. They have to work on different fronts simultaneously. According to their experiences, political advocacy will be strengthened by judicial actions and vice versa. Such an interplay would enhance public education. Likewise, domestic rights advocacy may be advanced by work in the international arena, which in turn needs to be informed by community advocacy.

Working within the parameters of the international legal regime is a critical part of an anti-poverty strategy on the part of social workers (Ife, 2008; Midgley, 1997). The use of international law does influence anti-poverty movements, providing avenues of justice for victims of social inequality. Social workers would become human rights workers at both the local and global levels, promoting the cause of vulnerable groups through their governments and the UN (Hick, 2007). Effectively, the HKCSS arranged for the concerned committee members of the UN Committee on Economic, Social and Cultural Rights to have a first-hand account of the poverty situation and social rights development by visiting Hong Kong prior to their review of the government report.

Individual complaints procedure (ICP)

The advantage of making an individual complaint is that one who believes one's rights have been violated has an opportunity to receive a determination from an international expert body and an entitlement to a remedy. The use of an ICP, including the right to food, as an avenue of redress for human right violations has a long history. The ICP under some human rights conventions has generated some successful cases of complaint against forms of discrimination such as gender and race (Tang, 2000). Any individual or group of individuals can lodge a complaint alleging a violation of all or any rights recognized in the ICESCR provided their government has ratified the Optional Protocol-ICESCR, which China has not.

However, some legal scholars, like Dennis and Stewart (2004), argue against such an international mechanism. First, they doubt the ICESCR Committee's ability to shoulder the responsibility to presume an adjudicative function. They further hold that some economic and social rights, which may be domestically justiciable, should not be considered because there is no convincing evidence that an international adjudicative body would have a better understanding of the relevant economic, demographic and statistical data than the government concerned.

Establishing the right to food

Kong (2009) argues that a right to food under international and national laws has been narrowly interpreted. The obligation of non-discrimination in existing international human rights treaties, which recognizes the right to food, focuses only on formal equality or special treatment to particular groups. There is no positive duty on the part of government to guarantee equality to food access.

According to Kong, the *Voluntary Guidelines* are most relevant to the right to food as these soft laws include much broader obligations on states than the ICESCR and *General Comment No. 12*. They reaffirm the indivisibility of all human rights and recognize the interdependence between civil and political rights and the right to food. They take into account a wide range of important principles, including equality and non-discrimination, participation and inclusion and accountability and the rule of law.

In the long run, the broader approach to the right to food in the form of a Code of Conduct and a Right to Food Convention should be adopted (Windfuhr, 2006; Kong, 2009). This supports the mainstreaming of equality as participation to re-conceptualize the right to food. In many countries like Hong Kong or India, one key reason for hunger lies in social and economic inequality which is the real obstacle to food security. Kong's argument is that social stratification blocks the equal and free distribution of economic and social resources and the means to access food. Inequality and discrimination cause this social stratification. The right to food should serve to break the wall of inequality through reconceptualizing equality by using the notions of participation and empowerment of the disadvantaged. At the state level, relevant policies are suggested.

Clearly, this approach requires social and political structures to be changed to eliminate obstacles to the participation of all people in the structures (Kimber, 1996). Importantly, the HKSAR Administration has a duty to provide for those who cannot access their minimum and essential food needs and to monitor how much of the budget is allocated each year to progressively realize socio-economic rights. There is much value in legislating the socio-economic rights more thoroughly, which helps in shaping public policy making and values (Kong, 2013).

Collaborative action at the local level

Over the years, local rights activities and NGOs in Hong Kong have used collaborative action to advance the cause of the hungry. They recently accepted an invitation to join the re-established Commission on Poverty and the Long Term Housing Strategy Steering Committee. They have used large-scale surveys to alert the public to the plight of the poor. They have also given their support to the new old-age means-tested living allowance. Regionally, the HKCSS and Second Harvest Asia (Japan) co-organized Asia's first Food Bank Forum in 2012, which included representatives from Korea, Malaysia, Singapore and the Philippines, to discuss the ways that food banking addressed hunger.

Globally, important lessons are drawn from food bank development in First World countries (Riches, 1997a): collaboration involves educating the media and food bank recipients on the cause of hunger and poverty; launching challenges at the local level against the demonizing of welfare recipients and the fallacy of neo-liberalism; building effective links between welfare, health, environmental and development education sectors at both the international and local levels; and making government accountable to international covenants monitoring committees. Additionally, coalition building by progressive bodies is the sine qua non of successful public action.

Meanwhile, some local Hong Kong solutions to the problems of poverty and hunger have emanated from food banks and NGOs, which call for a reconfiguration of food bank services. The five publicly-funded NGOs on food assistance maintain that every person is entitled to sufficient and nutritious food to meet their dietary needs and food preferences in order to live an active and healthy life. In light of this, the government should provide a meal allowance for low-income workers and immediately increase the meal allowance for children. Also, food bank services should be improved, including increasing the variety.

At the same time, Oxfam HK (2012b) has put forth a set of comprehensive policies as necessary to help working poor families escape from poverty, including establishing a poverty line and setting specific poverty reduction targets. They also suggest exploring the feasibility of implementing a low-income family allowance for the working poor as a supplementary provision to the minimum wage as well as urging the government annually to review and adjust the level of the minimum wage.

For the poor, the need for food often intertwines with housing needs that are not being addressed by the government which should double its current targets of 15,000 flats each year (Oxfam HK, 2011a). To lessen the burden on poor families, short-term rental allowances are being advocated as well as increasing the maximum level of the rent allowance under the CSSA scheme. Oxfam has also urged the government to adopt a new Earned Income Tax Credit system based on the US model (2011a, 2011b).

Adversarial politics

A successful case showing the operation of adversarial politics in civil rights could have implications for advancing the right to food in Hong Kong. Lessons can be learned from a recent Hong Kong protest organized by younger people against the introduction of 'national education' pro-Beijing propaganda into school curricula (Bradsher, 2012). In 2012, over 120,000 people (students, parents, teachers, grassroots and advocacy groups) protested against the programme, calling it 'brainwashing'. This set off huge demonstrations, sit-ins and hunger strikes at the Hong Kong government's headquarters. After fierce protests, the new Administration finally backed down. Remarkably, the key organizers were secondary school students organizing themselves through Facebook and other Internet communications. However, such confrontational politics is likely to be ineffective in exerting pressure on the government to adopt new policies that would realize the fulfilment of social rights for all. A recent example can be found in the failure of the use of filibustering by the radical democrats to prevent the passage of the Budget Bill to campaign for a universal old-age pension.

Conclusion

The challenges of hunger, poverty and inequities in Hong Kong are daunting. Judging from the *2013 Policy Address* of the Administration, the absence of long-term measures to resolve the poverty issue is worrisome (Mullany and Bradsher, 2013). This worry assumed greater reality after the Budget Speech 2013, with its long list of one-off subsidies for the poor and aging but lacking comprehensive long-term planning (Bradsher, 2013). Dowler and O'Connor (2012) caution that anti-poverty strategies are often implemented without monitoring for effects on food outcomes. Thus scant evidence exists even for First World nations in meeting their right to food obligations. Inevitably, continuing collaborative and adversarial actions with and against the government for anti-poverty policies are essential.

In this respect, Sen (2004, p. 356) reminds us of the need for conceptual clarity on the part of human rights and the richness of practice:

It is important to note that the conceptual understanding of human rights, in turn, can benefit substantially from considering the reasoning that moves the activists and the range and effectiveness of practical actions they undertake, including recognition, monitoring and agitation, in addition to legislation. Not only is conceptual clarity important for practice, the richness of practice...is also critically relevant for understanding the concept and reach of human rights. There is...no great deficit in the balance of trade between theory and practice.

8
Privatizing the Right to Food: Aotearoa/New Zealand

Michael O'Brien

Introduction

Aotearoa/New Zealand is a significant food exporter, a role which extends back for almost a century and a half since the introduction of refrigerated shipping in the late 19th century. The early exporting was primarily to the United Kingdom and it was the entry of the UK into the EEC in the 1960s which promoted significant reworking of the New Zealand economy as the guaranteed market, which existed at that time, disappeared. Farmers were significantly subsidized through a guaranteed prices scheme which operated for most primary products. The removal of those subsidies in the late 1980s was accompanied by the introduction of a neo-liberal framework into the country's social and economic policies (Kelsey, 1995).

The last two decades have seen substantial growth in New Zealand's export of milk and associated products into China and the increasing internationalization of those products through the creation of a multinational company, Fonterra, which is the world's largest dairy exporter (Fonterra, 2013). Primary products remain the core of the New Zealand economy, constituting 70 per cent of exports. Twenty five per cent of exports are milk powder, butter and cheese (Statistics New Zealand, 2013). It is, then, both ironic and tragic that food insecurity, hunger, the growth of food banks (all of which are provided on a charitable basis) and welfare grants for food have been major elements in the changing New Zealand social and welfare framework over the last two decades.

This chapter will explore these elements in the context of both New Zealand's changing economy and the human rights framework. In particular, it will examine the relationship between neo-liberal reforms and food insecurity by referencing data on the country's growing inequality and increasing poverty since the mid-1980s; the growth of food insecurity; and associated welfare measures related to hunger, nutrition and food insecurity. It will also consider welfare reforms throughout this period, focusing especially on the changing role of the state and changing relationships between the state, the family NGOs and the corporate sector in relation to economic and social wellbeing and social development. The chapter begins with a brief overview of inequality and poverty statistics, charting changes in welfare provision since the late 1990s. It then concentrates on food insecurity and related data, including the growth of food banks, locating this discussion within a framework of changing welfare relationships and welfare reform. The chapter concludes with a reflection on rights-based possibilities for change, consistent with the country's ICESR obligations. Significantly, New Zealand does not have a formal or official definition of food security.

Growing inequality, poverty and welfare reform

Any discussion of food security, hunger and nutritional inadequacy in New Zealand needs to be placed within the framework of growing inequality and poverty which has shaped so much economic and social policy in this country over the last 25 years. Income inequality has grown faster in New Zealand than in any other country since the late 1980s, with the possible exception of the United Kingdom (Perry, 2012).

Poverty has also increased substantially, irrespective of whether an income or living standards measure is adopted; New Zealand does not have an official poverty line. As is the international experience, both the widening income gap and growing poverty have not fallen evenly. Māori (the country's indigenous people), Pacific peoples, sole parent families and social security beneficiaries have borne the brunt of their impact. Retired people have not experienced such a heavy impact from the growth of inequality and poverty which, at 7 per cent (Perry, 2012) is significantly lower than for the other groups identified here.

A significant contributing cause of growing inequality and poverty has been the reforms to social security since the benefit cuts in 1991 and the subsequent failure by governments to increase benefit rates, other than regular increases reflecting changes in the Consumer Price Index (CPI). In brief, benefits (other than superannuation for pensioners) were cut by up to 20 per cent in 1991 (Stephens, 1992). As Mackay (1995) notes, significant growth in food banks occurred following the benefit cuts. Concerns about food security, food adequacy and hunger have become increasingly prominent in the subsequent decades. Since 2009 the welfare reform process has gathered further momentum, with the National-led government tightening benefit eligibility and entitlement and introducing a strong, almost exclusive, focus on participation in paid work as the basis for social security benefits.

The framework for the changes is set out by the Welfare Working Group (WWG) established by the government in 2010 to undertake a comprehensive review of New Zealand's welfare system. The WWG was asked to address three questions: reduction of long-term welfare dependency, welfare structures and incentives and whether the system was achieving the outcomes desired by taxpayers taking sustainability, fairness, access and improved social outcomes into account. The group was also asked 'to consider the fit of the current system with a flexible labour market and the modern roles and responsibilities within families'. It was explicitly instructed not to consider New Zealand superannuation, the tax-benefit interface, tax credits or income adequacy. Chaired by a former Commerce Commission Chair, 'dependency' framed the Group's work as is reflected in the title of its final report 'Reducing Long-Term Benefit Dependency' (WWG, 2011). Although the subsequent legislation has not followed its recommendations completely, the differences are minimal and not significant for the purposes of this discussion. This brief background provides the critical context for the discussion below on nutrition and hunger.

Nutrition, hunger and food expenditure

A range of research work has shown the extent and nature of hunger and food insecurity in New Zealand over the last two decades. Most of this work has been undertaken in academia, either directly or as part of wider research projects on nutritional standards. The national nutritional study undertaken by the University of Otago and the Ministry of Health (UOMH, 2011) gives a comprehensive overview of what is happening in New Zealand families. It shows that 'based on responses to a series of eight statements, 59.1 per cent of households were classified as being *Fully/almost food secure*, 33.7 per cent were classified as being *Moderately food secure*, and 7.3 per cent were classified as having *Low food security*. From 1997 to 2008/2009 the proportion of households classified as having *Low food security* increased for males (1.6 per cent to 5.6 per cent) and females (3.8 per cent to 8.8 per cent)' (UOMH, 2011, p. xxxii, italics in original).

Unsurprisingly, the rates were higher for more deprived areas. Households in these areas were five times more likely to report using food banks or food grants than those in more affluent areas. Approximately 20 per cent of those surveyed reported sometimes feeling stressed because of not having enough food, having less variety in their diets, eating less because of not having enough money and were five times more likely to report running out of food than those in more affluent areas. Sixteen per cent of the sample reported that they were only able to eat properly sometimes, while 80 per cent reported that they were always able to eat properly (UOMH, 2011).

Statistics New Zealand household food expenditure food data shows, *inter alia*, that for lower income groups, food expenditure constitutes a higher proportion of their budget than for the highest income group, although the actual expenditure is smaller in dollar terms. This applies even more strongly for those whose source of income is superannuation or a benefit, with food constituting, respectively, 21 per cent and 20 per cent of their expenditure, compared with 17 per cent for wage and salary earners (Statistics New Zealand, 2013). In order to gain some appreciation of how the living costs faced by a typical low-income household are changing, the Salvation Army's policy unit has developed a simple alternative measure known as the 'low income household living cost index', in which 'sub-categories are re-weighted to more closely reflect the spending patterns of a low income household'. The report notes that over the five years to December 2012, the cumulative change in the CPI was 12.7 per cent while the change in the low-income household index was 14.2 per cent (Johnson, 2013, p. 47).

In light of this different pattern of expenditure, changes in food prices have a more significant effect for lower income households than they do for more affluent households. Using different family structure and income scenarios, the Regional Public Health report (RPH, 2011) shows that households on low incomes needed to spend between 23–52 per cent of their income on food if they were to provide a basic healthy diet, using current nutritional standards. The consequence, they argue, is that these families are likely to spend less on food than is required and therefore they are at greater risk of obesity and nutritionally related diseases (see also Cox and Black, 2012). Taking up the issue of affordability of nutritious food, Hopgood et al., (2010, p. 251) show that 'providing diets for children that are nutritionally appropriate requires on average 33 per cent of the child related component of New Zealand Government provisions for low socio-economic families in 2007'. Calculating the cost of food for different family scenarios led the authors to argue that: 'low-income families in New Zealand need to spend a proportion of their income on food for children that is large by international comparison' (Hopgood et al., 2010, p. 256). Repeating the pattern in these studies, a study of 136 households for the Families Commission (Smith et al., 2010) noted that: 'the factor with the most impact on food security for New Zealand families included in this survey was economic'.

Almost half of the households in the low-income group of 38 families reported that food 'often' or 'sometimes' ran out because of a lack of money. Approximately 40 per cent of households experienced moderate and low food security, with 10 per cent experiencing low food security. The lowest-income group had the highest rate of food insecurity with 82 per cent of households with a low income stating that the variety of food they ate was 'often' or 'sometimes' limited by a lack of money. Highlighting the stress on families facing food insecurity, the report concludes its discussion as follows:

> It is reasonable to conclude that the greatest cause of food insecurity for New Zealand families included in this survey was economic in origin. For those families receiving a government benefit, in particular, food insecurity was predominant. Clearly, to enhance food security, relaxation of economic constraints in these households needs to occur. The social and economic determinants of food insecurity, such as income, housing and the cost of food must be considered in any interventions to address this issue. (Smith et al., 2010, p. 32)

In the context of food expenditure patterns, obesity, including child obesity, has been the subject of considerable public and professional attention over the last decade, with commentators noting that low-income households are more likely to buy less nutritional food because that food is cheaper and bulkier and therefore children in those households are less likely to feel hungry. This is in large part because highly processed, poor quality, calorie dense food is relatively satisfying when compared to fresh fruit and vegetables, and relatively cheap when compared to good quality protein (Wynd, 2011, p. 4).

Goulding et al. (2007) report that extreme obesity is more prevalent in the poorest areas and is significantly more likely amongst Māori and Pacific children than amongst Pakeha (non-indigenous New Zealanders) and other children, while adult females (but not males) are more likely to be obese or overweight than those in the least deprived areas (Russell et al., 1999; Smith et al., 2010).

The overall picture from the research work is consistent. Food insecurity and the financial inability to provide adequately for their household is a significant issue for a remarkable number of low-income households.

Their inadequate and inconsistent diets generate stress for these house-holds and are important contributors to higher rates of obesity. Māori and Pacific families are significantly over-represented amongst these households.

Responding to hunger

The evidence summarized and reviewed in the preceding discussion clearly identifies significant concerns about food security and the human right to adequate food as reflected in New Zealand's ratifica-tion of the ICESCR in 1978. What then has been the response? As is to be expected, given the neo-liberal frames which have dominated policy over the last three decades, individual responsibility, limited direct government involvement (with a strong focus on management and surveillance) and an emphasis on charitable and corporate provision, articulated frequently around a theme of partnership, have been the central features of New Zealand's responses to the evidence and experi-ence of growing hunger. While largely discussed separately below for reasons of clarity, these components are, of course, interconnected, a relationship which is considered at the end of the chapter.

Government: limited, managing and monitoring

Reflecting the welfare changes noted above, one of the important elements of government response has been the growth of hardship and Special Needs Grants, payments for which both beneficiaries and the low paid are eligible. Despite the tightening of the rules for eligibility, the number of payments increased significantly between 2007 and 2011, with food grants more than doubling from 272,514 in 2006/2007 to 553,854 in 2010/2011 (MSD, 2012, p. 142). The maximum available assistance was last increased in 2008. Rules around providing food grants have also been tightened with applicants being limited to a maximum of three grants annually and requests for assistance being met on the condition that applicants undertake budgeting advice. Budgeting serv-ices have reported delays of some weeks in making appointments for this purpose because of the increased demand on their services. The budgeting requirement means that beneficiaries and the working poor are being positioned in New Zealand as poor managers and 'bludgers'. Consequently, benefit inadequacy and poverty do not then need to be addressed.

The welfare reforms following the work of the WWG have included the introduction of government controls on food expenditure of some beneficiaries. The WWG had recommended the use of payment cards in particular circumstances and controls over the finances of teen parent beneficiaries under 18 years of age. The subsequent legislative changes in provision affecting these two groups included the introduction of cards for the purchase of food as part of the benefit provision. That is, part of the weekly benefit payment for these beneficiaries includes a card to be used in the supermarkets for food purchases with limits on what can be purchased. Fifty dollars in cash is given to the young person while the rest of the benefit payment is loaded onto the payment card, reducing the amount of cash over which the beneficiary has discretionary control. Young people are required to undertake a budgeting course as a condition for receipt of the youth support payment. The government argued that it was simply providing young people with the additional supports they need to develop the skills to become independent (Hansard, 2012a).

Payment cards were a response to articulated concerns that beneficiaries were not spending their money properly, resulting in particular in child hunger amongst beneficiary children. It might be argued that government action reflected a right to food for the children of beneficiaries. However, the coverage was limited to the groups mentioned above and not extended to other beneficiaries with children, despite the suggestion of the WWG that it could be used to help people on welfare 'who are at risk or have demonstrated they are unable to manage their resources without intensive help' (WWG, 2011, p. 124). The payment card is, then, part of government control of beneficiaries and their lives, rather than reflecting any commitment to the right to food security and adequacy.

Thus far there has been no evaluation of these cards and their effects. While in some respects they function as debit cards in that purchases from approved suppliers are debited against the card, the fact that they can only be used at approved stores and cannot be used for some purchases such as tobacco and alcohol, means that they discriminate against young people who will be readily identified as beneficiaries simply by presenting the card when they make a purchase. They represent a reduction in rights for these beneficiaries whose lives are subject to tight controls by the not-for-profit organization which manages the benefits and the state bureaucracy which oversees them. It is clear that the limited and managerial nature of government responses have been accompanied by, and to some extent built on, the contributions of charities (predominantly through food banks) and corporations.

Charities and corporations

While conceptually, organizationally and legally distinct, there are important connections between charities and corporations in responding to food insecurity. The relationships between the two are multi-faceted. For some food banks, for example, there is no relationship with goods being donated directly by individuals while for other larger entities there is an important connection as these food banks receive some of the food which they provide from corporate food suppliers with other food supplies being donated by individuals and/or church parishes. Further, as the discussion below indicates, some corporations supply goods directly to schools through 'community partnerships' with this model being drawn on by government in its recent decision on food in schools. The multifaceted nature of the relationship makes a simple discussion of roles and contributions impossible. Hence, the role of charities is first explored followed by a discussion on corporations, connecting the two where appropriate.

Food banks

Turning initially to food banks, these now have an entrenched place in New Zealand's social service and welfare provision. As Uttley (1997) shows, they have developed significantly since the benefit cuts in 1991. Their development reflects a turn away from citizenship rights to an adequate income, reflected in part in the development of social security in New Zealand (O'Brien, 2013). That right is replaced by an increasing reliance on charity, reinforced by the stigma of 'not managing money properly' and the demeaning experience of seeking assistance, undermining the very nature of being a responsible human, namely providing food for oneself and one's dependents. Public policy, including non-policy, and practice has implicitly encouraged charitable responses. Food security and the right to food have in many important respects been undermined by the growth and institutionalization of food banks.

Food insecurity creates significant dilemmas for charitable social services. On the one hand they are faced with responding to significant and basic human need while at the same time their existence and support through the food banks reduces the pressures on government to improve incomes and engage with income distribution and poverty issues. The dilemma was acute in the late 1990s when there was a proposal that food banks should strike in order to demonstrate their concern with poverty and state failure. The proposal did not proceed, in part because of these dilemmas.

Precise numbers using food banks are impossible to ascertain effectively: data is not consistently gathered; different requirements and policies in relation to eligibility for assistance apply; there is no system for gathering information about those who may seek assistance from more than one food bank; and there is no national data collection and collation. There is no national organization of food banks although some larger ones supply food to smaller entities. Food bank use is at best a proxy for food insecurity but it does provide a very useful indicator.

Compounding the data gathering difficulties is the diversity of food banks, which range from small local services to large regional and national organizations. Despite the lack of comprehensive aggregate data, NGO agencies which provide and support food banks continue to report growing use. For example, the Salvation Army which operates the largest national network of food banks, reports that demand increased dramatically between 2007 and 2010 with the volume of parcels increasing from just over 6,000 in December 2007 to almost 14,000 five years later. In 2012 its network provided 54,600 parcels to almost 28,000 families (Johnson, 2013). Some food banks also report a changing pattern of use, with an increasing number of requests for assistance from those in paid work, ironic given the emphasis on paid work as the core of social policy for beneficiaries.

When there is not enough money for food, families are left with little choice but to access food charities. The significance of sudden changes in family circumstances – unemployment, sickness, accident, debt, family violence, family death – as important influences shaping the use of food banks, has been noted as well as a local media observation that: 'many don't come until the last minute because they don't want to admit that they can't cope as they struggle to keep things together in tight times' (Cox and Black, 2012, p. 10). It has been observed that this sense of shame about seeking assistance has at times led to people going without food or creating debt by seeking assistance from loan sharks, frequently at very high interest rates and creating a sense of social exclusion and marginalization (McNeill, 2011).

Reflecting the ways in which food bank use stems from and is associated with issues of poverty, inequality and disadvantage, Wynd (2005) identifies inadequate income, housing and fuel costs, debt, childcare costs, medical and health costs and gambling as significant factors. Similar factors were noted by the New Zealand Council of Christian Social Services (NZCCSS) in its review of a four-year project gathering data from seven church social service agencies. Food bank clients, they noted: 'have a mix of issues and circumstances – from women in poverty, struggling sole parent families, single people in poverty, Māori in poverty, low wage incomes, inadequate income for those who receive a benefit' (NZCCSS, 2005, p. 61). Reflecting, *inter alia*, the data on household spending on food, social service providers have suggested that one of the factors in the increasing pattern of food bank use is that food is a discretionary item in household budgets. Accommodation costs and power have no flexibility: they have to be paid and food costs then form the major discretionary item with households treating the food bank as an alternative source of supply.

In its overview, the NZCCSS noted (contrary to some other experiences) that there had been some decline in demand at the agencies over the four years of the project, with most of the participants being beneficiaries (a benefit being their only source of income) and half or more of the households having children. Over 60 per cent of those interviewed were spending more than 30 per cent of their net income on food. Debt, especially debt to Work and Income (the government agency responsible for benefit payment and administration), was a dominant feature for many of those requesting a food parcel. Many special needs and hardship 'grants' are provided as a loan or benefit advance which has to be repaid.

In her work on food banks in Christchurch, undertaken before the devastating earthquakes of 2010 and 2011, McPherson (2006) also notes lack of income, household bills and unaffordable housing, along with personal considerations in relation to management of finances, as factors contributing to food bank use in that city. Single males and low-income workers were also important users. The research found clear geographical associations between neighbourhood deprivation and food insecurity, with those living in more deprived neighbourhoods more likely to use a food bank, although there was also significant use amongst those in less deprived areas. Tellingly, McPherson concludes that 'Several key groups were not utilising the food bank at a rate to be expected... As one social service manager noted about some of the people in need that they never see: ... *they would rather die than use a food bank.* This implies that, as a whole, food bank clients cannot always be taken to be representative of the most deprived and food-insecure members of the community.'

Furthermore, she notes that more than 75 per cent of the participants in her research were seeking assistance on more than one occasion 'enduring longer-term food insecurity'.

What, then, has the governments' response been to the growth and development of food banks? The Labour/Alliance government (1999–2008) established a food bank strategy, with the Minister of Social Development stating that he wanted to see them go out of business. However, no consistent or coherent strategy was ever published to show how this was to happen and the growth and development of food banks has received little effective attention from government. There has been no subsequent government attention given to the role of food banks. Rather, government policy and practice has been to refer applicants to them directly, implicitly reinforcing their role.

Food in schools

As noted above, children's nutrition and child hunger have been important considerations in the debates around food security, and the right to food has featured strongly in much of the discussion and many of the reports. A significant area of public and policy attention has been the possibility of developing a national programme for food in schools, with breakfast and/or lunch programmes receiving considerable attention. This has been recommended by the Expert Advisory Group on Solutions to Child Poverty (EAG, 2012), established by the Children's Commissioner to review the available evidence and provide recommendations to reduce the levels of child poverty in New Zealand.

Unlike many other OECD countries, New Zealand has no planned or systematic school meals programme. Further reflecting the reliance on charity and voluntary effort rather than a right to food, a number of schools have developed their own programmes, using whatever local resources and funding they can secure. A Waikato study (Cox and Black, 2012) estimated that in decile one and two schools (schools in the poorest communities) in that region, approximately 25 per cent of children were coming to school with some degree of food need and approximately 75 per cent of these schools were running a breakfast programme. One particular programme, KickStart, provided breakfast programmes in 72 of the 139 decile one to four schools in the region. Supported by Fonterra and a breakfast cereal maker, Sanitarium (discussed further below), KickStart provides 40,000 free breakfasts one to two mornings per week to children in these schools. Drawing on what it describes as a 'community partnership model', schools provide the facilities and the staffing.

As noted almost universally in discussions on these school programmes, the Waikato report (Cox and Black, 2012) commented that schools struggle with certainty and continuity in having the volunteers available to support the programmes. Both the Waikato report and Wynd's (2011) work emphasized the importance of a comprehensive approach to school food provision including nutritional and educational dimensions as part of the total approach. While noting the health advantages, it was the educational advantages that the EAG drew on to support its argument for the government initiative referred to above.

Another school-based food programme is delivered by the registered charity KidsCan which coordinates a number of programmes that support children, including the 'Food for Kids' Programme. A range of food – including bread, spreads, fruit pottles (yoghurt and fruit salad in plastic containers), muesli bars and spaghetti – is provided to over 23,000 children over the course of a week in 276 schools (planned to increase to 405 schools in 2014). The organization lists significant government and corporate entities as its sponsoring partners. The charitable focus is reflected in their mission statement: 'To meet the physical and nutritional needs of Kiwi kids less fortunate than others so they can be more engaged in their education and have a better chance of reaching their potential in life' (KidsCan, 2013). Wynd's (2011) research, KickStart and KidsCan all argue that breakfast programmes make a difference to children's health and learning and improve school attendance.

Importantly, reflecting the 'charity' dimension which some potential participants experienced as stigmatizing, the Waikato study reported some non-attendance, quoting one teacher aide who commented: 'Some children have been told (by parents) that they are not allowed to come to the breakfast. There is a stigma' (Cox and Black, 2012, p. 19), with the report referring to children being kept at home because their parents were unable to feed them. McNeill (2011) made similar observations. All of these illustrations point to the risks of relying on a discretionary or charitable approach in ensuring that children are adequately fed.

Corporations

Examples above highlight a growing dimension in responses to food insecurity, namely the role of corporations in supporting charities and/ or in providing food directly. Fonterra has announced a plan to eventually extend its current milk distribution scheme to all New Zealand primary (year one to year six) schools and, as noted above, charities such as KidsCan highlight the role of corporations in supporting their work. Corporate welfare and charitable welfare have become inseparable partners.

Reflecting the connection with corporations some large food banks have been exploring the possibility of a formal partnership with corporate food providers to guarantee food availability. As illustrated below, government lauds this as part of its response to poverty. However, in this way universal human rights, which promote the interests and needs of all citizens, are weakened and replaced by a partialized philanthropy or by corporations lauded, ironically, as good corporate citizens.

The reliance on corporate and charitable responses and the limited government response to the lack of food security were clearly illustrated in the government's decision in June 2013 to support the expansion of school food programmes. The two major companies currently involved in providing breakfast in schools (Fonterra and Sanitarium) are to be financially supported by government to extend their work to all decile one and two schools, with government meeting half the costs ($500,000) of the expansion. The public relations value of this to the companies is significant. It is able to position itself as a good citizen but food security is treated as a commodity, not as a human right. Government is seen to be acting but only in a narrow and limited way. In the same statement, the Government announced further support for KidsCan, allowing it to expand its charitable work in schools.

This reliance on corporate and/or charitable responses is the antithesis of a human rights approach to food security. While their contributions are for the time being gratefully accepted by recipients, neither are based on recipient rights. The goal for corporations is to advance their business profitability and engagement with food provision needs to be consistent with that goal. Significantly, for example, Fonterra's description of its work with schools talks of 'making sure Kiwi kids benefit from the goodness of dairy' (Fonterra, 2013). Corporate citizenship (a term often used in this context) does not provide assistance as a right. It is a contribution which in this instance has been allowed and used by Government as an alternative to comprehensive public action to reduce food insecurity.

Reliance on corporations and on charities, even if topped up by government financial assistance cannot be a substitute for a human rights framework. If a corporation's financial circumstances deteriorate or strategic directions change, then it will not sustain its interest and involvement, as illustrated in the supermarket example below. Charitable responses too are constrained by factors such as limited resources, availability of personnel, geographical coverage and strategic directions, all of which inevitably mean that assistance is provided based on criteria decided by the agency and not on the basis of universal human rights for all citizens. Despite their best intentions and aspirations, charitable organizations cannot guarantee the universal rights to food security of all citizens across New Zealand. This can only be guaranteed by active state participation, informed by human rights.

Future prospects: the right to food?

Neo-liberal constructions of the role of the state and neo-liberal approaches to state welfare provision and programmes have become strongly entrenched. In such a climate, extending citizenship rights, particularly to the hungry children of beneficiaries, is an anathema. Rather, a focus on individual responsibility, with an emphasis on individuals choosing a life of poverty, is likely to continue to dominate public discourse and policy making. This focus will be reinforced by emphasizing charitable and corporate involvement and residual state participation. The human right to adequate food and food security will, undoubtedly, continue to be articulated, especially by many of those individuals and groups committed to children's development and well-being. However, individual responsibility, with charitable support and provision and corporate engagement, is likely to continue as the dominant approach. In this climate, the prospects for reducing hunger and increasing food security remain weak. When the state has adopted neo-liberal public policies, the citizen has been transformed from a citizen into a consumer who is expected to exercise choice; in that transformation, rights have been replaced by charity.

While rights-based arguments have been well advanced by many of those engaged in research around food adequacy (Wynd, 2011; Cox and Black, 2012), the health and educational advantages of children being well nourished, supported by the corporate food charity model, are more likely to be the dominant discourse and to influence policy decisions. Such an approach fits with the targeting, partnership approach adopted by government and is reflected in the June 2013 decision on food in schools referred to above. The failure of such an approach was well illustrated in 2012 when a programme run by Countdown, a major supermarket chain, and the international charity, Red Cross, closed because the supermarket withdrew sponsorship. Only the state is able to guarantee funds and resources and to ensure that these are available to all, reducing stigma and widening coverage. Wynd (2011) estimates that a universal programme focused on decile one and two schools would cost between $7m and $19m, depending on coverage and whether food is included as a cost.

While much of the focus has been on child hunger, food insecurity and hunger for the adult population is also closely tied to government policy, especially in relation to the levels of poverty experienced by those receiving social security benefits. At the present time, there is no public policy commitment to improving core benefit levels. Current policy directions all point towards paid work as the route out of poverty and, there is little interest in attacking the poverty that lies at the heart of many of the issues of food insecurity. Significantly, in response to a parliamentary question about the government's response to poverty, the Prime Minister lauded the contribution of Fonterra and cited government contribution to KidsCan as evidence of its response, implicitly highlighting the role of charities and the corporate sector and the limited and reducing role for government (Key, 2013).

Food banks and charities are increasingly used by government to, effectively, substitute for government policies which would reduce food insecurity and hunger and are, to a certain extent, caught in the problem. McNeill (2011, p. ii) captures this well when she states that 'the socio-political environment in which formal food support takes place is characterised by the unwillingness of the state to fully realise its role in affirming the right of citizens to be free from hunger. At the same time, there is evidence of a corresponding willingness to delegate provision of food aid to charity based third sector organisations that receive no state funding.'

This raises serious dilemmas for NGOs and the role of food banks, which, as noted above, are now an integral part of the social service network. They have become both publicly and politically accepted, but as McPherson notes (2006, p. 90), writing prior to her appointment to the WWG, food banks 'are *not* a policy option' (Italics in original). The problem of food insecurity and poverty is largely structural; therefore improvements and changes need to be made to the economic and political system that has led to the emergence and growth of food relief from community organisations.

The difficulty they face is the same as that faced by schools providing food to their pupils, namely that not doing so means that those who come to the social service agency or to the school are hungry and the agencies feel a moral obligation to respond to the immediate needs of those with whom they work. In the context of food security, they have a potentially important role in supporting and supplementing state provision but ensuring basic human rights can only be met by comprehensive state provision.

Tragically, given New Zealand's welfare history and food resources, immediate prospects for strengthening the right to adequate food are, then, weak. Undoubtedly, the case for a broader and deeper response, based around the ICESCR and a central role for government in addressing food insecurity will continue to be argued in civil society and by key individuals. Enhancing food security and strengthening the right to food for all citizens can never be achieved by relying on strategies in which charities and the corporate sector are the dominant response. The argument for a universal approach to providing food is well supported by the evidence but the current political environment suggests that translating that case into effective action has a long and difficult road ahead.

9

Between Markets and Masses: Food Assistance and Food Banks in South Africa

Sheryl L Hendriks and Angela McIntyre

Introduction

Although food security is enshrined in South Africa's constitution, the pathways to claiming the right to food are made hazardous by poor coordination between social support and food and agricultural policies. While strides have been made in rolling out social benefits in South Africa, principally in the form of means-tested unconditional cash transfers or social grants (including child grants, disability grants and pensions), these and other arguably transitional measures (such as food parcels, drop-in centres, feeding schemes) fail to keep up with urbanization resulting from rural underinvestment, social decline and intractable unemployment. Moreover, the social and economic repercussions of the HIV/AIDS crisis have been far-reaching, with impacts on food security that are still poorly understood.

Recent food security policy (RSA, 2013) puts forward food safety nets as one of its five pillars, focusing on food assistance in various forms, including cash transfers, subsidized feeding programmes and redistribution of food. It is argued here that such palliative, short-term solutions to hunger fail to address and even exacerbate poverty, inequality and food insecurity where these ultimately result from neglected rural development and a fragmented food policy environment. For the moment, this creates a fertile gap in which the food charity response may grow and thrive for some time to come, under the dual guises of social protection and 'corporate social responsibility' (CSR) and accompanied by a gradual shift towards a more developmental state. The *National Development Plan* (NPC, 2011) illustrates state-led planning through regulation of the economy in an effort to reduce poverty, unemployment and inequality, with the emphasis on '(...) market share rather than profit, economic nationalism, protectionism, technology transfers and the existence of a large, insulated and competent civil service, a weak and subordinate civil society and an alliance between the state, labour and industry' (Dumon, 2012).

Recent history of food poverty

The African National Congress inherited in 1994 a country with inequality deeply entrenched by long-institutionalized racial discrimination, bolstered by spatial segregation that pushed people of colour to the margins of the rapidly-industrializing economy. Under Apartheid, the creation of autonomous tribal homelands relegated so-called 'Bantu' (black African) populations to the agriculturally least-productive areas of the country, where they quickly ceased to compete with English and Afrikaner settler farmers, becoming instead pools of migrant labour for a booming mining industry. The costs of social reproduction of mine labour were thus largely externalized, with the burden falling mainly on rural women.

In contrast, under the old regime, a welfare state for whites existed, both guaranteeing employment and offering means-tested grants for the poor, elderly and disabled, as well as occupational benefits. Only urban employment as migrant workers linked black Africans to retirement pensions and other limited benefits, reflecting the emerging power of black trade unions. Under Apartheid, 'less civilized' rural people were considered to have more basic needs and access to social support arising from 'traditional' extended family networks, even though the black homelands were incapable of supporting adequate subsistence farming, effectively making most of the black African population dependent on migrant labour for income (Van den Berg, 1997). Former Bantustans still contain the poorest and most food insecure districts in South Africa, with the highest HIV prevalence and lowest employment continuing to make the greatest contributions to urban migration. Urban migrants often have no guarantees of employment in cities, no guarantees of housing and little social support, effectively falling into the rift of urban-rural inequality.

Sevenhuijsen et al., (2003) argue that social welfare in South Africa has yet to move beyond an obsolete familialist ethic of social assistance, retaining 'an outspoken communitarian influence at play, stressing the family in the community (read women) as the primary location of care, which is potentially reinforced by invoking the principle of "Ubuntu"' (*human kindness* [author]) and 'elegated to the separate, private sphere of "households" and "families"'. Within this existing ethic, she argues, '[women] should be supported in their caring roles without the gender divisions in care being questioned in the light of gender justice or of promoting caregiving as an aspect of the quality of men's lives' (Sevenhuijsen et al., 2003). Children and the elderly are constructed as beneficiaries of care in either functional or dysfunctional families, ignoring the fact that many elderly people and children are sometimes, in modern, HIV-afflicted South Africa, principle caregivers.

Women make up the majority of South Africa's poor and economically marginalized, a point which Bentley (2004) argues further, suggesting that patriarchy's new guises under the democratic constitution – cloaked behind respect for cultural diversity, for example – perpetuate feminized poverty, especially where so-called traditional rule is strong. In many ways, the costs of social reproduction in South Africa remain externalized, both economically and constitutionally, to be borne by poor rural women, who are frequently deprived of rights to own land, access credit and technical support if not as someone's daughter, sister or wife (McFadden, 2001). Gender inequality contributes to the stagnation of rural economies, as does the HIV/AIDS epidemic. De Waal and Whiteside (2003) propose a 'new variant of famine', linked to HIV/AIDS, that has driven a regional food crisis, involving four interrelated factors, including household labour shortages brought on by adult morbidity and an increased number of dependents; the loss of skills and assets with adult mortality; high burdens of care created by sick adults and orphaned children and vicious interactions between HIV and malnutrition.

Prevalence of food insecurity

Classified as a middle-income country, South Africa is the worst performer in this category, with the highest income inequality, lowest human development index, lowest real growth and lowest growth per capita amongst its peers (Dumon, 2012). The evidence suggests that an unacceptably large proportion of the population suffers from food insecurity; 21.5 per cent of households (approximately ten million people) experienced difficulty in accessing adequate food in 2012 (StatsSA, 2013). These are typically the unemployed, infirm and those with disabilities (including people living with HIV, who are eligible for disability grants), children and the elderly who live in poverty, child-headed households, migrants from neighbouring countries, indigent people, those in remote areas and farm workers.

However, the proportion of households that reported experiencing hunger has reduced over time, with 11.5 per cent of households (just over

5 million people) surveyed through the annual *General Household Survey* in 2011 (StatsSA, 2012). While data on undernutrition is scant and irregularly collected, three national surveys conducted in 1999, 2005 and 2013 (Labadarios et al., 2005, 2011; Shisana, 2013) show that levels of child undernourishment in South Africa are exceptionally high for a middle-income nation and, in fact, child malnutrition (indicated by stunting, severe stunting, severe wasting and severe underweight) has increased since 2005. In view of publication date of 2014, one in four children were stunted and one in ten were underweight (Shisana et al., 2013).

Close to 16 million of just over 50 million people in the country receive social grants. This accounts for 3.4 per cent of the Gross Domestic Product (NTSARS, 2011). While social grants have significantly improved the living conditions of the poorest sectors of society by mitigating poverty, the grants are inadequate to actually lift households out of poverty (Financial and Fiscal Commission, 2013). To complement these, various national and provincial programmes including agricultural (smallholder development, input supply) and school (feeding schemes and early childhood development) programmes have also been initiated. These are aimed at supporting poor households – primarily grant recipients and those who qualify to be grant recipients but are unable to access support.

Many of these programmes amount to food charity. While some are funded through CSR programmes by major food retailers (e.g., Pick n Pay, Massmart and Woolworths), global food corporations (e.g., Unilever and Nestlé) and others through international (e.g., OXFAM and Save the Children) and national NGOs, the vast majority are implemented directly by government with public funds or through NGOs supported by public funds. One such agency, established in 2007, is FoodBank SA (FBSA), a non-profit organization, subsidized by public funds with operations in six of South Africa's nine provinces. FBSA is a member of the US based Global Foodbank Network (GFN), which has been advising on the development of a national food banking system in South Africa (Warshawsky, 2011).

Food assistance programmes

Food assistance is one of five pillars of the National Food and Nutrition Security Policy. It includes the availability of improved nutritional safety nets, including government run and supported nutrition and feeding programmes, emergency food relief, as well as private sector, Community-based Organisation (CBO) and NGO interventions. The other four pillars comprise: nutrition education; local economic development (including the provision or subsidization of inputs and support services for increased food production, as well as more effective food storage and distribution networks); market development (participation of the emerging agricultural sector through public–private partnerships, including off-take and other agreements; a government food purchase programme that supports smallholder farmers); and food security risk management, including research and investment in improving production (RSA, 2013).

Food assistance is essentially domestic food aid. Although not clearly defined in the national policy, it consists of a combination of:

- Public procurement of food distributed through a network of not-for-profit agencies, with several enterprises having sprung up to serve this purpose. These government-accredited agencies are essentially small businesses that cover their salary and distribution costs from government funds. Fresh produce is sourced from small producers through direct contracting as part of the food security promotion strategy.
- CSR programmes that distribute perfectly good food through FBSA as 'charity'. However, such donations are part of a CSR requirement in South Africa that is linked to tax incentives. CSR in South Africa first emerged as a response to the notion that many big businesses supported and thrived under the Apartheid system and therefore bear an additional responsibility to rectify historical disadvantaged. It is tied, under legislation, to Black Economic Empowerment (BEE), and requires companies to spend 3% of their after-tax revenue on social empowerment or charity programmes. With time, most corporations have chosen to use the alternative term 'corporate social investment' (CSI) rather than CSR, with its implicit admission of guilt (Skinner and Mersham, 2008).
- Redistribution of 'rescued' food – these are donations of food that is still edible but past its 'sell by date' but has not yet expired from large supermarket chains such as Pick n Pay and Woolworths.
- Citizen charity programmes run by various groups such as Rotary, religious groups and others that distribute food or host soup kitchens.
- Corporate marketing campaigns that induce customer loyalty in return for donations to charity.

Food charity and public–private partnerships

A number of food assistance programmes are in place in South Africa as part of both the National Development Plan and the National Social

Development Strategy. Apart from institutionalized care centres, public works programmes and the direct and unconditional cash transfer programmes available to pensioners, orphans, foster parents, people with HIV and disability grants, a number of CSR, charity and public–private programmes include food transfers as meals or food parcels through organizations such as:

- Drop-in Centres (for those in need of care including HIV/AIDS multi-purpose centres, street children and after-school care facilities);
- Early Childhood Centers that offer lunch;
- Luncheon clubs – social clubs for the elderly and poor where meals prepared from donated food are offered;
- Meals on Wheels – prepared meals for home-based care recipients;
- Popular restaurants (these were started in Gauteng province in 2013, based on the Brazilian model of subsidized meals and local farmers);
- Social Relief of Distress food parcels for people in emergency situations;
- Soup kitchens, including mobile units; and
- Subsidized food purchased in bulk with government revenue and sold at cost.

FoodBank South Africa: channelling corporate waste?

Oelofse and Nahman (2013) estimate the total food waste per year in South Africa is 9.04 million tonnes. Food retail waste accounts for 17 per cent (or 1.54 million tonnes), a portion of which is channelled by food businesses to food aid distribution. Using FBSA's estimations, this amounts to approximately 513 million meals per year or 1.4 million meals per day.

Other examples of donations to FBSA include:

- Regular corporate donations of food from companies such as Massmart Nestlé, Parmalat, Sunbake Bakeries and Unilever (FBSA 2011a, b, d);
- Rescued food donations from Woolworths, which donates over R250m of rescued food and clothing to needy charities each year (Woolworths, 2013) and Pick n Pay (FBSA, 2011c);
- Publicity-driven marketing such as Pick n Pay's 'Hampers against Hunger' campaign (FBSA, 2012a) and Denny which donated 50c worth of soup to FBSA for every 400g can of Denny soup sold in May and June 2011 (FBSA, 2011e).

Many of these corporate food donations are widely publicized in the media and on the printed labels on cans and bottles, pledging to donate a certain amount per item purchased of the product to FBSA (FBSA, 2011e).

An estimated 6,000 tonnes of rescued food is distributed each year by FBSA, which is said to translate into 18 to 20 million meals per year or, on average, 50,000 meals a day (McKenzie, 2012). As shown in Table 9.1, this food is distributed to six provinces: the Eastern Cape (Port Elizabeth); Gauteng (Johannesburg); KwaZulu-Natal (Durban and Pietermaritzburg); Limpopo (Polokwane); North West (Rustenburg); and Western Cape (Cape Town).

The number of beneficiaries reached per province represents, on average, just over half a per cent of the population. The distribution of FBSA benefits is not spread evenly across and within the provinces but is typically concentrated in certain targeted areas. The impact of this concentration is important to consider in terms of the impact on the local food system. For example, FBSA reaches 1.45 per cent of the population of the Limpopo province – where the highest proportion of households, that is, over 58 per cent of the population – are engaged in some form of agriculture and where the highest proportion of people receive social grants (StatsSA, 2013). It is not known whether the recipients of food charity are also recipients of social grants.

Food is donated to FBSA from a variety of sources including food producers, manufacturers, retailers, government agencies and individuals. In 2012, FBSA was sourcing just under 400 metric tonnes of food a month with a target of 2800 metric tons (FBSA, 2012a). This is supplemented by public funding, corporate and private citizen donations. In 2009, 60 per cent or just over $USD 2.1 million of the organization's funding came from the government, via the National Lotteries Foundation, plus an additional $440,000 from the National Department of Development (Warshawsky, 2011).

The agency dispatches the food to community-based organizations such as child and youth development programmes (pre-schools, foster care, shelters for orphans and vulnerable children and school feeding schemes); programmes for adults (nutritional feeding centres and soup kitchens serving unemployed persons, HIV-infected persons and pregnant women); and social welfare programmes (aged care, disabled care and care for the terminally ill).

Policy issues and debates

Whilst food charity may be an essential emergency measure for filling gaps in transitional economies it falls short of having real transformational effects. On the continuum of food security measures, emergency food distribution addresses the immediate hunger problem and little more. As institutionalized charity, this kind of food distribution de-politicizes hunger and stunts the structural transformations

Table 9.1 Number of households and beneficiaries receiving food assistance from FBSA by province, South Africa, 2012 and 2013

Province where FBSA operates	Number of households per province thousands (StatsSA, 2013)	Number of people per province thousands (Stats SA, 2013)	Proportion of population that benefit from social grants (%) (Stats SA, 2013)	Proportion of households that benefit from social grants (Stats SA, 2013)	Proportion of total population receiving FBSA support (%)	Proportion of households experiencing severely inadequate access to food (Stats SA, 2013)	Proportion of households experiencing inadequate access to food (Stats SA, 2013)	Number of FBSA agencies	Number of FBSA beneficiaries	Number of beneficiaries per Food Bank SA agency
Eastern Cape	1,631	6,586	40.3	58.1	0.86	8.6	19.4	84	56,729	675.35
Gauteng (excl. Tshwane/Pretoria)	4,153	12,464	16.5	27.2	0.08	5.3	13.1	155	2,979	19.22
Gauteng (Tshwane Pretoria)								717	7,245	10.10
KwaZulu-Natal	2,504	10,346	36.1	49.9	0.58	4.5	15.3	200	59,746	298.73
Limpopo	1,392	452	37.7	58.8	1.45	2.7	7.5	60	6,563	109.38
North West	1,105	3,547	32.6	46.7	0.28	13.2	21.4	39	9,789	251.00
Western Cape	1,619	5,904	20.1	34.2	1.19	7.6	13.7	245	70,178	286.44
Total South Africa	1,4631	52,275	29.5	43.6	0.58	6.5	15	1500	305,245	203.50

Source: Author's calculations from FBSA (2012a) and StatsSA (2013) data.

required for a more equitable society. That the poor depend on waste and corporate food players reap political capital from this is ethically questionable, to say the least. Commentators on CSI in South Africa often point to the cynicism of corporations, not only because of the conscious shift from 'responsibility' to 'investment' in the terminology, but also because of their lack of direct involvement and focus on reputation, management and public relations (Fig, 2005).

There is little information available on the targeting of beneficiaries of programmes. Are they reaching the people most in need, or are the supplementing existing social welfare programmes? The impact of these programmes on the local economy and the informal sector in particular has not been evaluated.

While such publicly funded and charitable food assistance and food provisioning is clearly a necessary, short-term poverty alleviation measure, its transformative potential needs to be carefully considered. The costs to the national budget are high and the impacts on the agriculture and food systems of food assistance programmes are poorly understood. Unless food assistance is part of a comprehensive national food security plan that is integrated with agriculture, rural development and broader social security goals, programmes can have negative effects on sustainable development, job creation and economic growth.

South African food assistance programmes are part of public programmes, although run through agencies accredited by the government. A network of over 1,700 NGOs and non-profit agencies is supported by the initiative (McKenzie, 2012). These agencies act as the intermediaries for procurement, acquisition and distribution of food purchased by the government and through private donations, including 'rescued' and redistributed food.

Earlier discussion documents for the National Food and Nutrition Security Policy (RSA, 2013) posed the intent to create a 'counter-food-value-chain' – a system that would use public resources to harness the cost savings of bulk procurement of food for distribution to the poor. The system proposed would undercut the current highly successful commercial distribution system and poses significant threats to commercial farm profitability and sustainability – the foundation of the country's food security. This aspect is underplayed in the final approved version of the policy, but the elements to induce this situation are still evident.

The 'counter-food value chain' is centred on using public and private food banks to distribute cheaper food staples to the poor. The current government lacks the institutional capacity and transparency to manage state procurement and distribution of food in an alternative food system, which may nonetheless unfairly compete with a well established and highly efficient commercial food production and distribution system. Furthermore, some configurations of corporate and state collaboration raise important questions around the right to food and food sovereignty, highlighting tension between the imperative to fulfil the constitutional right to food and the need for food policy to be democratic and socially transformative.

The right to food

Since the end of Apartheid, South Africa has seen new, but not always articulate or effective, waves of protest grounded in the material hardships of poor communities demanding access to housing, sanitation and education. These 'service delivery protests' bring into sharp focus the ANC's still-unfulfilled populist promises to redress inequality, underscored by unique possibilities for human rights litigation to mediate South Africa's changing social risks (Bonoli, 2005; Koelble, 2004).

Constitutional entrenchment

In this context it is important to note the entrenchment of the right to food (RTF) in South Africa's Constitution and the recent Cabinet decision in 2012 to ratify the UN *International Covenant of Economic, Social and Cultural Rights* (ICESCR) which includes the RTF (GCIS, 2012). Section 27 of the Constitution obliges the South African state to take 'reasonable legislative and other measures, within the context of its available resources, to achieve the progressive realization of: health care services, including reproductive health care; sufficient food and water; and social security, including, if they are unable to support themselves and their dependants, appropriate social assistance' (RSA, 1996).

With respect to children, section 28(1) of the Constitution determines that every child has the right, amongst others to: basic nutrition, shelter, basic health care services and social services; and to be protected from maltreatment, neglect, abuse or degradation (RSA, 1996). Sections 28(1)(c) and (d) concerning children's rights, including the right to basic nutrition, are not dependent on the availability of state resources; the obligation to ensure the full realization of these rights (and other section 28 rights) is unqualified. Cognisance must also be taken of section 2 (the right to equality) and section 11, the right to life (Hendriks and Olivier, 2013).

The justiciability of the right to food in South Africa holds possibilities, thanks in part to the precedents set by HIV/AIDS activism, and, for example, the Constitutional Court's broader approach to socioeconomic rights reflected in the Grootboom decision, which highlights the transformational nature of the Constitution in awarding damages to 900 people forcibly evicted from illegally-occupied land, including some 400 children (Government of South Africa v. Grootboom, 2000). Sunstein (2010) comments that the Constitution did not create a right to 'shelter or housing immediately upon demand', but it did create a right to a 'coherent, co-ordinated programme designed to meet' constitutional obligations. The obligation of the state was therefore to create such a programme, including reasonable measures specifically designed 'to provide relief for people who have no access to land, no roof over their heads, and who are living in intolerable conditions or [a] crisis situation, [opening] the possibility of providing that protection in a way that is respectful of democratic prerogatives and the simple fact of limited budgets' (Sunstein, 2010; Government of South Africa v. Grootboom, 2000).

The state in South Africa can clearly be compelled to progressively realize socio-economic rights and has in fact implemented a large number of wide-reaching programmes to address food assistance (FAO, 2006), but can food banks be considered a step towards progressive realization of the right to food, or are they actually side-tracking social progress?

Challenges to fulfilling the right to food

The challenge of fulfilling the right to food in South Africa was most recently articulated by the United Nations Special Rapporteur on the Right to Food during a visit to South Africa in July 2011. Olivier De Schutter lauded existing social assistance programmes but also described a moribund rural economy where smallholders and subsistence farmers go unsupported, land reform processes are truncated by a lack of technical support and droves of migration to cities leave swathes of the population to fall into the trap of urban dispossession, where food banks play their critical palliative role. While internationally recognized for its progressive legal frameworks, policy initiatives and wide-reaching social assistance programmes, South Africa still struggles with deeply-rooted inequalities that call for a rights-based approach to improving food security and nutrition. They also necessitate rights-based approaches to agricultural support schemes that target the most vulnerable of the 'three worlds of farming', namely the 2.5 million households, mostly in the Apartheid-era former homelands, which practice small-scale subsistence farming (De Schutter, 2012a). This, according to the United Nations Special Rapporteur, means favouring the participation of these groups in the design of policies, defining beneficiaries as rights holders who can claim services from the government, and moving towards a more bottom-up approach to agricultural support – in other words promoting food sovereignty as well as food security.

A rights-based approach also demands the integration of the gender dimension into agricultural policies. This is particularly important in former homelands where, under traditional authority, women face greater cultural obstacles to land ownership, access to credit and extension services and, varyingly, exclusion from household and community decision-making (Rangan and Gilmartin, 2002).

Food charity and food democracy

Instead of creating a more responsive food system, food charity in South Africa displaces informal market supply through state-funded distribution mechanisms. This suppresses local demand, creating disincentives for production and the development of local food markets and defies the notions of food citizenry (Wilkins, 2005), and food democracy (Lang and Heasman, 2004). A parallel, state-controlled food economy will put control over food systems firmly out of democratic reach, undoing liberalization and introducing distortions in favour of low consumer prices, while corporate dumping distorts markets and undercuts small producers and suppliers.

Food handouts are vulnerable to political expediency, for example, being used as a political tool by way of the distribution of food parcels at election time. Reports and allegations of vote buying by political opposition parties, civil society organizations and the media accompanied nearly every one of South Africa's local and national elections since 1994. This often takes the form of the distribution of food parcels and articles of party-branded clothing in poor areas (see Quintal, 2013). While the actual quantities may be insignificant, for unemployed, hungry shack-dwellers and impoverished rural people stretching meagre social grants across a month, the impact of a well-timed few kilograms of maize meal and sugar is disproportionate, suggesting that the capabilities of poor South Africans to participate meaningfully in politics, including the much-needed reform of food and agriculture policies, is impaired.

Political as well as economic vulnerabilities must be highlighted here. With massive youth unemployment, a weak education system and high dependence on social assistance, poor South Africans have little frame of reference beyond the conditioned acceptance and low expectations generated by poverty and marginalization (Nussbaum, 2000). Under the guise of a developmental state, there is the risk of government resorting to manipulation through the selective and opportunistic bestowal of what should be the basic rights of all South Africans – including food, housing and healthcare.

Conclusion

The question arising here is whether food charity amounts to progressive realization of the right to food or simply entrenches dependence and poverty and exacerbates already troubling populist political manipulation. While social assistance is obviously a necessary part of the post-Apartheid transformation agenda, no exit strategies involving significant job creation and well-paid employment exist. The proportion of grant recipients to taxpayers (over 15 million grant recipients vs 13.7 million registered taxpayers (NTSARS, 2012)) high levels of unemployment (25.6 per cent, StatsSA, 2013) and the proportion of the national budget supporting them raises questions of sustainability. The direct use of state resources to procure and distribute food seems to contradict long-term sustainable development goals.

Using state power to develop a food counter-economy also raises many concerns. Popular opinion amongst officials is that distributing 'waste' food from up-market urban supermarkets in rural areas does not compete with local businesses but there is little recognition of how it affects demand in rural areas or how it affects struggling rural entrepreneurs. While the food products may never be bought by the rural poor, the distribution of these goods amounts to domestic dumping. Rural entrepreneurs are already undercut by the insurgence of supermarkets and competitive foreign shop owners. They face significant business barriers, including access to finance, long distances to wholesalers and consumers with constrained purchasing power. They have no say in the negotiation of terms related to the dumping of food through means such as FBSA.

Warshawsky (2011) questions, also, the impact of Food Bank SA in Johannesburg's urban areas, pointing to an entire enterprise of intermediaries that has materialized to distribute food, essentially middlemen who respond to opportunities created by FBSA. Cases of nepotism and favouritism in the award of contracts are reported frequently in the media. This does not imply that there is no place for surplus food in South Africa. Instead of being dumped into rural economies and poor urban centres where it not only displaces demand in the formal retail sector, but also cripples the vital informal sector, it could be used, for example, to reduce budgetary requirements for the provision of institutional systems such as prisons, hospitals and other state institutions.

Following the 2008 world food price crisis and the concomitant focus on food prices, too much emphasis has been given to reducing food prices rather than raising incomes and purchasing power for a broader sector of the economy. Low consumer prices mean under-cutting the farmer (primarily rural) and squeezing out informal sector retailers. When the government itself starts to compete with essential sectors in which the poor find opportunities, a distorting force is at play that falls neither within economic growth nor developmental objectives. From a policy perspective, the creation of a parallel food economy demonstrates serious incoherence. Both farming and the informal sector offer significant broad-based growth opportunities for African countries, including real labour and income possibilities for poor rural and urban households. In the current environment of political neglect, these are relegated to survivalist activities.

It is essential for South Africa to review the role of FBSA and, more generally, the distribution of cheap, rescued and surplus food in the country. FBSA should operate as a charity agency and should not receive government funding nor be an agent for the distribution of 'free' corporate food. It should run off donations from corporations and wealthy consumers with a social conscience regarding food waste and reaching out to those in poverty. Corporations could play a much more productive role in channelling surplus food into government institutions in regulated ways that support the overall food security programmes, without compromising the livelihoods of the very people such charities are meant to assist. Finally, it is essential to distinguish emergency food transfer programmes needed to respond to hunger (which should provide a balanced basket of nutritious food to households requiring short-term support) from the creation of a shadow food economy that serves neither rational economic nor transformational purposes. Food charity should not become a salve, applied haphazardly to South Africa's corporate conscience, policy lacunae and huge equality rifts, which, in the end, may keep the gaps from closing.

10
Erosion of Rights, Uncritical Solidarity and Food Banks in Spain

Karlos Pérez de Armiño

Introduction

In recent years food banks in Spain have been playing an increasingly important role in meeting the basic needs of vulnerable people in order to face the current economic and social crisis, the worst in decades. This is taking place in the context of a weakening of the welfare state, which has been affected by structural shortcomings, cuts in funding and neoliberal privatizations.

Between 1986 and 2008, Spain experienced a long process of economic growth ('the Spanish miracle'), which came to a virulent end with the international financial crisis that broke out in 2008. This created the greatest fiscal deficit in the country's history, an increasing level of debt, and a clear economic recession, with a 7 per cent fall in GDP over the last five years. In response, the government has imposed harsh austerity measures and cuts in public expenditure to reduce the state deficit, but at the cost of contracting economic activity.

Impoverishment and livelihoods

Both the economic crisis and the austerity measures have generated a disproportionate increase in unemployment, reducing incomes but also the social protection of people, which largely depends on their occupational status. The number of unemployed in July 2013 was 5,977,506, amounting to 26.26 per cent of the active population, against 1,927,600 at the end of 2007 (INE, 2013). The current percentage is 2.5 times higher than that of the average of the European Union.

Amongst the hardest hit social sectors, young people under 25 stand out, with 55.1 per cent unemployment, a rate without comparison in Europe. Equally grave is the high percentage of long-term unemployment: at the end of 2012, 55 per cent of unemployed had been without work for over a year, while a million had been jobless for three years, having exhausted every benefit. The high percentage of households where all active members are unemployed is also having a great impact on the inability to meet basic needs; while in 2007 the figure was 2.5 per cent, at the end of 2012 it rose to 10.6 per cent (FOESSA, 2013, pp. 9, 11, 12).

In this context, the income of the population has fallen in recent years. In 2011, the average annual incomes of households were 24,609 euros, against 26,500 in 2008 (INE, 2013). Similarly, the relative rate of poverty at the end of 2012 was 21.8 per cent – while the European average was 16.9 per cent – against a figure of 19.7 per cent in 2007, which represents a significant increase (FOESSA, 2013, pp. 12, 21). What is most worrying is the fact that this increase has been especially pronounced in the case of severe poverty, referring to incomes below 30 per cent of the median; this has risen one point, reaching 5.2 per cent, which reflects a collapse of lower incomes and an intensification of poverty (Laparra, 2012, p. 181). It should be added that the rates of poverty in the 17 Autonomous Communities or regions show great disparities.

One of the most alarming data is the sharp increase of households without income, that is, those which do not receive salaries, unemployment benefits or other social security benefits. While before the crisis, in 2007, these amounted to 2 per cent, in 2012 they had climbed to a historical maximum of 3.67 per cent (FOESSA, 2013, pp. 13, 22).

Another characteristic of the impact of the crisis in Spain has been the increase in inequality, making it the EU country with the third highest rates: the richest 10 per cent of the population has five times more income than the poorest 10 per cent, with the difference rising by 16.3 per cent since 2007, principally due to the loss of income amongst the poorest (Laparra, 2012, p. 181). This reveals that the crisis is not being borne equitably by all social strata and that, on the contrary, a transfer of income is at present taking place from the lower and middle classes towards the upper classes (FOESSA, 2013, p. 7).

Food insecurity

The crisis is involving a serious erosion of the livelihoods of the more vulnerable families, which reduces their capacity to access essential goods, not least of which is food. However, it is striking that neither the official statistics nor prestigious reports by different social organizations include hardly any specific data on the deterioration of the nutritional situation.

One of such few data was offered by the Center of Sociological Investigations (CIS) in its survey of December 2011. It recorded how, since the start of the crisis, 41.1 per cent of the interviewees and their families had altered their habits of food consumption to save money (CIS, 2011), a practice that sometimes consists of a reduction of fresh products, resulting in an impoverishment of the diet (UNICEF, 2012a, p. 37). Along these lines, a recent study by the Ombudsman of Catalonia indicated that the percentage of Catalan households that who did not have access to meat or fish meals at least every two days was multiplied by almost six between 2008 (1.7 per cent) and 2011 (9.8 per cent) (Síndic de Greuges, 2013). Similarly, a report of the Government of the Basque Country indicated that between 2008 and 2012 the percentage of people in households affected by very serious food consumption problems grew by 45.7 per cent, rising from 2.1 per cent to 3.1 per cent of all households (Gobierno Vasco, 2012, p. 17).

In addition to the scarce existing statistical figures, some other data and indications provide testimony to the growth of this problem in recent years. One of them is the denunciations made by associations of teachers and parents concerning an increase in the undernourishment of schoolchildren from poor families, to which the reduction of public grants to school canteens has contributed (*El País*, 6 June 2013). A second indication consists in the growing assistance in the form of free daily meals provided by different institutions and civil organizations, such as the Red Cross, to disadvantaged people (*El País*, 6 June 2013). In the same way, Cáritas points out that in its provision of economic assistance since 2008, there has been an increase of interventions involving food, which have become the most important, accounting in 2011 for 39 per cent of the value of its total assistance (Cáritas, 2012, p. 8).

The welfare state in Spain: a weak system under attack

In response to the crisis, the Spanish welfare system has proved weak and unable to respond satisfactorily to Spain's growing needs. Furthermore, the budget austerity policies are contributing to its progressive erosion. The crisis and the budget deficit seem to have provided, from the perspective of neoliberal postulates, an ideal excuse for weakening public welfare policies, favouring the provision of some services by private companies, as well as by charitable organizations.

The Spanish welfare state rests on four great pillars: (i) Education; (ii) Health; (iii) Income transfers (pension and unemployment incomes; subsidies for people without means and in situations of need); and (iv) Social services, consisting of a system of monetary benefits and programmes of prevention, integration and social rehabilitation, regulated by public administration but also implemented by private companies and social organizations.

Therefore, the Spanish system is a mixture of the two great welfare systems, the Bismarckian and the Beveridgean, as it combines social benefits and services, both selective or occupational (based on the contributions of those affiliated to the social security system), and universal coverage (social assistance, education, health, and old age and invalidity pensions) (Moreno, 2012, pp. 8, 52).

Another important characteristic of the Spanish welfare model, as in other Catholic countries of southern Europe, is a strong family microsolidarity that meets material, social, educational and other needs, providing welfare and social cohesion. Nevertheless, this entails two problems. First, such provision is basically carried out by women, which gives rise to a difficult balance between domestic work, care, and their growing insertion in the labour market. And, second, taking for granted such family solidarity, government interventions towards households tend to be passive and meagre (Moreno, 2009, pp. 9, 102, 266).

In Spain these links of intra-family solidarity have been reactivated with the crisis. They provide the main strategies facing the crisis, followed by the activities of the submerged economy and, in the third place, the search for support from social organizations (Cáritas, 2012, p. 16). Thus, they are proving to have a key role in cushioning the high level of youth unemployment and avoiding social fractures.

Nonetheless, the function of the family as a social safety-net has been weakening in recent decades due to several structural and demographic factors, such as the decline of the matrimonial institution, the increase in one-person households and single parent families, the increase in separations (Cáritas, 2012, p. 16), as well as the incorporation of women into the labour market (Moreno, 2012, pp. 106–107).

Territorial decentralization

Another characteristic of the Spanish welfare state is its strong institutional and territorial decentralization, given the quasi-federal structure of the state. The pension and unemployment protection policies correspond to the central state, while the rest (health, education, social services) are managed by the Autonomous Communities, in collaboration with the municipalities in the case of social services. In this way, the Autonomous Communities have been a key factor in the expansion of the welfare state, although there are great disparities in their resources and services (García et al., 2013, p. 17).

Until the crisis erupted in 2007, the welfare state was gradually being built in Spain, although with weaker levels of coverage than in other European countries. In recent years however, the weaknesses of the Spanish welfare state have become more pronounced due to the crisis and, since 2010, the austerity measures which have reduced the funding of social policies and basic services. In addition, in 2012 harder conditions were established for gaining access to unemployment benefit, resulting in an increase in the percentage of unemployed people without benefits.

The cuts in social policies are excluding determinate sectors of the population from certain basic services and damaging their socioeconomic rights. There is a well-founded fear that this 'progressive differentiation of citizens in the access to basic rights will mark our social structure in coming years', which could be based on greater inequalities than in past decades (FOESSA, 2013, pp. 8, 14). Such exclusion of vulnerable sectors from basic services could have irreversible effects for social cohesion even after the crisis.

The right to food

When it comes to judging welfare policies and anti-crisis measures it is important to bear in mind that Spain was one of the countries that signed and ratified, in 1977, the *International Covenant on Economic, Social and Cultural Rights* (ICESCR), which includes amongst others the right to food, as well as the Optional Protocol to that Covenant in 2010. In May 2012, Spain sent its latest report on the advances made in applying that agreement to the United Nations Committee on Economic, Social and Cultural Rights (CESCR). Shortly afterwards, the CESCR published its *Concluding Observations*, expressing its concern at the fact that the government's austerity measures and the lack of political palliatives to the crisis were reducing the protection of rights such as health, education, work and housing, especially amongst the most vulnerable and marginalized sectors. This document recalls that the essentials of such rights must be preserved even in crisis contexts, which is why it recommends revising such austerity measures and adopting a national programme of integrated struggle against poverty and unemployment (CESCR, 2012).

In conclusion, the signing and ratification of the ICESCR has had no real effect on the design of policies and the protection of socioeconomic rights in Spain. As the CESCR itself observes in its *Concluding Observations*, the deterioration of socioeconomic rights is not only due to the crisis, but also to the fact that the Spanish Constitution does not give them the juridical status of rights that can be claimed in the law courts, a status that it does confer on civil and political rights. On the other hand, although the criticisms formulated by the CESCR have been received with satisfaction by different social organizations, they have found little echo in the mass media and have not given rise to social or political debate.

Facing this diminishing capacity of public welfare policies, there has been an increase in the provision of help by social organizations, some of their programmes being specifically focused on confronting food insecurity by distributing food or, on occasion, money. Thus, for example, the Red Cross has a programme providing help to 1.4 million people, including food aid provisioned with surpluses provided by the European Union. Similarly, Cáritas attended to 1,015,276 people in 2011, when in 2007 it had attended to 370,251 (Cáritas, 2012, p. 4, 7). In some provinces this Catholic organization distributes food, while in others it has chosen to provide cash instead. Another increasingly important social initiative, specializing in food assistance, is that of food banks.

The spread of food banks: between a service to corporations and solidarity

Food banks have undergone a strong expansion in Spain in recent years: they have been established in all the provinces, with a constant increase in beneficiaries and volume of food distributed. Similarly, they have acquired a notable presence in the mass media and, thanks to their popular food collections, they are becoming increasingly well-known to public opinion.

Spanish food banks show characteristics that are common to the majority of European food banks: they are non-profit making organizations, the majority of the people who manage them are volunteers, and their function is to collect food that is freely donated to be voluntarily distributed to people in need. However, this is never done in an individual and direct way, but instead it is delivered to different affiliated organizations and care centres. They seek to avoid the waste of food that is surplus or that cannot be sold for different reasons, but which is consumable, collecting it to be distributed to charitable organizations that work with people in need.

Organization and functioning of food banks

After France and Belgium, Spain was one of the first European countries where food banks were established. The first was created in Barcelona in 1987, which was inspired by the Paris food bank, the oldest in Europe that had been set up three years previously. It was a personal initiative of Jordi Peix, at that time the General Director of Agri-food Industries of the government of Catalonia, who has made a decisive contribution to the spread of the banks and to the elaboration of a technical, social and ethical discourse on their function.

The Barcelona food bank has become the biggest in Europe and in Spain it is outstanding because of the introduction of innovative management initiatives and its links with the civil society of its setting, and also because it has the most elaborated discourse concerning its aims and social usefulness. Besides, it served as a model for the spread of banks throughout the country and for the foundation in 1996 of the Spanish Federation of Food Banks (Federación Española de Bancos de Alimentos – FESBAL).

At present there are 55 food banks in Spain, one for each province. Each bank is an independent body, although all have subscribed to a Code of Good Practices and form part of the FESBAL, which carries out functions of coordination, interlocution before national and international authorities, exchange of information and food, and representation before the European Federation of Food Banks (FEBA). The Spanish banks are managed by some 2,000 volunteers, the majority retired professionals, with the support of a very small number of wage workers and tens of thousands of occasional collaborators for specific campaigns.

Spanish food banks have several mechanisms for provisioning themselves:

- The main source is donations, made by some 3,000 companies that produce and commercialize food, of surpluses or products fit for consumption but not for commercialization for different reasons (defects in packaging or labelling, end of seasonal campaigns, close proximity of sell-by date, etc.).
- The European Union's 'Food Distribution Programme for the Most Deprived Persons of the Community' accounts for nearly 40 per cent of the banks' supplies. It was established to eradicate surpluses, but as these have been reduced, most of the food is now bought in the market with EU funds. Several countries question the plan arguing that social policies correspond to each country, not to the EU, and therefore its continuity is under discussion, a substantial funding reduction being foreseeable for the coming year (FESBAL, 2013a, p. 26)
- The European Union's programme for the market withdrawal of fruit and vegetables subsidizes the removal of those products from the market to avoid a fall in their prices. The produce is then distributed as food aid through charitable organizations. The banks of Catalonia

in particular have made active use of the programme, obtaining nearly 3,000 tons of fruit and vegetables in 2012. Besides this, since 2009 they have used the programme to carry out an innovative initiative, consisting of withdrawing fruit surpluses during the high season to produce fruit juices that the banks distribute (Banco de Alimentos de Barcelona, 2012; Peix, 2012).

- Food donations by citizens are another source of provisions, through mass collections mainly at the doors of supermarkets, as well as, for example, in schools, at sporting events, and from companies. In 2009, the Food Bank of Barcelona organized the first great collection, an initiative that was subsequently imitated by nearly all Spanish food banks and that is carried out on the same day at the end of November. The collections contribute a relatively modest percentage of the supplies of the banks: in 2011 in Barcelona, for example, 1,095 tons of food were collected. Nonetheless, they have two advantages: they provide basic non-perishable food (pulses, oil, rice, powdered milk, sugar) of which there is no surplus and of which the banks tend to have a low stock; and they promote a wide mobilization and raise social consciousness, supported by the work of thousands of occasional volunteers and broad coverage in the mass media (Banco de Alimentos de Barcelona, 2012; interview with Jordi Peix).

With respect to the range of food distributed, this was initially very reduced, as it depended above all on European surpluses, but with time it has diversified, making it possible to support more balanced nutritional diets. Donations by companies and distributors have enabled them to increase the availability of fresh food, like fruit and vegetables, dairy and meat derivatives, as well as frozen products. However, this has posed new logistical problems, forcing them to acquire more sophisticated infrastructures and distribution mechanisms.

As mentioned above, Spanish banks have grown appreciably in recent years, both in terms of the volume of food, and in the number of distributing organizations and people benefitting from them, although the people in charge point out that their resources do not meet the demand that they face. The volume of food managed has increased annually in recent years by approximately 20 per cent, the greatest increase amongst European banks, reaching 120,000 tons in 2012, against 104,000 tons in 2011 and 83,272 tons in 2010. Thus, in 2012 the Food Bank of Barcelona, the biggest in Europe, distributed a total of 10,162 tons, and the bank of Madrid 9,377 tons. The number of people benefitting throughout Spain was 1.5 million in 2012, against 1.3 million in 2011, and 700,000 in 2007, before the start of the crisis.

In 2012, distribution was carried out through 7,106 charitable organizations (e.g., soup kitchens for the homeless, parishes, school canteens). According to FESBAL (2013a), the main recipients are immigrants (28 per cent), elderly people (21 per cent), drug addicts (12 per cent), homeless people (10 per cent), long-term unemployed (9 per cent), children and teenagers (7 per cent) and terminally ill people and their relatives (6 per cent). With the current crisis, the spectrum of recipients has widened to include people who formerly had jobs and were not at risk of social exclusion.

The charitable organizations associated with food banks use different methods of distribution, although they are always free: for example, the direct provision in canteens, distribution of packets to families to be cooked at home, and of breakfasts in schools. Some mechanisms are based on the mere provision of assistance; in others, however, the donation of food is linked to processes of accompaniment to provide the beneficiaries with more autonomy and empowerment. In some food banks, like that of Biscay, there is an open debate on the most suitable distribution mechanisms, and some voices warn of the social stigma generated by distribution that does not respect confidentiality, such as the distribution of packets after waiting in a queue. For these reasons, in some provinces the Catholic organization Cáritas has decided not to distribute food issued from banks, opting instead to distribute money to people in need.

On the other hand, it should be stressed that the food banks have been gaining growing support and recognition: they are increasingly well-known to public opinion, they frequently appear in the mass media, they receive support from an increasing number of companies, and they have a growing recognition from the different public institutions at the national, regional and local levels. Thus, many institutions have supplied financial support to pay for their infrastructure and management costs, including warehouses, vehicles and workers made available temporarily from employment offices.

Aims and discourses of the food banks

The visibility and social incidence of the food banks does not only rest on the material and quantitative dimension of their activities, but also on the discourses with which they formulate their aims and functions. In the light of the documentation used and the interviews held, two differentiated discursive lines can be appreciated, one focused on functional and pragmatic arguments, and the other more focused on ethical arguments, with components relating to values, human rights and public policies. The first line is a robust one, and is clearly rooted in the Spanish food banks as a whole and their federation, the FESBAL; while the ethical discourse has a weaker presence and is more geographically uneven.

As mentioned above, Spanish food banks place an emphasis on functional and pragmatic arguments to justify the utility and efficiency of their activities, arguments that are without doubt decisive for mobilizing donations and institutional aid. Such ideas stress the benefits that accrue to companies that collaborate with them, to public administration and to society in general. The main arguments are as follows:

- Making good use of food surpluses in order to avoid 'waste'. Significantly, the Founding Charter of the European Federation of Food Banks states that its main aim is to 'fight against waste'.
- The technical, professional and efficient management of the logistic chain of collecting and distributing provisions, with workings characteristic of a company.
- The provision to producer and distributor companies of a 'management service for their surpluses'. The destruction of surpluses involves a significant logistic effort and cost for the companies, which accounts for an average of 10 per cent of the value of what is produced. The food banks help them to avoid this, by offering them a network extending through Europe that can take charge of their surpluses, and by issuing them with certificates for technical and tax purposes (Peix, 2009, p. 38; Peix blog, 29 April 2012).
- Providing companies with a space for their activities of 'solidarity marketing' and 'corporate social responsibility', with which to transmit the fact of their adopting certain attitudes and values desired by society, in order to win consumer loyalty and improve their results. Moreover, the food banks help to avoid the deterioration caused to the image of the commercial brand of companies and supermarkets by the elimination of food in incinerators or dumps (Peix, 2009, p. 38). In this respect, according to the FESBAL (2013a), numerous companies (like Nestlé, Unilever España, MRW, etc.), including financial institutions like Banco Santander, have made commitments to collaborate with the food banks.
- The tax relief that companies obtain because of their donations, which Spanish law sets at 35 per cent of the value of the latter.
- The contribution to preventing a fall in the prices of fruit and vegetables in seasons when there is a surplus, helping to maintain farmers' incomes.
- The reduction of environmental damage and the greenhouse effect, since the destruction of one ton of surplus food generates 4.5 tons

of CO_2. This also entails an economic saving, since on the market of permanent CO_2 emission rights, each ton is priced at 12 euros.

• The high economic profitability of the banks' activity, since the value of the food they distribute multiplies it to a figure one hundred times higher than the banks' costs (280 million euros and 2.8 million euros respectively in 2011). One of the keys to explaining this lies in their being based on voluntary work, which saves the state the costs that would be involved in providing such aid with paid personnel.

Besides this functional discourse based on efficiency, Spanish food banks have also elaborated, or are in the process of elaborating, a discourse with a more ethical content, focused on the defence of values and even on the right to food in a generic way. In relation to this, two basic conclusions may be drawn. The first is that this is a weaker discourse than the one linked to functional arguments. Indeed, in the best of cases the food bank documents include some allusions to, and figures on poverty, but it is clear that their work is not based on a reflection on, and much less on a critique of its causes, nor of the working of the agri-food system and the corporate food sector and neither of the management of the crisis by the institutions or the erosion of the welfare state. However, some sectors within the food banks, such as those of Catalonia and the Basque Country for example, have been arguing for the need to articulate a more elaborated discourse on poverty, going beyond mere efficiency in logistics and assistance.

The second conclusion is that this discourse containing ethical elements is not something uniform amongst food banks and provinces. The most elaborated discourse in this respect is that of the Bank of Barcelona, which is largely due to the intellectual leadership of its founder and current vice-president, Jordi Peix, who is very active in the spread of arguments based on values. It is also related to the characteristics of Catalan society itself, which has a stronger and more dynamic associative network than other areas in Spain. On the contrary, in the documentation of the FESBAL and other banks, like that of Madrid, that ethical discourse is much weaker, in favour of the discourse on technical efficiency; which would seem to indicate a more traditional conceptualization of social assistance.

The ethical discourse, linked to determinate values, revolves around the following ideas:

• The appeal to solidarity and human values. According to FESBAL, the banks 'have organized a new concept of solidarity', linking industries with charities, 'making a commitment to a more prosperous world' (FESBAL, 2013a).

- The need, and civic moral obligation, for each citizen to involve him/herself personally in the collective fight against hunger. The idea is frequently found that, even though responsibility falls to the state, given that the latter and the social services do not reach everywhere, it is necessary for society to involve itself in palliating those deficits by organizing a 'solidarity network' to act in the nearby milieu. In this respect, the banks contribute to a 'participatory democracy', according to Jordi Peix (Peix blog, 2 November 2012 and 18 October 2012).

- The fight against food waste, as a moral response to hunger and as a way of reducing the environmental harm entailed in its destruction. Unlike others, the Food Bank of Barcelona in particular includes amongst its aims the promotion of a more sustainable development and the fight against climate change, making efficient use of unmarketable food.

- Social justice: Peix inscribes the banks in an effort to achieve a world that is more just, for a reduction in inequalities and an improvement of social cohesion and integration, and for environmental sustainability (Peix blog, 18 October 2012). However, the truth is that these ideas barely have a presence in the documentation of the banks.

- The allusion to the human right to food is present, although with unequal intensity, in the discourse of the Spanish food banks. In fact, in the annual Assembly of 2008 held by FEBA in Madrid, consideration was given to this. A document of the FESBAL on this right declared that 'states therefore have the obligation of guaranteeing, as a minimum, that their inhabitants should not be victims of hunger, and of doing everything possible to fulfill' such regular access to sufficient food that is adequate from the nutritional point of view and culturally acceptable. And it continues by declaring that food banks, in cooperation with the charities, 'constitute a point of support for the realization of this right' (FESBAL, 2013b). The Bank of Barcelona in particular indicates in its Mission and Values that its 'effort thus points towards fulfilling one of the most basic human rights: that of sufficient and healthy food for everyone'.

It is well known that a large part of the international debates on the right to food revolves around its enforcement and the obligations this places on states. In this respect, the appeal to state obligation is not something frequently found, it is generic and does not give rise to messages of protest or political criticism. Nonetheless, as a personal proposal, Jordi

Peix writes that 'suitable public services must be defended that make it possible to fulfill the right of every person to have access to healthy and nutritional food', and to oblige governments to fulfil the basic rights of the person (Peix blog, 13 November 2012; FESBAL, 2013b).

- The implicit criticism of the institutions: the social mobilizations encouraged by the banks, in particular though mass food collections, is interpreted by Jordi Peix (Peix blog, 13 November 2012; and personal interview) and other people interviewed as an act of indignation and warning and as a criticism of governments because of their incapacity to put an end to poverty. Nonetheless, such positions are not explicit, since the campaigns, publicity and documents of the banks lack any criticism of the institutions and their public policies.
- The need to spread values and raise the awareness of society, especially amongst children and young people, about hunger in the nearby milieu, food wastage, the right to food and environmental sustainability, in order to achieve their active involvement. This is one of the aims of the popular food collections, as well as of the consciousness-raising campaigns in schools.

Conclusions

Compared with the welfare systems of neighbouring countries in Europe, the Spanish system is a late one, not fully universal, fragmented into different levels of protection, decentralized in its territorial management, and lacking sufficient capacity to equitably include all people in need (Moreno, 2012, p. 64; Laparra, 2012, p. 189). To these structural shortcomings must be added the attrition it has lately been suffering from due to neoliberal privatization initiatives, and budget cuts aimed at confronting the current economic crisis.

In this way, in the present context of crisis, in which there is an increase in poverty, social precariousness and food insecurity, it is clear that public institutions are reducing their capacity and commitment to meeting their obligations to respect, protect and fulfil social and economic human rights, such as the right to food. This means that the contribution of different charitable organizations, together with the food banks that work with them, is of growing importance.

Food banks have grown considerably in Spain in recent years, with a substantial increase in the volume of food they collect, the number of receiving organizations and people benefitting from them. Similarly, they have won an increasing presence in the mass media, backing from public institutions and recognition and support from society. To support their activity the banks present a discourse that essentially focuses on the logistical and technical efficiency of their management, the services they provide to companies by helping them to get rid of their surpluses, the saving in economic and environmental costs to society, and the utility of reconverting food waste into a resource for alleviating hunger. Moreover, occasionally and in a weaker form, some banks and sectors of banks have elaborated a broader discourse, invoking ethical arguments, the right to food, environmental sustainability, democratic participation and social mobilization in response to the problem of hunger. In any case, in the documentation and campaigns of the food banks – unlike the case of other social action organizations involved in the fight against hunger and poverty – no analysis at all can be found on the causes of the latter, nor any criticism of the institutions, their public policies in the framework of the crisis, or the economic system. We could conclude that food banks are, therefore, a way of uncritical solidarity.

From the documentation consulted and the interviews held, it is possible to verify in certain progressive circles involved in the fight against poverty and the defence of the welfare state from a human rights focus, a certain reticence towards the food banks. This reticence is chiefly due to the latter's charitable and palliative character, their substitute role in performing functions that should be assumed by the state, their collaboration with institutions without criticizing their policies on welfare matters, and their willingness to make a space available for the corporate image of food and distribution companies (ignoring the questionable activities of some of these latter in the food chain or in labour rights) and of banking organizations (strongly questioned by public opinion due to their responsibility in the economic crisis and the repossession of homes).

However, even those sectors and people tend to leave such doubts and reticence in the background given the gravity of the present crisis. The opinion normally found amongst all types of organizations, one that is shared by the food banks themselves, is that the response that they give to poverty and hunger is neither sufficient nor the most suitable, as it is merely palliative, but that it is nonetheless useful in a context where public policies are not sufficient. As the European Anti-Poverty Network EAPN-ES (2012) states, 'food distribution does not take people out of poverty and thus does not achieve their social inclusion', which is why it should be seen as 'a resource with a temporary character'.

In short, in the context of a reduction in both welfare policies and the state's commitment to guarantee the human right to food and other socioeconomic rights, food banks are making a significant palliative contribution. At the same time, they provide other benefits, such as: the net contribution of resources to charitable organizations and families, since the donation of food enables them to redirect resources to other programmes and needs; the reduction in environmental costs by avoiding the destruction of food surpluses; and the consciousness-raising and social mobilization they generate around the existence of hunger on one's doorstep.

In any case, Spanish food banks still have a margin for improvement on several fronts. First, the impact of their activities could be strengthened with a greater analysis of the causes and dimensions of poverty, as well as with the maintenance of more links with the social organizations that reflect and work on the question, taking part in campaigns in this respect. Second, in line with the above, food banks should pay more attention to the discourses and messages that they project on key questions (the right to food, obligations of the institutions, etc.), as this is decisive on whether or not they contribute to raising awareness and arousing consciences. And, third, although the distribution of food to people is done through the collaborating charitable organizations, both these and food banks should reflect on the different forms of distribution and their impact with respect to reducing vulnerability. In particular, it is necessary to avoid those forms of distribution that do not guarantee confidentiality and can generate the stigmatization of recipients, and priority should be given, where possible, to those mechanisms that are linked to processes of training and empowering recipients.

11
Food Banking in Turkey: Conservative Politics in a Neo-Liberal State

Mustafa Koc

Introduction

Food Banking is a relatively new form of charitable access to food in Turkey. Introduced in 2004 by the government in an omnibus bill, food banks spread rapidly in the following decade, claiming to provide food for thousands of food insecure families. The Turkish law provides 100 per cent tax exemptions to those who make donations to food banks, yet there is no publicly available data on the numbers of people receiving food assistance, nor the amount of donations and income tax benefits received by the donors. This chapter examines the socio-economic and political context in the early 2000s in Turkey that has led to the formation of food banks. It reviews the conditions of food insecurity, and the role of food banks as charitable organizations in food provisioning and electoral politics across the country. The chapter claims that the introduction of food banks during this period reflects the politics of religious conservatism and neo-liberal economic strategies adopted by the governing Justice and Development Party (AKP) during this decade.

The chapter first provides an historical account of the Islamic tradition of almsgiving in the Ottoman Empire and discusses how this tradition was replaced later in the 20th century by the modern welfare state model. It then reviews the conditions of neo-liberal transformation of the Turkish economy throughout the 1980s and 1990s and its consequences for social welfare. The politics of the AKP era when neo-liberal economic policies continued side by side with religious conservatism are then discussed including the reasons behind the adoption of food banking as government policy in Turkey. The conclusion provides some final observations helping to make sense of why food banks emerged in an era where the Turkish economy seemed to be growing rapidly and in which there was a decline in poverty and levels of food insecurity.

Historical legacy of faith-based charity: the Turkish example

Although food banks in Turkey emerged during the era of neo-liberal reforms, charitable social assistance has a long tradition extending back to pre-welfare and pre-nation state periods. Faith-based charities, for example, have served their communities for millennia. As 'civil society organisations that have a commitment to moral and altruistic values', faith-based charities have assisted vulnerable people experiencing social exclusion and poverty (Morvaridi, 2013, p. 309). Originating in the pre-modern era, many traditional practices of faith-based organizations would not necessarily reflect the legal–rational practices of modern bureaucracies and in most cases modern welfare states would replace them or marginalize their functions in the 19th and 20th centuries. What the modern state provided was a sense of entitlement for citizenry (though this was not always universal) as opposed to the personalized relations of charity. The Turkish example, where faith-based philanthropic tradition under the Ottoman Empire was replaced by the modern nation state and its social services is a typical example of such transition from a faith-based charity model to a state-based welfare model.

Founded in 1923, the Republic of Turkey aimed to cut its historic, linguistic and cultural ties with the Ottoman Empire, Middle Eastern geography and Islamic tradition, and tried to establish a modern nation state. While the Turkish Republic was praised as one of the most successful experiments in modernity in the Middle East, this was not a completely smooth transition. The tensions between the imperial past and republicanism, secularism and Islam, modernity and tradition have bedevilled Turkish politics throughout the 20th century and have been clearly pronounced in the political rhetoric and practices of the Justice and Development Party (AKP) that has been governing Turkey in the first decade of the 21st century.

In its classic age (1300–1600), the Ottoman Empire created a centralized state structure with a sophisticated bureaucratic organization by adopting the past practices of the former Eastern Roman Empire, combined with the Islamic sharia law. While private property rights did not exist in the legal sense, peasant families were allowed usufruct rights as long as they continued to cultivate land and pay taxes.

Distributive systems of almsgiving

Highly suspicious of potential threats by local gentry, the Ottoman state used forced appropriations combined with distributive mechanisms which resulted in a relatively egalitarian social structure. For the Muslim majority, state taxation on land was combined with *zekat*, a distributive system of almsgiving required to be paid by all Muslims. Despite it's highly centralist tendencies, the Ottoman Empire provided a semi-autonomous system to religious minorities. The Ottoman Millet system allowed each recognized religious community (Jews, Armenians, Orthodox) to have a semi-autonomous existence with their courts, social justice networks and religious and linguistic autonomy as long as they continued to pay *jizya* tax required by non-Muslims.

For the Muslim majority, state taxation on land was combined with *zekat*, a distributive system of almsgiving required to be paid by all Muslims. The giving of the *zekat* was considered a means of purifying one's wealth and soul and all Muslims who could afford it (about 1/40 of capital assets) were obliged to pay. Based on Qur'anic specifications, categories of people qualified to receive *zekat* included the poor, the needy, the *zekat* collectors; non-Muslims whose hearts were to be reconciled; wayfarers, homeless children and travellers; debtors, people who were unable to pay their debts while attempting to satisfy their basic needs; those working in God's way; and for freeing slaves or prisoners of war (The Qur'an, Tevbe 9:60).

Combined with *sadaqa* – voluntary almsgiving – a broader category for the purpose of doing good to please Allah, *zekat* was an important redistributive mechanism of social justice as well as a means to accommodate social frictions in the Ottoman Empire (Ergin et al., 2007). Many pious individuals, contributed by establishing hospitals, schools, libraries, mosques and soup kitchens to help out the less-fortunate. Imarets, the public kitchens, handed out food, free of charge, to specific groups and to individuals, to be consumed in the premises.

However, not all who would benefit from imarets were destitute, as 'charity instituted a patron–client relationship between benefactor and beneficiary, regardless of whether the latter was a destitute person in need of sustenance or a member of the patron's retinue' (Ergin et al., 2007, p. 16). Singer (2006) points out that by the 16th century, Fatih imaret in Istanbul, for example, was feeding up to 1500 people twice a day. The clients included 'visiting dignitaries, travellers, scholars and students from the prestigious colleges attached to the mosque, the door-keepers and guards of these colleges, the students of three other nearby colleges and four local dervish lodges (*zaviyes*), 600 student candidates and their eight proctors, fifty-six members of the imaret staff, forty-seven hospital staff members and fifty-one other functionaries of the complex, including employees serving at the mosque and tombs. Finally, after all these people finished eating, what was left over was distributed to the indigent poor'.

The need for social assistance became even more apparent as the Empire declined in the 19th century. The loss of territories resulted in millions of refugees going in different directions. Hunger and poverty killed possibly more people than the wars and ethnic massacres. Dealing with millions of refugees proved to be increasingly difficult for the state as well as faith-based charities as many felt the impacts of these social disturbances. Instead of faith-based charities, new social organizations such as Hilal-i Ahmer (1868) to assist wounded soldiers, or Darüşşafaka Association (1863) to assist war orphans were formed.

Republican modernization and reforms

The Republic of Turkey was the outcome of the struggle for sovereignty and nationhood of the Anatolian peoples who sought a homeland in the ruins of the old empire. The modernization programme that was implemented in the first decade of the Republic was exemplary in the history of social revolutions that brought comprehensive changes in virtually all aspects of everyday life. The modernization package included radical reforms at political, legal, religious and cultural levels, including the abolition of the monarchy and caliphate, establishment of laicism as the official ideology of the state, emancipation of women, banning of polygamy, adoption of the Latin alphabet, Gregorian calendar, metric system, European numerals, and changes in dress code. The speed of the introduction of these changes, the top-down approach by which they were introduced, the inability to address existing patterns of social and regional inequalities, and distrust towards the masses created grounds for future social tensions. The political turmoil during the multi-party years and frequent military interventions reflected not only the growing pains, but demonstrated tensions between republicanism and democratic priorities.

Reforms also included the closing of institutionalized convents and the dervish lodges and replacing Sharia law with a new constitution and civil, commercial and penal codes based on European models. Likewise, modernist secular policies also brought to an end some of the autonomous organization of non-Muslim religious groups as regulated by the Ottoman Millet system. These changes also affected the Vakıfs (foundations) by restricting their ability to purchase new properties aimed to further weaken the power of religious charities (Kurban and Hatemi,

2009). With Vakıfs and faith-based charities in decline and religious convents and dervish lodges closed the state emerged as the new patron in job creation and social welfare. This was seen as the right step towards the modernization and rationalization of social services and cutting the power base of religious organizations. Organizations such as *Kızılay* (The Turkish Red Crescent Society) would work closely with the government in assisting natural disasters and other emergencies.

Through various programmes, the Turkish state aimed to fulfil its social welfare functions. Support policies provided assistance to small family farmers in rural areas, government subsidies offered cheap food and energy for urban consumers and state economic enterprises created infrastructure and employment. Especially since the 1960s public health and social security organizations have provided assistance to ever increasing numbers of people in need. While both the scale of the economy and the functions of the welfare state could not be a match with Turkey's neighbours in the West, in many ways, Turkey presented the profile of a welfare state until the accumulation crisis in the mid-1970s.

Nevertheless, the inward looking import substitution industrialization model and agricultural modernization in the post-World War II era resulted in a significant trend of rural-urban migration and unemployment threatening the sustainability of the welfare regime in Turkey. Between 1950 and 1960, the urban population rose by 83.2 per cent. This was followed by another 77 per cent increase between 1960 and 1970 (Koc, 1994, p. 214). Many newcomers to the city settled in shanty towns called *gecekondu*, surrounding major cities (Keles, 1983). The population of Istanbul rose from 983,000 in 1950, to 1,466,000 in 1960 and reaching 2,132,000 in 1970. While rising demand for foreign labour in Western Europe absorbed part of the 'surplus' population, the 'Oil Crisis' of 1973, economic hardships following the Turkish military intervention in Cyprus in 1974, and declining remittances from migrant workers in the second half of the 1970s led to a serious balance of payments crisis.

The neo-liberal era in Turkish politics

The economic crisis aggravated social and political conflict in the second half of the 1970s. As inflation rose, real wages started declining. Austerity measures dictated by the International Monetary Fund (IMF) resulted in cuts in social programmes. Strikes, work stoppages and political unrest became commonplace. In an inflationary environment, hoarding and black marketing in basic staples such as sugar, margarine and rice resulted in long line-ups. Municipal governments in many cities organized staple stores to fight against hoarding and provide affordable food to urban populations (Koc and Koc, 1999, pp. 115–121). While retired workers, and returning migrant labourers dreamed about opening a small grocery store or a restaurant to provide food to this growing population, many newcomers survived in the informal sector as urban farmers, street pedlars, greengrocers providing goods and services that the state and the markets could not. Urban and peri-urban agriculture (Kaldjian, 2004; Eloglu, 2012), public markets (Dökmeci, 2005; Duru, 2012), street vendors (Dana and Dana 1999) and domestic workers (Cinar, 1994) contributed significantly to the everyday food security of urban residents.

In January 1980, following IMF recommendations, Turkey accepted an export-oriented economic recovery plan, privatization of state economic enterprises, and cuts in social programmes and real wages. Increasing protests brought the third military intervention in two decades. The military coup in September 1980 dissolved Parliament, banned political parties, unions and associations with restrictions being placed on freedom of expression, freedom of press and rights to assembly. These measures were accompanied by a sharp decline in real wages and agricultural subsidies (Margulies and Yildizoglu, 1988; Aricanli and Rodrik, 1990; Koc, 1994). A new constitution adopted in 1982 introduced severe limitations to democratic rights and political liberties. Elections in 1983 brought a civilian regime under military tutelage eager to implement a neo-liberal economic development model.

Throughout the 1980s and 1990s political coercion went hand in hand with economic liberalism. Measures were taken to reduce the state's role in the economy, allowing market forces to operate with fewer restrictions. Financial incentives aimed to promote exports while restrictions on imports were reduced significantly. Customs Free Zones were established; price controls were eased; subsidies were reduced; and public spending on social programmes continued to be trimmed. Deregulation went in parallel with and privatization of state economic enterprises.

Food security in the neo-liberal era

For the urban and rural poor, the neo-liberal era in the post-1980 era meant significant cuts in real wages, a decline in farm prices, high unemployment, and higher rates of part-time employment. Cuts in agricultural support programmes, and armed conflict in Turkish Kurdistan brought even more impoverished people to big cities such as Istanbul. Istanbul's population rose from 2,772,000 in 1980, to 7,620,000 in 1990 and 10,923,000 by 2000. As old *gecekondus* were turning into multi-storey apartments, small grocery stores began to be replaced with supermarket chains. Major global retail chains such as Metro, Carrefour; and fast food restaurants such as McDonalds, Burger King and KFC entered the Turkish market, mostly targeting the prosperous urban middle class.

For those who were seeking self-employment, demand for affordable food created opportunities as street pedlars, urban gardeners, or food retailers in public markets. They provided relatively affordable food for the urban poor, the precarious workers, the unemployed, and pensioners. Throughout all these changes possibly the only constant that did not change in the Turkish food scene was the role of bread as the main staple. Highly subsidized by the state and monitored by local governments, bread remained as the main source of calories for the Turkish population. FAO has estimated that the major percentage of energy for Turkish people comes from bread (44 per cent) and bread with other cereals (58 per cent) (FAO, 2010; Bilgic and Yen, 2013). For many of the urban poor, bread was not a side dish but most likely the only source of food, with a touch of margarine, or a few olives and some tea. As reported in a recent Hunger and Poverty Line study of a Turkish labour union confederation (Turk-Is, 2011) many low-income families could not make sufficient income to obtain an adequate and balanced diet and they would often consume food items that are lower in price and nutritionally inadequate.

Conservative neo-liberalism of the AKP

Neo-liberalism emerged as a hegemonic discourse in the 1980s. In a short time, it captivated the imaginations of people and political parties of diverse stripes from the conservative right to the social democratic left. It was no surprise, therefore, to see that the AKP, a political party that has been associated with traditional Islam and a critique of secularism and modernism in Turkey, could also be an effective adaptor of neo-liberal policies after their election victory in 2002. The AKP had its ideological origins in the earlier religious conservative parties, some of which managed to form a number of coalition governments in the 1970–1990 period and were banned by the courts for violating the secularist articles of the Turkish constitution.

Aware of the faith of previous pro-Islamic parties and feeling threatened by secular opposition and civilian and military bureaucracy, the AKP adopted a liberal discourse internally, while reiterating its desire to become a full member of the European Union and adopting a series of policy reforms to improve human rights. The ratification of the *International*

Covenant on Economic, Social and Cultural Rights (ICESCR) on 4 June 2003, including the right to food, led to changes allowing community based *Vakıfs* to purchase land. These were also necessary steps taken in unison with the Copenhagen Criteria as required for full EU membership.

If religious conservatism has been one of the ideological strains of the AKP governments, the other was the pragmatism. Working with Turgut Ozal and his Motherland Party (ANAP) in the previous decades, many members of the AKP had been impressed by the success of Ozal's pragmatic populism, combining neoliberal economics with religious conservatism during the 1980s and 1990s (Cosar and Yegenoglu, 2009). Ozal aimed to replace the old import substitution industrialization model with an export promotion model. This was also a political strategy for creating a business-elite friendly to the regime, benefitting from public contracts, privatization bids and cheap credit from public banks. Controlling municipal governments for securing financial as well as electoral support and the controlling of the media were the other aspects of Ozal's winning formula (Öniş, 2004; Patton, 2006).

A similar thinking would likely explain why the AKP was so quick and keen in adapting the food banking model in 2004, only a few months after signing the ICESCR. Even though food banking was an untested model, it offered a unique potential to provide financial gain to friendly businesses, a chance to strengthen the public profile of religious NGOs, foundations, and municipal governments involved in food banking. Following the Ozal model, AKP governments at the national and municipal levels used public contracts to revitalize the economy while at the same time creating opportunities for businesses friendlier to the party ideologically. The AKP established a symbiotic relationship with various municipal governments, charitable foundations and business associations who shared the same political stripe.

This formula seemed to work during the early 2000s where Turkey managed to survive the global financial crisis that had devastated some of the EU economies. Speaking at a panel on Turkey-EU relations in Brussels, Olli Rehn, EU Vice President in charge of monetary and financial matters, would praise Turkey for effective financial policies and reforms in responding to the global economic crisis in an 'extraordinary' fashion. 'After the crisis, Turkey's quick growth spurt allowed its economy to become the 16th largest in the world and as a result Turkey was accepted into the G-20,' said Rehn. He also stressed that Turkey's inflation rate had dropped from an average 75 per cent in the 1990s to 11 per cent today, its public debt had been halved, and its banking sector reformed (Hürriyet Daily News, 2012).

Food insecurity under the AKP

Yet this economic miracle could not be shared equally. While Turkey was the 16th largest economy in the world, it was 56th in terms of per capita GDP. Allocation of public social expenditure as a proportion of GDP (12.8 per cent in 2009) would show a significantly lower place in comparison to the OECD average of 22.1 per cent, as well. The State Statistical Organisation TUIK's calculations in terms of the income gap, as reflected by the gini coefficient, showed that between 2000 and 2012 the score moved from 0.40 to 0.46, indicating a widening gap.

Even the most conservative estimates provided by the Global Food Banking Network indicated that there were 340,000 people in 2011 living below the 'hunger line' in Turkey (monthly income of US$185 for a four-person household). The same report estimated that about 17 per cent of the total population of 75 million people were living below the 'poverty line' (US$520 a month for a four-person household) (GFN, 2011).

Economic growth relied, at least partially, on lower wages. Government aimed to reform existing social welfare and health care agencies. However, these were costly reforms and would require years to deliver significant outcomes. In this environment, charities provided a quick and historically familiar model similar to *vakifs* and *imaret*. Charities, collecting funds from the pious individuals also created an opportunity for legitimizing the re-institutionalization of the *zekat*.

Legalizing food banks

One of the earlier acts of the AKP regime was the legalization of food banks. Decree (no. 5035) adopted in 2004 allowed all associations and foundations to set up food banks, provided that this was explicitly stated in their charters (TBMM, 2004). Companies were allowed a 100 per cent tax deduction for donations to food banks and were exempted from value added tax. Municipal governments were also allowed to set up food banks in 2005.

Speaking to a delegation of Global Foodbank Network representatives, Turkish FoodBanking Association (TFA) Board Chair Serhan Suzer said that 'as a group respecting traditional values and involved in various food businesses, we thought it is particularly fitting that we should be involved in the founding of the (TFA).' He continued 'Our objective...is to expand food banking in Turkey and make sure it is done according to certain operating standards and on a much larger scale' (GFN, 2011). Interestingly while donations to food banks originally included only food items, they have now expanded to include cleaning materials, clothing and heating material such as coal. The fact that food banks are providing assistance beyond food indicates that food banking is not simply seen as a measure to alleviate food insecurity but as an instrument of public social assistance to address poverty and the gap created by the neo-liberal restructuring of the state's role in this area.

The 2004 law allows any association or foundation (*Vakıf*) to receive donations as long as they mention assisting people in need of food, clothing, cleaning and heating materials in their bylaws. Many municipal governments provide electronic membership cards similar to credit cards. Clients whose eligibility is accepted by the authorities may use these cards to receive food, clothing, shoes, cleaning and heating materials according to the funds they have on their card. Modern food banks looking like mini supermarkets provide comfortable space for clients to make their selections as to their needs from well organized shelves. By imitating the supermarket environment, food banks replicate commodity relations of the marketplace.

Interestingly, however, finding data on the number of people benefitting from food banks, or on the amount of tax deductions due to donations is not easy to find. An interview with businessman Mustafa Suzer provided some ideas as to the level of operations of food banks: 'We are making donations to organizations that have identified the people in need. There are food banks in the Silivri and Beyoglu districts (where) hundreds of people receive food every day. We give food to schools and dormitories.' Amongst the type of donations and donors, he lists 2 tons of bulgur, 50 blocks of cheese, frozen fish, meat, chicken, cheese, and yogurt, and products from brands such as Banvit, Beşler Gıda, Altınkaya Meat Products, Baktat, Bahçıvan Cheese products, Ay Işığı Gıda, Torunlar and Nestlé, an odd list of food processors national and transnational.

A study conducted by the İstanbul Serbest Muhasebeciler Mali Müşavirler Odası (ISMMMO, 2009 – Istanbul Chamber of Public Accountants and Financial Advisors) indicated that as of 2007, 20 associations had been authorized by the Ministry of the Interior to operate as food banks, and claimed to receive 897,051 TL worth of goods as donations. Between 2003–2008, the amount of donations to food banks reached a total of over 7 billion liras' worth (ISMMMO, 2009).

The ISMMMO report also provides a regional distribution of food bank members between 2004–2007. The total number of food bank members (clients/recipients) rose from over 5 million to 8.5 million in the four-year period although it is suggested that a significant number of people might belong to multiple food banks, keeping their membership even if they do not continue to pay membership fees. The reports indicated potential for abuse of donations estimating that about 10 per cent of donations end at the wrong addresses, that some people are receiving donations from more than one food bank, or that some are selling the donations (particularly coal) in the marketplace (ISMMMO, 2009, p. 6).

The details of donations and the number of beneficiaries are not listed clearly by individual organizations. Other than figures, such as in the Beyoglu municipality in Istanbul, where close to 20,000 people receive food donations from municipal food banks, one can find hardly any evidence, neither by government representatives nor available statistics (GFN, 2011). As Morvaridi (2013, p. 316) states, 'no data are available in the public domain on how much funding [faith-based organizations] raised through specific kinds of donations or how donations are spent. Thus, little attention has been paid to the roles and responsibilities of politico-religious organisations in both directing charitable activities and in defining who the appropriate recipients should be.' Many of these organizations, including the Turkish Red Crescent Society now accept *zekat* and *fitre* (a form of *sadaqa* in Ramadan). The collection of *fitre* and *zekat* represent acts that could not even be imaginable only a decade ago in a modernist secular Turkey. This demonstrates the hegemony of the AKP government that has ruled the country since 2002, and their ability to move a political agenda closely associated with the Islamic past of the country.

Fear of bread waste

It is no wonder that in a country that satisfies 44 per cent of its caloric needs with bread alone, one can find on almost every city block at least one bakery providing various combinations of flour, sugar, salt and fat. In terms of conservative neo-liberalism this would be considered as an opportunity in creating employment and providing affordable food through market forces.

The consequences of this dietary transformation was reflected in a recent study by the *Turkish Diabetes Epidemiology Study* (TURDEP). Measuring fasting glucose and biochemical parameters of 26,499 randomly sampled adults, the TURDEP study concluded that the prevalence of diabetes in Turkey was 16.5 per cent, obesity 36 per cent and hypertension 31.4 per cent. Compared to the previous TURDEP study conducted in 1997–1998, these figures show a 90 per cent increase in diabetes rates and 44 per cent in obesity (Satman et al., 2013).

However, rather than the ever increasing numbers of bakeries and rising obesity rates, government would address bread waste as a food security concern. A circular released by the Prime Minister's office on 2 April 2013 declared a campaign against wasting bread (Resmî Gazete, 2013). A booklet prepared by the Foundation to Prevent Waste in Turkey identified the waste of food and bread as a serious national security concern and provided recipes to utilize stale bread (Akgül, 2008). The foundation also defended food banking as a tool to avoid food waste.

This concern with avoiding food waste also reflected increasing divergence from secularism of the republican past increasing references to religious text in social policy design. Referring to various verses from the Quran, Mert, a professor of theology from Hitit University in Çorum, argued that the causes of poverty and hunger could be found in 'idleness and indulgence, greed, immodesty and extravagance, and lack of mutual assistance and solidarity not in lack of food or over population' (Mert, 2010). This conservative interpretation while questioning popular myths of hunger, would also lead to a 'blame the victim' attitude that would provide religious justification to neo-conservative policies.

Conclusion

Poverty and hunger are not new to Turkey. Even though Turkey reached a level of economic development where it is now assisting less developed countries in Central Asia and Africa, and to victims of civil war in the Middle East in countries such as Syria and Libya, Turkey has its own poor in need of assistance. While considerable progress has been made in recent years in lowering the number of people living in absolute poverty, millions still need social assistance to survive day by day.

The fact that within months of its 2003 ratification of the *International Covenant on Economic, Social and Cultural Rights* (ICESCR) and the right to food, Turkey would choose charitable food banking as a solution to deal with poverty should not be a surprise. Food banks provided a model developed in the West during the neo-liberal era (Riches, 1997a; Poppendieck, 1998). It was a tried and true model that fitted well into the commodified food economy increasingly dominated by modern food processors and supermarket chains.

Adaption of food banks of course cannot be explained simply within the context of a neo-liberal agenda. This issue must also be understood as part of the Islamic conservatism of the AKP that wanted to replace the agencies of the welfare state with faith-based philanthropies reminiscent of the country's Islamic past. The charitable model seemed like a comfortable fit with the AKP leadership's pro-Islamic politics. Charitable solutions to hunger provided a comfortable continuity with the Islamic almsgiving tradition that had been undermined during the Republican era.

Charitable food banking provided a legitimate venue for re-establishing *fitre* and *zekat*. Food banking also fit well with the Party's local organizing efforts in various municipalities, where providing particular social services (such as free health services, tutoring for university or high school examinations, donations of food, clothing and coal) brought positive results in elections. Success of local community-based efforts of the Ikhwan movement (Muslim Brotherhood) in Egypt, an organization that the AKP closely followed, has most likely demonstrated to the AKP leadership the importance of philanthropic work in political organizing (Toth, 2003).

Furthermore, tax exemptions provided desired incentives and benefits to businesses that were politically closer to the AKP. While only 5 per cent of donations to foundations were tax deductible, 100 per cent of donations given to food banking associations would receive tax deductions (ISMMMO, 2009, p. 2). Likewise, donations to food banks in municipalities where the governing party has the majority would be seen as a smart investment with the expectations of favourable results in receiving government contracts; and this is how food (and other commodities) are used for political ends in Turkey.

As Morvaridi correctly points out, the Turkish government's current policy 'operates on the basis of fragmentation and clientelism' instead of a system based on 'social rights and entitlements' (2013, p. 318). While those who could manage to establish closer relations with political and influential bodies gain privileges, others who cannot have such ties have to rely on their kinship networks or charity. In this environment of clientelist politics, supporting friendly businesses through tax benefits could also be seen as smart politics. Like previous regimes in the past, the AKP, too, has seen the importance of controlling the media and establishing a friendly bourgeoisie for its hegemony.

The fact that food banks donate not only food but clothing, shoes, cleaning and heating materials indicates clearly that food banks operate not only frontline food security organizations but as civil society-based social assistance networks, filling the gap left by the shrinking welfare state. It is however not a system facilitating income redistribution but instead aid in kind rather than cash transfers. In this sense it is not about the right to food, which respects the right of all citizens to make their own food choices.

This fragmented welfare system not only makes accountability and transparency difficult, but also diminishes the citizenship rights of participants (Bugra and Candas, 2011). What the faith-based food banks provide is something akin to the old imaret system where '[h]and in hand with the image of imperial generosity is that of strictly-run establishments, which carefully regulated the movements of their clients and the sustenance that each received. Existing social hierarchies were reinforced, perhaps even taking their basic definition from the order in which people were served and the quantity and quality of the food that they received.' (Singer, 2006)

Turkey's achievements in recent years in providing food security and eliminating hunger for its citizens, its global commitments, and the role played by food charity need further scrutiny not only in terms of gaining a transparent account of what has actually been achieved but who is benefitting and why. This scrutiny also requires an investigation of the usefulness of current measurements of hunger and food security. Providing packaged cookies of flour, sugar and margarine, and pops sweetened with high fructose corn syrup may curb hunger momentarily but is already presenting the new profile of hunger in the form of rising obesity and diabetes figures, while lacking integrated measures for food, agriculture, trade and public health policy.

Finally, there is a need to question the limits of establishing a rights-based approach to food security in an authoritarian state and clientelist politics. As the Turkish case demonstrates, recognizing rights on paper, and specifically the right to food, is only an important first step but needs to be fully backed up by democratization of the state and all social institutions, respect for law, transparency and civil society based advocacy.

12
Food Banks and Food Justice in 'Austerity Britain'

Elizabeth Dowler

Introduction

'Twenty years' after documenting poverty and hunger in the United Kingdom and the inadequacy of the state's response (Craig and Dowler, 1997) we find an astonishing and previously unimaginable situation unfolding in the UK. Growing number of households are apparently having to use emergency 'food aid' systems, largely from the charitable sector, and increasingly this practice is not only recognized by the state at national and local levels, it is also being endorsed, enshrined and encouraged. How has such a situation arisen, especially following years of economic prosperity and government attempts to address low-income and diet problems, and to reduce inequalities in health (which is where food and nutrition initiatives have largely been located)?

This chapter explores the UK's political and social practice, ideological approaches, and the current challenges that face civil society and citizens alike, in enabling people to eat sufficiently, sustainably and appropriately for a healthy life. It begins with a brief review of food system problematics, including rising prices, and the impact on low-income households particularly. A summary of recent policies to address inequalities and food poverty, broadly defined as the inability to afford, or have access to, sufficient food for a healthy, acceptable diet, then leads to the examination of current circumstances and responses.

Challenges to the economy and the food system

The UK is no exception in currently facing times of economic austerity, following fall-out from the collapse of the US sub-prime market and subsequent banking crisis; as economic anxieties have spread across

Europe there have been severe losses of job and income security and at times a near collapse of social fabric. Some attribute the major English riots in 2011 in part to intense social dissatisfaction and frustration at high youth unemployment, continuing deprivation and loss of social security support (Rogers, 2011). The previous Labour Government had tried to use fiscal action to stimulate aggregate demand in response to the recession, but lost the 2010 General Election; the Coalition Government which emerged set out to reduce the economic deficit as fast as possible, and seeking to reduce public spending, brought in a series of increasingly harsh social security reforms aimed at strategic and systematic reductions. Indeed, reducing the 'welfare costs and wasteful spending' was an explicit aim (HMT, 2010, p. 5), along with rejection of the previous administration's approach (Powell, 2013).

Social sector impact

Among public sector cuts, those that applied to social security, in particular the support for working-age adults and/or families, was argued to be disproportionate (IFS, 2010). The reforms led to major reductions in social security provision and increased application of 'sanctions', where people's benefits are cut or refused because they are said not to be following rules correctly, particularly for the unemployed. In addition, other public sector cuts included both direct job losses and indirect support for community level needs, such as children's centres and Sure Start, home care and voluntary sector activities. These belt-tightenings have particularly affected part-time workers, increased job insecurity and many variations of 'zero hour contracts', whereby employees are on-call but with no set minimum hours or definite schedule, and who are only paid if actually employed.

These cuts have marked gendered effects: two thirds of the public sector workforce is female, and many of these women work part-time (often involuntarily); the majority of lone parents (whose benefit entitlements have been changed) are female; women are more likely to be in poorly paid, precarious employment which is harder to sustain, given changes to child benefit, child and working tax credits (a means-tested cash benefit which brings inadequate wages up to a notional minimum). Furthermore, women are much less likely to have adequate old-age pensions. Women also make up the majority of claimants for Housing Benefit (which itself is now harder to obtain as both access and the amounts have considerably tightened). Finally, it is women who are primarily experiencing hardship through the withdrawal of support services such as Sure Start (for parents with young children), anti-domestic violence centres and youth support (Women's Budget Group 2010, 2012; Stephenson and Harrison, 2011).

Food sector impact

These economic and social policy austerity measures, put in place in response to the international fiscal crisis, added to existing challenges faced by the food system (CFPA, 2010), from rising oil prices, loss of biodiversity, climate change and rising demand for meat. In addition, problematic harvests, support for biofuels and financial speculation following the economic crisis, had major effects on food prices; these rose considerably from 2007–2008 onwards, and despite some fluctuation, are unlikely to come down to pre-2007 levels in the near future (De Schutter, 2010).

UK food policy responses

In the UK, anxieties about the food system led the Department for Environment, Food and Rural Affairs (Defra) to use the framing of 'food security' to review the sustainability and reliability of food supply chains and consumption assurance (Defra, 2006), a departure from previous views that food security was largely a global issue concerning the needs of developing countries (MacMillan and Dowler, 2012). A small team drew on wide consultation to analyse the complex factors affecting national- and household-level food security. Partly as a result, social aspects of sustainability were acknowledged alongside the environmental and economic aspects (though the work began before the economic crisis) and the 2006 *Evidence and Analysis* paper briefly discussed issues of 'access' and 'affordability', including whether 'low-income individuals [can] afford decent food, and to what extent "food poverty", like "fuel poverty" exist[s in the UK]' (Defra, 2006, p. 7).

In its subsequent report on UK food security, Defra stated 'Every Briton should have access to an affordable, healthy diet; achieving this is at the core of Government policy. [...] Defra already keeps a close watch on movements in real food prices and food's share of spending in low-income households, but the *UK Food Security Assessment* brings this data together with other evidence on the affordability of fruit and vegetables, and household access to food stores' (Defra, 2009, p. 11). The focus was thus on affordability, and recognition of its importance to prevent or address 'food poverty'. Of course, 'affordability' relates to both price and effective demand: what a householder can afford to put towards food expenditure.

Defra (2012, 2013) has since published regular summary data from the Family Food Statistics annual dataset on food consumption experiences of the lowest tenth and fifth of the income distribution. There has, however, been no systematic data on physical access to food stores, and the proposed additional measure of consumers' self-reported food insecurity is yet to be developed.

Meanwhile, the Strategy Unit of the Cabinet Office (which answers to the Prime Minister) published a review of issues and overarching policy document, *Food Matters* (TSU, 2008), which also briefly addressed the problems facing low-income households. Partly as a result of *Food Matters*, a Council of Food Policy Advisors was set up under Defra, to develop further understanding and offer advice to the then Minister (Hilary Benn). Their subsequent report (CFPA, 2010) sets out ten immediate priorities for the then Labour Government's newly published food policy for England: with the third listed being to reduce inequalities of access to healthy, 'low impact' diets, in order to avoid increases in diet-related health inequalities. The report stressed that access to a decent, environmentally and socially sustainable diet should form part of the understanding of poverty in the UK in a similar way to the need for decent housing and affordable heating. This was an important recognition of the need for affordable sustainable food.

However, the 2010 Coalition Government (Conservatives and Liberal Democrats, both with a neo-liberal agenda) was less interested in food security, certainly at the household level. Thus there have been few policy initiatives or pronouncements concerning low-income households. However in January 2013, Defra called for a rapid scoping review and evidence assessment on the use of 'food aid' (which includes what are known as food banks) across the UK (Fell et al., 2013, p. 7). There has also been recent interest in 'food poverty' from the Food Standards Agency (which is no longer responsible for nutrition as it was under the previous administration, where it had a strong strand of research on low-income households). There have been a number of briefings for parliamentary groups on food poverty and recognition from the Church, the media and by politicians (see also Fell et al., 2013), of the rising use of emergency charitable systems, and some regional meetings. There is as yet no coordinated policy response.

Nevertheless, two important points remain from earlier Defra work on food security and food policy: first, recognition that, where possible, consumers' responses to rising prices can be quite nuanced, with many trying to express their continuing concerns about food quality, provenance, environmental and ethical issues. Secondly, however, that rising prices do have a disproportionate effect on those in the poorest households, both because food is a higher proportion of household expenditure, and also because many in such households live in places where food which is appropriate for health and reasonably priced is harder to find. They may also live in homes which are poorly insulated and more difficult to heat, so that rising fuel prices compete starkly with food for priority in expenditure.

Thus while the need grows for UK food policies which take account of environmental, economic and social sustainability, the policy spaces and opportunities to focus on structural determinants of improving access for all to healthy, low-impact, affordable diets, seem more remote than ever. Individualized 'informed choice' has largely been reinstated, with the state's role merely a light-touch regulation of the food supply and retail sectors, rather than wages or benefits in relation to the cost of food. There is no recognition of the human right to food, where 'accessibility' is of central importance, along with the maintenance of human dignity and sustainability across generations (Dowler and O'Connor, 2012).

Impact on food in low-income households

Ideological context

These policy shifts fail to address the needs of those living on low, or even low to middling incomes and/or in areas of multiple deprivation, who face a double or even triple challenge: rising costs of fuel and food, alongside major cuts in social security benefits, stagnant wages and/or rising unemployment. Such policies result from an economic, austerity strategy located in neo-liberalism and individualism in the political sphere. New Labour failed to reverse this trend from the Thatcher agenda of the 1980s – indeed, some argue they embraced it – but it has accelerated under the Coalition Government from 2010.

The implications for understanding and responding to food system problematics at the household level are profound. First, while the private sector is obviously the main source of food and nutrition, responsibility for choice being located at the individual level means that people's ability to manage expenditure so as to obtain appropriate food for health and social wellbeing is also seen as 'private' in terms of duty, necessity and culpability. Questioning poor people's individual-level competencies in knowing how to budget for, choose or cook healthy food, is the default position: they have only themselves to blame.

Second, there has been a systematic dismantling of the post-war consensus on the need for and maintenance of a welfare state, to support people through times of need. People claiming benefits are increasingly demonized by the Government as 'skivers not strivers' (though in reality many hold down two jobs, or are living with disability, or are carers, or forced in and out of short-term work) (Reid, 2013); and as part of the 'something for nothing' generation (though many have contributed to entitlement through National Insurance). In addition, the value of benefits is being eroded, partly by actual cuts in levels, and partly because uprating now uses the Consumer Price Index (CPI) rather than the Retail Price Index (RPI). Since the RPI is rising faster, social security benefits and the National Minimum Wage are falling further behind actual costs of food and other necessities as well as average income (Hirsch, 2013). These and other structural changes such as access to child care for those in work, compound the problems from increasing food (and fuel) prices, but are located by the state and much of the more right-wing media at the level of the individual, both to shoulder blame for them and to solve them. Sometimes media comment can be particularly virulent and personalized in attacking individuals who speak out (usually on blogs) about their own experiences of living in poverty and trying to manage food; such demonization of character, skills and even the right to have a voice is consonant with a neo-liberal agenda of individualizing culpability (Monroe, 2013).

Impact on household food management

Although there has been little purposive research on how the global economic crisis has affected poor households in the UK, useful, largely qualitative, evidence is available (Hossain et al., 2011; Dowler et al., 2011; Kneafsey et al., 2012). It shows that, even by 2010, the impacts of rising food and fuel prices were quite severe on low-income households. Growing hardship in daily living and future prospects were documented, despite people's resourcefulness in managing on increasingly limited means. Family, friends and local communities were vital for social and economic survival; when people somehow 'got by' they did so at considerable cost to their present and future health and social well-being. People reported many adaptive practices, such as buying food which was cheaper than they were used to, of poorer nutritional or social quality (including 'fast food' because it did not need cooking) or broadly unacceptable to their cultural food patterns, with many making the effort to travel to cheaper supermarkets rather than their local shops.

Where possible, some had begun growing food; many mentioned having to spend considerably more time and effort to obtain and prepare food; several had ceased bulk buying and, because of living 'hand-to-mouth', were purchasing simply what was needed for that day or even just that meal, rather than their usual economies of scale (in money and time). People saw themselves as victims of rising food prices, and that food choice was largely shaped by the ability to pay, which they saw as primarily outside of their control. Cost and availability shaped dietary practices, notwithstanding skills and nutritional knowledge; those with less to spend on food enjoyed less choice and ultimately a less healthy diet. A substantial proportion taking part in the research, carried out before the advent of the Coalition Government and austerity cuts, felt they had poor food security themselves, and saw things getting worse in the future.

Impact on food outcomes

In the absence of systematic monitoring, there are no official data on numbers of households living in food insecurity, or in food poverty. These have to be inferred. Almost 13 million people, about 21 per cent of the UK population, are living on incomes which define them as poor (using data after deduction of housing costs). Half of poor children and working-age adults live in households in paid work (Aldridge et al., 2012). About five million in poverty are in workless households; of these, 3.6 million are adults and the majority are looking for work, claiming Jobseeker's Allowance (JSA). In addition, about 1.4 million part-time workers want full-time work. Many are only offered short-term jobs which are poorly paid and non-unionized, and often below their skills level. A high proportion of those on low incomes, whether in work or not, are likely to see their incomes reduced from welfare benefit changes, through a combination of income-related disability and housing benefit changes (Aldridge et al., 2012). The inferred impact on food budgets and nutritional outcomes comes from large datasets, and observed effects from smaller scale studies (for example, Craig and Dowler, 1997; Dowler et al., 2007; Maslen et al., 2013). Broadly speaking, those with insufficient money and/or living in areas of multiple deprivation are more likely to eat monotonous, less healthy diets, with little dietary variety and low intakes of fruit and vegetables, especially fresh produce. Institutional food, including at school, is also likely to be of poor quality.

Defra's *Family Food Survey* is the only source for systematic monitoring of the effects of current economic austerity on food patterns or dietary intakes. These data, produced annually, measure what households actually purchase at different levels of income, in relation to the likely healthiness of the diet, but are not presented in terms of the poverty indicators cited above. In the last five years, falling incomes and rising food prices have reduced food affordability by more than 20 per cent for the lowest income decile (Defra, 2013). Between 1998 and 2009, the average income of low-income households increased by 22 per cent, but average food prices went up by 33 per cent (Defra, 2012, p. 29). The average expenditure on food in UK households was 11.2 per cent of total expenditure, but for low-income households, it was 16.6 per cent, reflecting continually increasing prices of food and fuel (Defra, 2013).

Those who are now in the lowest income households are buying fewer fruits and vegetables than five years ago. The data show that even those in average income groups are buying less meat, fish, tea, fruit; some are trading down (buying cheaper versions of usual commodities) to cope with rising prices; but those in the lowest income group are not trading down because they have less opportunity to do so, being already on the most basic of diets. Although this group are buying less food, particularly fruit and vegetables, they have to spend nearly a fifth more to do so, than in the previous year (Defra, 2012). The nutritional impact of these changes in purchasing patterns can be profound (Griffith et al., 2013), particularly in households with young children and pensioners. Significantly, Defra's surveys do not monitor households where there is acute hunger or food budget crises, since they record expenditure rather than experience, and households in real financial difficulties tend not to take part in surveys.

Defra does not have responsibility for reacting to potential health consequences of people having insufficient money for food or living where healthy food cannot readily be obtained. Inequalities in health have profound effects, not only on the incidence of coronary heart disease, type II diabetes, cancer and obesity all shown to be associated with poor dietary intakes and meal patterns (Lawlor, 2013), but also on the capacity to resist infections or mental confusion, and ultimately on mortality. Children's ability to concentrate and study effectively is also damaged by insufficient food and/or food of poor nutritious value – which tends to be cheaper, particularly where public procurement is driven by falling budgets, as in the provision of school meals (Morgan and Sonnino, 2008). These inequalities in health consequences, exacerbated by economic conditions, carry serious costs to individuals and society.

Money needed to eat healthily

A way of addressing the implications of reduced income on food budgets is to examine what it would theoretically cost to meet standardized expenditure needs, including food, for households of different sizes and compositions, where the dietary component has been calculated to meet minimal nutritional requirements in ways which fulfil social norms. Consensual budget standard methodologies are a systematic and objective way of establishing such estimations and are produced and uprated annually in the UK (Minimum Income Standards). They consistently show that those who live in households with incomes at or below the National Minimum Wage (NMW), or on state benefits, or with incomes below the relative poverty threshold, do not have enough money to meet basic needs. Food expenditure is where people often cut back, partly because there are no fines or immediate negative consequences (other than hunger or a depressing dull diet); thus, however carefully people budget, shop and cook, they cannot afford a healthy diet (Hirsch, 2013). This is particularly true if people cannot get to mainstream supermarkets, where prices tend to be lower (Dowler et al., 2007; Lloyd et al., 2011), so that they therefore have to spend even more on food than MIS costings. The most recent MIS report shows that state benefits for those who are unemployed but seeking work cover less than 60 per cent of the needs of couples with children, and less than 40 per cent of those for single adults (Hirsch, 2013). Families with children are particularly squeezed, and women are more likely to deny their own intakes where there are food shortfalls, in favour of other household members (Attree, 2005).

Policy responses to emergent food austerity

There is almost no discussion of the current severe problems many people are facing in terms of food, outside charities, the broadsheet press and efforts of campaigning groups. Despite some acknowledgement in specific departmental publications such as the Family Food Survey (Defra), there has been very little comment from the Government on the challenges from sudden shocks (loss of employment; loss of Tax Credit) or the ongoing erosion of wages or benefits against expenditure needs.

Government responses: policy neglect?

In central government, there is little evidence of policy coherence over the issues. A few debates and questions have been raised in the House of Commons, in the Welsh Assembly Government and in the Scottish Parliament. For instance, in January 2012 the Hon. Member for Wakefield, Mary Creagh, introduced the impact on poor households of rising food prices, and the increase in usage of food banks, during an Opposition (unallotted) Day. The long, heated debate which followed included graphic accounts by MPs from constituents about their problems (Hansard, 2012b). However, little practical response from government ensued; on the contrary, the response was to deny that changes to, or problems with, the social security system have led to people using food banks (e.g., Hansard, 2013). During 2013, the government devolved responsibility for Social Fund crisis loans to local authorities, some of whom intended to use these funds, themselves more limited than hitherto, to support local food banks (Hansard, 2013; Royston and Rodrigues, 2013).

Central government in turn takes no responsibility for food banks, which are seen as wholly in the charitable sector: 'My Lords, I must emphasise to my noble friend that food banks are absolutely not part of our welfare system [...] There is local provision, and following the devolution of part of the Social Fund to local authorities, local authorities are now responsible for setting up local welfare provision. To the extent that they are interested in using third-sector groups, including food banks, that is entirely up to them.' (Lord Freud, Parliamentary Under-Secretary of State, Department for Work and Pensions: Hansard, 2013)

In the same debate there is reference to food banks being a free good, with the implication that they generate a supply-led demand (this claim was subject to considerable scorn on social media).

Economic access to sufficient food for health is once again off the policy agenda. Despite their promotion by the respected Joseph Rowntree Foundation, no central body uses MIS to judge the adequacy of the NMW or levels of benefit. Campaigning for a 'Living Wage' (which is above the NMW and broadly sufficient to meet MIS) has met with some successes, for instance in London (Grover, 2008), although even this level does not allow for the now marked differences in housing costs in different parts of the country. There is also no central Government response to the loss of community services, which are seen as Local Authority responsibility. Response to people's increasing inability to secure food is constantly located 'downstream', both through reliance on charitable food, which is now put squarely into local authorities' and the food industry's courts, and from longstanding tacit encouragement of local food interventions. There is no recognition by the central state of the problems associated with, nor acceptance of responsibility for, the growing number of households unable to survive economically, and who are using charitable and emergency food sources. Waged work is the only response to poverty (as under the previous Government), low wages, temporary or zero-hour contracts notwithstanding, even where it is available; and the growing lack of affordable housing particularly in south-east England compounds the problems.

There is some evidence that public policy at local levels has some potential to effect change. Some local authorities have begun documenting evidence of food poverty, underlying drivers, and initiatives to address them. For instance, in late 2012, the Greater London Authority Health and Environment Committee set up an open consultation to investigate the scale and causes of food poverty in London, and how the Mayor and partners could support people and address risk factors (GLA, 2013). Critically, the Report highlighted the risk that food banks would be overwhelmed as the economic downturn persisted and living costs rose, and called for concerted action across Greater London, including the provision of universal free school breakfast and lunch. At the time of writing, the (Conservative) Mayor's response included a number of growing and provisioning initiatives and lively research, but little which addressed insufficiency of income or access to shops. Bristol City Council similarly called for evidence (Maslen et al., 2013). Whether local authorities have the capacity or resources to fully address underlying causes of rising food poverty is a moot point; they can, and in some instances do, demand that all contractors for public work use the Living Wage, and can support schools in improving school meal quality. Indeed, several London Boroughs successfully sustain the cost of providing universal free primary school meals. However, neither they nor the devolved territories have jurisdiction over fiscal policy or social security, which are Reserved Matters.

Charitable and civil society responses

The UK, as elsewhere, has a long history of charitable and local community support for households and people in need, whether in direct meal provision or initiatives which address lack of food availability and decent shops, skills in cooking, or growing food (Dowler and Caraher, 2003; see also CFHS, 2013). What seems to be different is the growing demand for emergency and ongoing food from people with nowhere else to turn. In the UK these are often called 'food banks' (these are similar to 'food pantries' in North America): places where those in need can receive a parcel of food sufficient for their household (and sometimes checked by a nutritionist). These operate a variety of structures and management systems; some link to other activities such as cooking clubs, free meal provision, or community cafés; some are part of a formal, networked franchise system run by the Trussell Trust, a Christian charity. Some source food from communities (the Trussell Trust is the most well known here, working through local churches); others draw on food from FareShare, a charity which enables judicious usage of 'surplus' or 'waste' food from the food and drink industry; yet other, more independent, charitable systems source food directly from local businesses and individual gifts. Volunteer training to handle food well and diminish people's sense of shame in claiming such benefits is supplemented in many instances by signposting advice and further help out of extreme emergency need.

Charities also vary in how food bank access is managed. The Trussell Trust and some others require claimants to present vouchers, obtained from gatekeepers in the local area: registered professionals in Health and Social Services, the Probation Service, schools and churches, and, since 2011, formally through JobCentre Plus, which has responsibility for helping the unemployed into work. This latter relationship has been problematic at times, but is evidence that the state is in fact looking to the charitable sector specifically to ensure people do not go hungry (at least in the short term: under the Trussell Trust scheme claimants receive three days' food for their household, and can only claim three times a year).

The numbers of food aid initiatives and claimants/recipients involved is hard to document accurately because there are many small, non-networked activities and because free food is distributed via many different mechanisms. In 2012–2013, Trussell Trust (2013) state they fed nearly 350,000 people (almost triple the number in 2011–2012) from almost 400 food banks (there were only 80 in January 2011). Nevertheless, however fast food banks grow, they could not meet the scale of the need, either in geographic coverage or length of time that support would be needed, as a recent trenchant report from Church Action Poverty and UK Oxfam, *Walking the Breadline*, made clear (Cooper and Dumpleton, 2013). This used evidence from around the UK to estimate that, in May 2013, more than half a million were already reliant on charitable food aid, arguing that 'the social safety net is failing in its basic duty to ensure families have access to sufficient income to feed themselves adequately' (Cooper and Dumpleton, 2013, p. 3) and should not be replaced by food banks, whose increasing deployment is a 'national disgrace' (2013, p. 3). The report links the growth in charitable necessity both to increasing social security benefit delay, administrative error and application of sanctions, and to the much publicized growth in tax avoidance, of which the latter is argued to contribute to reducing public sector revenue. It called not only for better monitoring of the usage of charitable food aid but also for an urgent formal inquiry into the evidence for its growth and appropriate response. A rapid evidence review for Defra, published after nine months' delay, also supported the link between growth in demand for charitable food and household income crises from job losses or social security problems, compounded by low income and increasing indebtedness (Lambie-Mumford et al, 2014).

The *Walking the Breadline* report generated widespread coverage and comment, if initially little official response, and contributed to emergent profound debates about social justice hitherto unarticulated. Until recently few understood the role food banks were increasingly being required to play; the poverty and desperate need behind them is hidden, and the realities they aim to address have simply been unacknowledged or dismissed as purely people's incompetence or temporary problems (and this line is often taken in online comments). Inevitably, people find it shameful to admit to not having enough to eat, and food banks and distribution points document how hard many find it to approach them. What is of interest is that in line with its recommendation and growing MPs' concern an All Party-Parliamentary Group Inquiry into Hunger and Food Poverty has since been established (FPI, 2014 http:foodpovertyinquiry.org/).

However, the charities, not government, are also the main source of information as to why people are in the position of requiring such help since there is no systematic centralized documentation (for the past few years, Job Seekers Plus would record on a form the reasons why they were referring people to a food bank, but this notification has recently been stopped by the DWP). Charities' websites, interviews with food bank managers, and growing social and spoken media coverage increasingly state that inadequate wages and benefits, along with sanctions, delays, reassessments and chronic indebtedness, are the reasons most claimants give; this analysis is rejected by the Government. At the time of writing, the implementation of benefit receipt capping, and the new 'removal of spare room subsidy' from Housing Benefit (the so-called 'bedroom tax') (DWP, 2013) is said to be triggering further urgent need. Lambie-Mumford's (2013) research is rare among academic questioning of current policy response, in terms of possibilities, effectiveness and morality.

Food justice and food rights?

The framing of food poverty in terms of justice and rights is not new in the UK but also not widely explored; the increasing visibility of, and concern over, charitable food as the main current response is spawning more recognition of the unfairness of blaming claimants and of how undignified and inappropriate this solution is. Campaigners are calling for 'upstream' focus, with less emphasis on reskilling households, individual behavioural change and responsibility, and direct provision, and more towards generating sustainable livelihoods, and state recognition of the income required for meeting minimum needs and monitoring how food costs can be met. Practical provision of, for instance, universal free school meals (which eliminate stigma, avoid targeting inefficiencies and benefit all children), and systematic resourcing of more 'hybrid' local food initiatives, would also help the majority of households, many of whom are deeply under-capitalized to withstand economic shocks or continually squeezed budgets.

Challenge in charitable and local responses

The challenge in the increasing institutionalization of charitable responses, particularly in the linking of 'food waste' as a solution to 'food poverty', is that the fundamental issues become de-politicized, and solutions are located in the responsible use of resources at local levels, enabling both the state to retreat from responsibilities and food businesses to gain from improving corporate social responsibility (CSR) and reduced landfill taxes. Some of the major brands who work with FareShare, for instance, include Tesco, Sainsbury's, Nestlé, Unilever, Cargill and Sodexho, and FareShare promotes itself as 'an increasingly recognised UK charity brand, leading the drive to tackle two of the most urgent issues facing the UK – food poverty and food waste' (FareShare 2013). Those who partner it gain skill recognition for their staff working as volunteers, as well as considerable social and environmental responsibility recognition.

Of course, volunteers can also gain inspirational insight into poorer people's lives, but in general, claimants are confirmed as lower status, needy and voiceless. Charitable agents are trapped in the dilemmas of seeking to support and empower the marginalized, while acting as proxy deliverers of state services, dependent on uncertain funding and facing increasing logistical tasks (of securing and training volunteers, as well as appropriately sourcing and managing food stocks). These dilemmas remain even in newer, creative initiatives, which try to address the social value of food in drawing people in to help cook and prepare meals in which any can share – not only the resource poor but also the socially isolated (for instance, Foodcycle). This enables the pleasure in food, from variety, taste and shared eating, to be the focus, along with making friends, even if only a temporary respite from the usual need to fill up and avoid hunger.

Other campaigning movements which enjoin more environmentally sustainable and simpler food practices (Tudge, 2011; Pollan, 2009) with more vegetables and less but better quality meat, are primarily aimed elsewhere other than poverty. Although those who are poor use fewer cars to shop, may eat simply and throw less away, they also seldom have cooking equipment or even tables, often have to eat while working or travelling, and spend so little that their diets lack sufficient diversity. Circumstances vary, but the poorest usually subsist on cheap, highly processed foods; even those relying on charitable food have to take what is provided, which may be far from ideal from a health or sustainability perspective. However, those lacking money or cultural capital may in fact share the desire to eat in ways which enhance sustainability or challenge corporate capitalism, even though their immediate priorities are avoiding hunger. There are good UK examples of inclusive initiatives (for instance, in Bristol and Brighton) and, before the current recession, of people on low incomes specifically joining a community supported agriculture scheme, or using a Farm Shop, because they thought the food was better value for money and enabled them to avoid cheap products based on exploitative production or employment systems (Kneafsey et al., 2008).

Indeed, many local food initiatives have important roles to play in re-engaging a largely distanced population with 'food' in all its nuances, offering capacity building, self-confidence and immediate provision to those who need all three (Kneafsey et al., 2008). However, they struggle to sustain patchy resourcing through continual reinvention of aims and practice to match changing funding demands, as well as considerable logistical and volunteer skills (Dowler and Caraher, 2003) – characteristics they share with food banks and other food aid initiatives. More critically, both are increasingly being required to fill gaps left by state retreat, that meet immediate and stark need but with unclear lines of accountability and potential for advocacy. The emergence of 'hybrid' initiatives, which engage networked members in policy analysis and advocacy as well as practical, ground level response, has potential to offer voice, creative ideas and shared possibilities for action (e.g., Scotland's Community Food and Health).

Potential for rights-based approaches?

The UK use of a household food security lens offers mild opportunity to frame issues in terms of rights and responsibilities, despite the unfamiliarity in a rights-based approach (Dowler and O'Connor, 2012). Indeed the incorporation of the *International Convention on Economic, Social and Cultural Rights* (ICESCR) into law has been resisted, despite a recommendation by the Joint Committee on Human Rights of the Houses of Lords and Commons that doing so would assist the government in addressing poverty, and Parliament and civil society in scrutinizing their performance (JCHR, 2004). Such a framing would not only bring the obligation to protect, respect and fulfil the rights to food, but also a coordinated and concerted approach through the designation of a specific institution with responsibility to oversee implementation, and development of a national strategy for household food and nutrition security, including indicators and benchmarks to assess progress and monitor and document violations (Dowler and O'Connor, 2012).

It may be that there is potential in the approaches of some charitable initiatives in the UK to act as the focus for people's voices to be heard. Church Action on Poverty, for instance, works from the ground up, always seeking to enable those experiencing poverty to speak to those with power on changes in structural elements – in this instance, over the need for sustainable livelihoods, sufficient wages, and monitoring/redressing the cumulative negative effects of current changes to social security benefits (levels, entitlement and administration). Ironically, the food system itself is notorious for low wages, insecure jobs and zero-hour contracts – particularly for women – as well as a tendency to promote unhealthier foods at bargain prices. The tie-up between grassroots campaigning on food poverty, and those working for more ethically, sustainably produced food at affordable prices is beginning to emerge, but the issue represents a key component of realizing the right to food: that people be enabled to engage and feed themselves in ways they see fit, and so as to achieve well-being and potential for themselves and the planet (FEC, 2010).

At present, however, the possibilities seem slim for effectual engagement over critical 'upstream' issues in the UK, particularly with central Government refusing to accept any evidence that changes in social security are jeopardizing people's capacity to sustain household food security. As noted above, this is powerfully gendered in effect: women often carry the heaviest load from benefit changes, as well as being more likely to work on zero-hour contracts, and/or on low wages within the food (and catering) system. Many also, of course, sustain voluntary community support networks, as well as the majority of unpaid carer roles within families and neighbourhoods.

The Government's resistance to acknowledging structural contributions to household food insecurity, to monitoring their effects or to addressing causes, is a clear dereliction of duty to implement the human right to food. Instead, a country which is one of the world's richest, and which, in hosting the 2012 Olympic Games, demonstrated creativity, generosity and the best of human nature, seems slow to grasp the realities of how many of its citizens are having to live because of harsh programmes of enforced economic austerity and the systematic undermining of its social safety net. It is time that food injustice in all its forms is challenged.

13
Food Assistance, Hunger and the End of Welfare in the USA

Janet Poppendieck

Food assistance, poverty and income support

Forty-seven million Americans, one in every seven, are currently enrolled in the Supplemental Nutrition Assistance Programme (SNAP), formerly known as Food Stamps. On a typical school day, 32 million children consume federally subsidized and regulated school lunches; nearly two-thirds of these meals are served free or at a drastically reduced price. More than 12 million children eat a school breakfast each school day, and together, the National School Lunch Programme (NSLP) and the School Breakfast Programme (SBP) serve 7.5 billion meals a year.

Nine million pregnant women, new mothers, infants and preschool age children are enrolled in the Special Supplemental Nutrition Programme for Women, Infants and Children (WIC); indeed, half the babies born in the United States each year are born into WIC. Nearly three and a half million people receive meals through the Child and Adult Care Feeding Programme (CACFP), which provides meals in day care facilities. These are the 'big five' of the food assistance programmes administered by the United States Department of Agriculture (USDA), and together they account for 96 per cent of the department's food assistance spending, but they are by no means its only food programmes. In fact, USDA administers 15 separate food and nutrition assistance programmes, and one in four Americans participates in at least one of these (Oliveira, 2012, pp. 2, 3). Food assistance outlays now exceed other USDA spending, accounting for more than two-thirds of the agency's budget, and totalling more than 100 billion last year. Nor is the USDA the only federal agency administering food assistance. The senior nutrition programmes, both congregate and home delivered meals, are administered by the Department of Health and Human Services (HHS). In 2008, these two programmes together served more than 2.5 million participants (Collelo, 2010). Food assistance is alive and well in the US.

The US differs from virtually every other OECD nation in its heavy reliance on food assistance rather than income transfers to aid impoverished families. While both social insurance and modest cash income guarantees are available to elderly and disabled Americans, able-bodied adults and their dependent children receive very limited cash assistance. Federal expenditure for SNAP in 2011 was 11 times the meagre cash provided through the Temporary Assistance to Needy Families (TANF) programme, the programme most frequently thought of as 'welfare'. Adults without children are not included in TANF and if they have not qualified for disability payments, they must turn to the states and localities when their unemployment compensation and savings run out. Only 30 of the states offer any cash assistance at all for non-disabled adults without children.

The programmes that provide such aid are collectively known as 'General Assistance' (GA), and the payments they offer are extremely low. Most provide a benefit that equals less than a quarter of the already low federal poverty threshold of $11,170 annually for a household of one. The entire social assistance sector in the US, in the aftermath of the 'welfare reform' of the mid-1990s, is designed to encourage paid employment. While welfare support for families headed by able-bodied adults has declined sharply, benefits tied to earnings have risen. The Center for Budget and Policy Priorities calculates what it calls a TANF ratio. For every one hundred officially poor US families with children, how many are receiving cash benefits from welfare? In 1979, under the much-maligned Aid to Families with Dependent Children (AFDC) programme, that number was 82. By 1996 when TANF first replaced AFDC, it stood at 68. By 2010, it had dropped to 27 (Trisi and Pavetti, 2012). Meanwhile, a federal programme called the Earned Income Tax Credit (EITC) and an associated programme called the Additional Child Tax Credit function to raise the incomes of impoverished households with earnings. The EITC is structured so that it encourages work as an alternative to welfare and rewards those with jobs for working additional hours.

In this complex context of very limited income transfers, food assistance programmes are often a major source of household support. SNAP is far and away the largest of these programmes, accounting for about three-quarters of total public food assistance expenditure. SNAP eligibility is directly tied to the nation's official poverty threshold. In order to be considered for the programme, applicants must have a pre-tax gross income below 130 per cent of the federal poverty line. In 2011, 20 per cent of SNAP households had no gross income at all. Applicants are entitled to a series of 'deductions' based on their circumstances: a standard deduction, a work expenses deduction if they are employed; a child care deduction if they must pay for child care in order to work; and an excess shelter cost deduction if their rent and utilities exceed half their income. In order to qualify for a benefit, their net income after deductions must be below the official poverty threshold itself, and the size of their benefit is based on how far below that line their income falls. In 2011, 39 per cent of SNAP households qualified for the maximum benefit because they had no net income after allowable deductions.

The Great Recession

Anything that raises the nation's poverty rate expands the pool of people eligible for SNAP, and anything that increases the depth of poverty increases SNAP expenditure per capita. SNAP participation tends to track the federal poverty rate very closely, and the immediate explanation for the current very high numbers of SNAP participants in the US is the Great Recession that began late in 2007. A shrinking economy impacts all of the primary causes of poverty. Unemployment rises, and in the context of high unemployment, wages stagnate or even decline.

The impact of the Great Recession on SNAP participation was immediate and dramatic. Average monthly participation in SNAP grew by 70 per cent between 2007 and 2011, because the SNAP programme is profoundly countercyclical. Programme participation figures have fluctuated with the business cycle, with few exceptions, since the programme reached its modern form in the early 1970s (Hanson and Oliveira, 2012, pp. 8–15). Typically, however, the official end of a recession, when GNP begins to rise, does not immediately spell a decline in unemployment at the bottom of the income distribution, so SNAP participation frequently shows what economists call an 'asymmetrical lag' in the aftermath of recession. This lag has been particularly pronounced in the current 'jobless recovery', when poverty rates have remained near their recession peak.

Overall participation figures, however, reflect not only the number of people in the population whose incomes make them eligible to receive benefits, but also the combination of barriers and incentives that determines the 'take-up rate', the percentage of those eligible who actually apply for and obtain benefits. The *American Recovery and Reinvestment Act* (ARRA), commonly known as the stimulus, temporarily increased SNAP benefit levels, thus increasing the incentive to seek them. This heightened incentive has interacted with a series of actions taken by the states in the early years of the 2000s that had the net effect of reducing barriers to participation: simplification of applications, longer certification periods and elimination of some components of an 'assets screen', notably the fair market value of a vehicle, that in the past had rendered many impoverished households ineligible for the programme. The take up rate for SNAP rose throughout the recession and has continued to rise during the painfully slow recovery (Hanson and Oliveira, 2012, pp. 12–14; Super, 2004, pp. 16–18, 24–25).

Other public sector food assistance programmes have also expanded in response to the condition of the economy, as they typically have in the past. Recent USDA analysis of the performance of these programmes over four complete cycles of growth and decline concluded that 'all of the major nutrition assistance programmes are countercyclical, responding to increased demand for their services by needy families during economic downturns' (Hanson and Oliviera, 2012, p. 35).

The fairly robust performance of food assistance in response to the recession comes into sharper focus when it is compared to the response of cash assistance through (TANF), the major family welfare programme in the US, and to the various state assistance programmes for indigent adults. While the number of SNAP cases rose 61 per cent between December 2007 and December 2010, the number of TANF households increased only 15 per cent, (CBPP, 2011). Similarly, GA has also failed to expand. After the recession began, many states found themselves strapped for cash, trying to make limited resources stretch. They tightened eligibility and time limits, even during the recession. As a report by the Center on Budget and Policy Priorities summarized, 'an increasing number of needy individuals are left without any cash assistance or similar income support' (Schott and Cho, 2011, p. 7).

Low wages and inadequate public assistance are visible in the portrait of SNAP beneficiaries. Eighty-three per cent had gross incomes below the FPL of $23,050 for a family of four. More revealing, 43 per cent of SNAP households in 2011 were considered to be in 'deep poverty', that is, they had gross incomes below *half* the federal poverty level. Employment is the largest single source of income for participants, and 30 per cent of SNAP households have income from work, but only 8 per cent have income from TANF, and only 4.1 per cent from state General Assistance programmes (USDA, 2012).

Food insecurity

With incomes so low and assistance benefits so scarce, it is not surprising that many Americans are at risk of hunger. The Federal Government measures this risk annually in its *Household Food Security Survey*. In 2011, 50 million Americans, one in six, lived in households classified as 'food insecure': they could not always afford adequate food. Of those, 17 million lived in households with 'very low food security,' the federal euphemism for hunger. In these households, people had to reduce the size of their meals, skip meals or sometimes go an entire day without eating. The rate of food insecurity was higher, 20.6 per cent, for households with children and higher still for households with children under six, (21.9 per cent). It was still higher for a household with children headed by a single man (24.9 per cent) and even higher for a household with children headed by a single woman (36.8 per cent).

Food insecurity does not treat all racial and ethnic groups alike. It characterizes 11.4 per cent of white households, 25.9 per cent of Black non-Hispanic households, and 26.2 per cent of Hispanic households (Coleman-Jensen et al., 2012, p. 11). The Federal Government does not routinely report rates for Native Americans, but an analysis of data from the 2001–2004 Household Food Security Survey found rates twice to three times as high as those for non-Native American households (Gundersen, 2008). Finally, as one would expect, food insecurity rates vary with household economic status. More than two-fifths (41 per cent) of households with incomes below the federal poverty line were food insecure, compared with only 7 per cent of those with incomes above 185 per cent of the federal poverty threshold. The near-poor, however, suffer very high rates of food insecurity; more than a third (34.5 per cent) of households with incomes below 185 per cent of the poverty line reported food insecurity.

One might expect that families participating in the SNAP programme would have greater food security than similarly poor families who are not SNAP participants, but the food security data do not confirm this expectation. In fact, amongst households with incomes below 130 per cent of the poverty line, the cut off for SNAP eligibility, 51.7 per cent of those who had received SNAP benefits during the previous 12 months were food insecure, compared with 27.7 per cent of those who did not receive SNAP benefits during the previous 12 months. Similarly, amongst households with school-aged children and incomes below 185 per cent of the federal poverty line, the cut off for reduced price meals in the national school lunch and breakfast programmes, 48.7 per cent of those who had received free or reduced price school lunches during the previous 30 days were food insecure, compared with 27.7 per cent of those who did not receive free or reduced price lunches in the preceding 30 days.

As the USDA economists comment in explaining these results, 'it is the more food-insecure households, those having greater difficulty meeting their food needs, that seek assistance from the programs' (Coleman-Jensen et al., 2012, p. 25). Overall, about 57 per cent of households classified as food insecure received assistance from at least one of the three largest programmes, SNAP, school meals, or WIC. These findings lend great credibility to advocates' assertions that SNAP benefits are too low to enable participants to achieve food security, and that eligibility thresholds are too low to make the programmes available to all in need (International Human Rights Clinic, 2013, pp. 12, 13). They also help to explain why so many Americans, an estimated 37 million in 2010, have turned to food pantries and soup kitchens in search of help. Charitable food assistance, while small in comparison to federal outlays, occupies a large place in the American anti-hunger landscape.

Food charity

Despite the extent of US federal expenditure on food assistance, and the breadth of participation, if you type 'fighting hunger in America' into almost any search engine, you will be guided to the web sites of private, charitable organizations or those of corporate philanthropies, not to the government programmes that provide the vast majority of the nation's food assistance. The nation's network of several hundred large, warehouse style 'food banks,' and the thousands of food pantries and soup kitchens that they supply, is highly visible, but small compared to the public provision of food assistance. Indeed, the Christian anti-hunger organization Bread for the World has recently calculated that amongst meals based on food assistance, only one in 24 is derived from private giving; the other 23 come from government sources. That is, $4.13 billion worth of food was distributed through charities in 2011, while USDA spent $96.88 billion on food and benefits (Bread for the World, 2013). The gap between perception and reality is enormous.

This brief overview of food assistance, income supports and poverty in the US raises many questions. How did the US come to provide so much of its assistance to poor people in the form of food rather than cash? In most other affluent nations this would be regarded as inefficient and stigmatizing. Why does the relatively small amount of private charity tend to obscure the much larger public effort in the nation's consciousness? And what are the practical and political consequences of this situation for efforts to establish a human right to food in the US? The next section will turn to history to explain how the unique US food assistance system came to be such an essential component of the survival strategies of poor Americans.

Food assistance: a brief history

Agricultural policy background

Federal food programmes in the US have their roots in the Great Depression of the 1930s. Enormous agricultural surpluses had troubled the farming sector throughout the 1920s and when the depression struck, the resulting contrast between hunger and waste demanded action. Both the Hoover and Roosevelt administrations responded to this embarrassing contradiction with programmes to transfer surplus farm products to people in need. USDA donated agricultural products to schools, a forerunner of the NSLP, and to relief agencies for use by the unemployed. An innovative food stamp programme allowed poor people to obtain surplus products through their local grocery stores. The programmes were drastically cut back with the onset of World War II, when shortages replaced excess, but the practice of using food assistance to dispose of farm surpluses was firmly established and remained the dominant policy for 30 years (Poppendieck, 1986). In the long run, the farm programme origins of food assistance meant that these programmes were administered by the USDA and overseen by the agricultural committees of the Congress.

Eventually, this led to the establishment of the sort of legislative bargaining that American political scientists refer to as a 'log-roll'. Congress members from rural areas needed urban support to pass the agricultural commodity subsidies and other components of farm support legislation. These were matters about which urban constituents understood little and cared less, so urban representatives were free to give or withhold their support. Urban members, on the other hand, needed the support of rural conservatives to fund and expand food programmes, especially within the Agriculture Committees where these long-serving rural members had much seniority and power. A classic trade in the early 1960s established the modern Food Stamp Program in exchange for support for wheat and cotton subsidies (Ripley, 1969). Due in part to the anti-welfare attitudes of the agricultural establishment, the programme was designed with the interests of farmers in mind, and proved inadequate in preventing poverty-related malnutrition.

When hunger became a public issue in the United States in the late 1960s, anti-poverty activists in the US made a strategic decision to pursue the reform and expansion of food programmes, rather than the more adequate cash assistance that might have made such programmes unnecessary (Kotz, 1984, p. 22). Working with Congressional allies, they successfully bargained for the creation of new programmes and substantial expansions of eligibility, increases in benefits, and the estab-lishment of protections for the rights of applicants and recipients. The success of food assistance, especially when compared with cash welfare, was not simply a result of the peculiar Congressional politics of agricul-ture. It also reflected advocates' ability to mobilize widespread objection to hunger amid the nation's fabled plenty, and to tolerate coalition with those who feared the poor would spend cash unwisely and therefore preferred to distribute assistance in kind.

Cutbacks and food banks

The election of Ronald Reagan in 1980 spelled the end of the period of expansion and ushered in an era of cutbacks. Not only food assist-ance, but virtually all programmes of aid for impoverished Americans were reduced. Coming as they did in the midst of a deep recession, these cutbacks contributed to widespread hardship. One result was a prolifera-tion and expansion of private, charitable food assistance in the form of food pantries and soup kitchens, referred to in the US as 'Emergency Food Providers'. The invention of the 'food bank', a large, warehouse style facility that receives bulk donations from food manufacturers and retailers, and sometimes from government, and redistributes them to kitchens and pantries, fuelled the expansion of the charitable food system. Food banking, in turn, was nourished by its capacity to absorb products fit for human consumption but cosmetically challenged or otherwise unsaleable in the American market. Further, the organization of a national association of food banks, first called Second Harvest and now known as Feeding America, promoted the expansion of food banking. Because food banks and their member agencies raise their resources through food drives and fundraisers that bring them into constant contact with the public, private, charitable food assistance gradually became the recog-nizable face of anti-hunger activity in the US (Poppendieck, 1998). The public programmes did not wither away; in fact they grew, but their growth was somewhat obscured by the highly visible activities of food charities. A culture of charity, in which gifts replaced rights, troubled many observers (Riches, 1997a; Popppendieck, 1998).

A new recession in the early 1990s sent Food Stamp participation numbers sharply upward, demonstrating the admirable countercyclical character of the programme, but simultaneously catching the attention of fiscal conservatives. The rise of neoliberal ideology fuelled a new attack on welfare programmes of all sorts. A group of 'insurgent' Republicans ran for office on the basis of a unified platform called the Contract With America, which called for a balanced federal budget, deep cuts in social spending, a virtual end to public assistance for able-bodied people, rigid time limits for assistance to families, a reorientation of all such programmes to emphasize work, and 'devolution,' or transfer of control of many social programmes to the states through a procedure called 'block-granting' in which the federal government provides the states with lump sums of money for general policy areas, to be used as the states see fit. When the Republican Party took control of both the House of Representatives and the Senate in the 1994 mid-term elections, the Contract With America group was able to elect its leader, Newt Gingrich, Speaker of the House, a position of great power in American policy making. The threat to both food and cash assistance was real and immediate.

What happened next laid the foundation for the very different responses of food assistance and cash welfare programmes to the 'Great Recession' that were described above. Congress replaced the Aid to Families with Dependent Children (AFDC) programme, a modest entitlement for children in need dating back to the Great Depression, with block grants to the states for the work oriented TANF programme. The block grants were a fixed amount – they would not vary with economic conditions. While the Contract conservatives, with the active collaboration of the President, succeeded in block granting cash assistance to families, their efforts to block grant the Food Stamp and school food programmes were effectively countered. Emergency food providers joined with the Washington based 'hunger lobby' to condemn the proposed block grant process as a betrayal of the nation's traditions of compassion, an attempt to 'balance the budget on the backs of poor, hungry people'.

Food aid as a bargaining chip

The congressional politics of agriculture proved decisive once again. As political scientist Ronald King has observed, the Agriculture Committees of the Congress, like all other committees, use the programmes under their control, and the budgets attached to these programmes, as bargaining chips in the ongoing budget negotiations that have long been central to American politics. If the food programmes were block-granted, the proponents of the traditional commodity surplus management and price support programmes would have nothing with which to trade in their periodic bargaining with urban members of Congress who tended to be food assistance supporters. Further, no committee wants to see the size of its budget shrink. By the time of the Contract With America, food assistance was already a major share of the USDA budget and thus a major share of the fiscal power of the Agriculture committees. Further, without the food programmes, the Agriculture Committees would govern issues and expenditures that were of concern primarily to farmers, a very small and declining share of the US population, and to a small number of the nation's congressional districts. Both Food Stamps and school food were spared the block grant fate (King, 1999, pp. 370–374, 379–380).

Reductions and restorations

This does not mean that they escaped unscathed. In the Personal Responsibility and Work Opportunities Reconciliation Act (PRWORA) of 1996, commonly known as 'welfare reform', food stamp funding was cut, primarily as a means to find funds for the new TANF block grants. The cuts were large – $27.7 billion over six years – and the savings were obtained by reducing benefits across the board, by declaring virtually all legal immigrants ineligible for the programme, and by limiting the eligibility of able-bodied unemployed adults without dependents (ABAWDS) to three months out of every three years. Finally, in an effort to control fraud and modernize administration, PRWORA directed all states to replace paper food coupons with Electronic Benefits Transfer (EBT), generally a plastic swipe card used at checkout like a debit card, by the end of 2002.

In the aftermath of PRWORA, food stamp participation fell rapidly, from more than 27 million people in 1994 to 17 million in 2000. While some of the drop was a welcome countercyclical response to increasing employment in an expanding economy, some of it came from widespread misunderstandings as the states replaced AFDC with TANF and began removing families from the welfare rolls and redirecting them to job training and employment (Berg, 2008, pp. 78–81). As research mounted showing that families in great need were being denied food stamps, advocates made a strategic decision to reframe the Food Stamp Programme as 'work support,' and to build upon rather than oppose state-level discretion in administration. They sought and obtained a substantial simplification of the rules governing food assistance to employed people, especially by lengthening the certification period and reducing the reporting requirements that burdened both families and welfare offices (Super, 2004, p. 21).

In keeping with the emphasis on state autonomy, they succeeded in obtaining legislation that allowed states to substitute for the food stamp 'assets screen' the rules that they used in their TANF programmes, and advocates pointed out to states a little-noticed provision in the TANF law that made anyone receiving services from TANF, not just cash assistance, 'categorically eligible' for food stamps. By the time Congress honoured the end of paper coupons ('stamps') by changing the name of the programme to the Supplemental Nutrition Assistance Programme (SNAP) in 2008, many states had figured out that they could make millions of residents categorically eligible for benefits by providing them with some low-cost service – a brochure with information on domestic violence assistance, for example, or a phone number for information and referral. This enabled them to bypass the complex and time consuming initial screening for SNAP (Super, 2004, pp. 16, 17). Benefit levels would still be determined by calculating a series of deductions from gross income, and some 'cat-el' (categorically eligible) clients would find themselves with a zero benefit level, but being 'eligible' for SNAP would still entitle them to free school meals for their children.

It did not take cash strapped state governments and mayors long to figure out that by simplifying access to SNAP in this way, they could draw federal dollars into their local economies. USDA fuelled this process by calculating the broader economic activity associated with food stamp benefits (Hanson and Golan, 2002). This multiplier effect obtained wider publicity when a prominent private sector economist, Mark Zandi, founder of Moody's Economy, analysing options for a stimulus, reported that the fastest way to infuse money into the economy would be by expanding the Food Stamp programme. He estimated that each dollar spent on Food Stamps generated $1.73 throughout the economy. Governors and mayors became vocal advocates for SNAP participation, helping to de-stigmatize it, and invested state and local funds in outreach efforts. Emergency Food providers in many communities became active allies, providing information on the programme and assisting clients with SNAP applications.

Governors and mayors were not the only 'strange bedfellows' promoting SNAP expansion. While the corporate sector in the US is generally regarded as 'conservative', food assistance in general and SNAP in particular have had the effect of enabling food manufacturers and grocers to see clearly their own interest in protecting and preserving federal food assistance spending. Thus the Food Marketing Institute and the Grocery Manufacturers of America have long weighed in on the side of liberalizing both eligibility and benefits, and more recently big food retailers like Walmart have become major donors to anti-hunger organizations. Large food donations to food banks have been supplemented by cash assistance to the organizations that use lobbying and policy analysis to protect and expand food assistance benefits.

Obesity and the new politics of food assistance

As obesity has gained prominence as a social issue in the US, the alliance between anti-hunger advocates and the manufacturers and purveyors of junk foods, especially sugar sweetened beverages, has drawn increasing criticism from groups that approach food (and food assistance) from a public health perspective. A proposal by the Mayor of New York City, Michael Bloomberg, to remove sugar sweetened beverages from the items for which SNAP recipients could spend their benefits, created a rift between long-time anti-hunger advocates who saw the proposal as stigmatizing, and public health activists who pointed out that spending SNAP dollars on soda constituted a large public subsidy to the soda industry. While the hunger lobby viewed its stance as a principled defence of the rights of SNAP participants, activists from the health community and other critics wondered publicly if anti-hunger organizations were being bought by the financial contributions of the American Beverage Association and food retailers to their work (Gunther, 2012; CSPI, 2013).

The dependence of anti-hunger groups on philanthropic contributions from Wal-Mart and other retailing giants has also raised questions. As Andy Fisher, former director of the Community Food Security Coalition, has pointed out, even Walmart's apparently large pledge of $2 billion in food and cash grants over a five-year period is small potatoes compared to the billions that American taxpayers spend subsidizing Walmart, whose employees earn so little that many of them qualify for SNAP and Medicaid (the average Walmart 'Associate' earns $8.81 per hour). Further, an unreported but significant quantity of SNAP benefits is redeemed at Walmart. No wonder Walmart wants to invest in organizations that can help to keep SNAP alive and well. A real end to hunger, however, would require higher wages, adequate benefits, and full employment, policies that are not in the immediate corporate self-interest.

Fisher focuses on the role of corporations on food bank boards of directors as one means by which corporate donors to anti-hunger organizations make their priorities felt. While he recognizes that corporate participation on boards confers respectability and increases access to corporate donations, he is distressed by its impact on the food banks' ability to fight for policies that would actually confront hunger. As he says 'on the other hand, the policy changes needed to reduce or eliminate hunger are anathema to the wealthy and the corporations on food bank boards. These changes might result in increased operational costs or federal taxes for businesses. Thus the high degree of corporate participation on food banks' boards serves as a prophylactic measure to these entities advocating for redistributive policies that go against the interests of the business sector...'. Fisher goes on to urge Feeding America and the Food Research and Action Center to lead a campaign to 'insist that their affiliates and partners will only lend their legitimacy to potential corporate donors by accepting their money, if the company commits to paying their employees a living wage with full benefits and allowing them to unionize' (Fisher, 2012).

Looking backward, then, over the whole history of food assistance in the US, a unique picture emerges, unlike that of any other western, industrialized nation. In the broader context of income support, the US has relied particularly heavily on means-tested programmes, with the notable exception of Social Security and Medicare for senior citizens. Thus the US has no universal children's allowance or family allowance, though it does have a child tax credit. A deep suspicion of cash welfare, and an abiding concern about work disincentives, has resulted in the near disappearance of cash support for able-bodied adults or their dependents. Food assistance, on the other hand, has expanded rapidly, both in response to the Great Recession and in response to the efforts of state governments to draw federal dollars into their economies. In the current situation, SNAP is essential to the survival of poor Americans.

In this context, the relationship between private charitable food assistance and public sector programmes is more complex than it appeared when this writer wrote about it in an earlier edition of this book in the late 1990s (Poppendieck, 1997). In theory, such programmes may undermine rights to food, both because they embody and promote a culture of charity and because they enable lawmakers to cut public programmes with impunity. The critique still holds, I believe, for the casual donor to a canned goods drive, but the staff and core volunteers of many emergency food providers have become essential allies in the fight to preserve and expand public sector food assistance provisions. At the local level, they have helped to enrol emergency food clients in the public programmes, and at the national level, they have spoken out repeatedly against threats to funding. Pondering the contrast between SNAP and TANF, one cannot help but wonder if the public preoccupation with food charity has worked quite differently than predicted. Perhaps it has created a sort of 'safe space' in which advocates could do the hard work of expanding benefits and reducing barriers to participation in SNAP. The very de-politicization of hunger, which appeared to be in substantial peril at the time of welfare reform, appears now in hindsight to have played a sort of protective role. That is, by diverting the attention of legislators and would-be budget cutters from the growth of public sector food assistance, the charitable food network may have functioned as a veil behind which public food entitlements could continue to grow.

This is all of immediate concern, because food assistance programmes face a new set of threats. Although the Congressional budget office has predicted that SNAP participation will fall as the economy improves, and that SNAP spending will decline by 23 per cent by 2022 (CBO, 2012), the very sharp rise in both participation and expenditure has caught the eye of Congressional deficit hawks. Both the House and the Senate are considering legislation that would curtail eligibility and shrink benefits. At the same time, food assistance and the entire food system are being subjected to a critique and reassessment that focuses upon the nutritional quality of the diets of Americans and the environmental impact of the food system (CSPC, 2012). This nutritional critique, while probably long overdue, has food assistance advocates worried that Congress will use the nutritional shortcomings of food assistance as an excuse to curtail the programmes rather than a push to improve them (FRAC, 2013).

The prospects for a human right to food in the US

A fact-finding mission to the US by Olivier De Schutter, the United Nations Special Rapporteur was planned for the Fall of 2013. Because such a visit required an official invitation through the Department of State, advocates of a human rights approach to food have expressed some cautious optimism that at least a conversation might begin in the US. If such a visit were to take place it would however, be an uphill battle for at least three reasons.

First, the US has never ratified the United Nations *International Covenant on Economic, Social and Cultural Rights*, nor the Convention on the Rights of the Child, the two documents most widely used as the basis for legal human rights claims to adequate food. This is not some sort of oversight; it is a consistent policy linked to American interpretations of the nature of sovereignty. Anyone imagining that this archaic assertion of national independence is weakening in the face of the obvious growing interdependence of the world has surely been disabused of such a fantasy by the recent failure of an effort to get the US Senate to ratify a treaty on the Rights of the Disabled that had been negotiated by the Bush administration and signed by President Obama. Despite assurances that the convention is non-binding and would not change or challenge US law, the Senate was unable to muster the two-thirds majority needed for ratification. As the *New York Times* reported, 'A majority of Republicans who voted against the treaty...said they feared that it would infringe on American sovereignty' (Steinhauer, 2012).

Second, while there are elements within the US anti-hunger movement that take a human rights approach to hunger very seriously (Anderson 2012; Messer and Cohen, 2009; M. Chilton and D. Rose, 2009) there is simply not much discourse, in the larger American culture, about human rights in the US, and especially not about economic, social and cultural rights. The US has a long tradition of focusing human rights talk on negative rights, freedoms from various forms of oppression, and particularly on the establishment of due process and other procedural rights. When it comes to positive rights, as Ellen Messer and Marc J. Cohen (2009) have noted, the 'United States increasingly finds itself an outlier to an emerging global consensus'.

Third, despite growing 'food justice' and 'food sovereignty' components in the alternative food movement, and long-term assertions of food as a right by many anti-hunger organizations, the mainstream fight over rights to food at the moment is over the preservation of the SNAP programme. While SNAP does not create a fundamental right to food, it does confer a justiciable entitlement on eligible people. With the virtual disappearance of cash assistance, the defence of SNAP is so urgent that it is likely to displace more abstract considerations, at least for the near future. In the long run, the US will not live up to its designation as the 'Land of Plenty' unless it addresses the shortage of jobs and the erosion of wages and establishes an incomes policy that makes reasonable provision for people who cannot or should not work, but in the short run, the protection of food assistance seems both more politically feasible and more immediate.

14

Hunger and Food Charity in Rich Societies: What Hope for the Right to Food?

Tiina Silvasti and Graham Riches

The early 1980s to mid-1990s

First World Hunger: Food Security and Welfare Politics (Riches, 1997a) offered the first cross-national study of the emergence and entrenchment of food aid and charitable food banking from the early 1980s to the mid-1990s. It consists of five case studies from advanced industrial countries with developed 'liberal' welfare states: Australia, Canada, New Zealand, the UK and the USA. All of the countries were food exporters and food secure through national production and imports, suggesting that domestic hunger could not be caused by the failure to provide sufficient food and nutrition, but rather was a matter of distributional justice and human rights – that is a fundamentally political issue.

Cross-national comparative analysis exposed the intertwined character of neo-liberal social and public policy, pursued by the strengthening New Right, and concurrent government denial of increasing domestic hunger or food insecurity. Harshening and constantly more punitive welfare reform policies aimed at disciplining labour, put into practice by cutting and freezing benefits and/or tightening the rules of eligibility for allowances, not only intensified but also produced food poverty. People living outside or on the fringe of the labour market as a result of unemployment, underemployment or low-paid jobs were especially at risk to descend into situations where they could not provide adequate food and nutrition for themselves and their families. The analysis indicated that household food expenditures were the most elastic part of family budgets: often, the only way for individuals and families living in vulnerable positions to be able pay for all the basic necessities of life (e.g., housing, gas, electricity, medications and so on) was to limit their diets or go without eating.

In spite of alarmingly growing poverty rates governments continued to run down their welfare states and gradually dismantled social security networks. They pleaded the case of fiscal restraint and social spending cutbacks as necessary responses to the weakening economic and political power of nation states and their need to ensure international market competitiveness in the face of global labour market deregulation, economic restructuring and free trade. It led, inevitably, to the vicious cycle of further social spending cutbacks.

Work was announced to be the best social policy and welfare benefits were attached increasingly to labour market participation. The problem was that these societies were not able to generate sufficiently well-paid jobs for ordinary people to earn a living wage, and many were unable to put food on the table.

With governments failing to recognize and take any effective measures to combat increasing food insecurity, space opened up for a myriad of different kinds of charity operations. Nevertheless, however strong human compassion or the moral imperative to feed hungry people, charitable food aid as a practical and effective response to hunger and poverty presented disturbing dilemmas. For example, by substituting for, or taking over the role of failing public welfare systems, increasingly institutionalized charity food distribution programmes actually allowed politicians to neglect the problem of food poverty and, consequently, de-politicized the hunger issue. It deflected public discussion and media attention away from governmental responsibilities and the human right to food. After all, in spite of good will, charitable food aid is nothing more than a gift. It is not a collective right or entitlement that can be claimed by a hungry person or a family in need of food.

Accordingly, the conclusion reached was that if food security is understood as 'the right of access to affordable and nutritious food and obtaining it in normal and socially acceptable ways (i.e. through supermarkets, corner stores, food co-operatives and so on) it must be acknowledged that charity and food banks are not part of the long term answer to hunger' (Riches, 1997c, p. 174). The book's final comment refers to the social democratic Scandinavian welfare states as an optimistic alternative and as proof of the fact 'that hunger need not exist'.

The mid-1990s to 2014: domestic hunger –
trends and issues

Has anything changed?

Now, more than 15 years later, *First World Hunger Revisited*, an expanded and updated trans-continental cross-national study of 12 wealthy nation states, further exposes the deepening and damaging impacts of ever stronger neo-liberal economic ideology on the most vulnerable people in the rich world, and their right to food. With one notable exception (see Brazil) this is despite the growing global right to food debate articulated and promoted by domestic and international NGOs, the UN FAO Right to Food Unit and the UN Special Rapporteur on the Right to Food.

Indeed, these new national case studies may suggest little has changed. Domestic food insecurity in wealthy societies has increased in recent years particularly since the 2007–2009 global economic recession; food charity continues to expand and become more deeply entrenched; and governments continue to look the other way, progressively ignoring their obligations under international law to realize the human right to adequate food.

What then are the lessons, indeed are there newly emerging trends and issues to be considered regarding domestic hunger and food charity? What is the role of public policy in terms of achieving food security for all: watching from the sidelines or taking charge? What are the possibilities for 'joined-up' food policy and progressive change informed by the RTF?

Prevalence of food poverty

The general absence of official, exact and timely data makes exploring the prevalence and causes of food poverty in wealthy first world countries challenging. At the same time there is plenty of valid indirect information available. Nevertheless, the lack of official national food security data, systematic collection and reliable time series analyses in the majority of the countries reviewed, makes the provision of comparable empirically-based cross-national findings regarding the prevalence of food insecurity not possible. This is itself an important finding, meaning it is only possible to estimate, sometimes with great difficulty, the prevalence of food insecurity or food poverty within each country under study.

However, as each county's national data demonstrate, food insecurity is widespread and increasing with only Brazil signalling significant progress in its struggle against domestic hunger. The passivity and direct

reluctance of governments to collect, distribute and act upon any official data of the hunger issue confirms not only neglect but also actual
denial of the problem. Even in those countries, for example in Canada
and the USA, where reliable information regarding food insecurity is
available, the state authorities fail to take advantage of it in the fight
against hunger.

Significantly, the national case studies comprising high income OECD
and emerging upper income states, each of which are food secure either
by internal production or import, indicate the increasing prevalence
of domestic hunger and food insecurity. There is no uniform pattern
of change, but surprisingly enough, the result seems to be congruent:
demand for, and the supply of food aid is growing. There is strong
national evidence to support this including the rapid expansion of
food aid and charitable food banking since 1997, and especially taking
account of the period during and after the 2007–2009 global economic
recession with soaring unemployment rates, food price increases, and
the accompanying austerity measures so dramatically impacting the
lives of the poor. These impacts were most marked in Estonia, Spain, the
UK and in the emerging economies.

In this context it is of interest that the *State of Food Insecurity in the
World 2013* report noted that undernourishment in developed regions,
while accounting for only 2 per cent of global hunger, rose by 15 per
cent from 13.6 million in 2005–2007 to 15.7 million in 2011–2013 (FAO,
2013), doubtless a consequence of the Great Recession.

The most reliable food insecurity data are to be found in the USA
and Canada. The USA's annual National Food Security Survey in
2011 classified 16.6 per cent of the population as food insecure with
17 million Americans experiencing 'very low food insecurity', which
as Poppendieck states, can be interpreted as the official euphemism for
hunger. For the same year, Canada's national population health survey
estimated that 3.9 million people, 11.6 per cent of the population, an
increase of 450,000 people since 2008, were food insecure. While these
two countries are further along the track in collecting reliable national
food security data, the reality is that in all high-income countries the
prevalence of food insecurity has largely to be inferred from national
poverty or household expenditure data or smaller scale studies.

For example, in the UK, in the absence of systematic monitoring
there are no official data on the numbers of households living in food
insecurity, or in food poverty. This has to be inferred from the almost
13 million people, about 21 per cent of the population, living on incomes
that define them as poor. Similarly, in Spain the relative rate of poverty

at the end of 2012 was 21.8 per cent. The increase has been especially pronounced in the case of severe poverty, referring to incomes below 30 per cent of the median reaching 5.2 per cent, which reflects an intensification of poverty. In South Africa household survey data suggest 21.5 per cent of households (10 million people) experience food insecurity.

At the lower range Booth cites the national *Australian Health Survey* (2004/2005), the most recent available data, which reports a 5 per cent rate of food insecurity or one million people but judged likely to be an underestimate. In New Zealand, a recent national nutritional study between the University of Otago and the Ministry of Health reported 7.3 per cent of the population experiencing 'low food security'. In cash rich Hong Kong SAR there are no official estimates of poverty let alone food insecurity, and even Finland lacks timely official statistics of those receiving food aid.

However, there is one exception. In Brazil the RTF is a constitutional right and the state is committed to integrated policy to combat food and nutrition insecurity through the *Zero Hunger* strategy. As a rule income poverty is the cause of domestic hunger. Unlike in other countries of this comparison, income disparities in Brazil have decreased due to implemented policies especially benefitting lower income households.

Primary causes

The growth of income inequality and the failure of work and social security policies to address the issue of income poverty have caused and exacerbated the issue of domestic hunger for populations at risk of food insecurity. Certainly, the general trend in this comparison is growing income inequality. As a consequence of globalization and neo-liberal economic policy there is an accelerating polarization of labour markets. The share of middle-income jobs is decreasing at the same time with the increase of the number of high- and low-paid jobs. In addition various disadvantaged and vulnerable population groups become more often permanently surplus to the requirements of global and local labour markets. Stubborn long-term unemployment, continuous or repetitious underemployment and growing numbers of low-paid jobs again force people to live in vulnerable economic situations.

Some population groups, for example Aboriginal peoples in Australia, Canada and New Zealand continue to experience 'Third World' conditions, facing exorbitant food prices in rural and remote communities and deprived of food sovereignty in their traditional territories. Those excluded from the labour market, families with many children and single-parent families, remain especially vulnerable and, hence, have a considerable risk of income poverty. Significantly though, as a result of recent economic and labour market policy development, including the promotion and expansion of low-paid labour markets, not even employment always guarantees a living wage and the ability to feed oneself or one's family.

However, the most common governmental claim throughout the case studies is that work is the best and/or the only right way to practice social policy even though it is self-evident that the increase of low-paid work at the expense of middle-income jobs boosts poverty rates. Most of the countries have implemented neo-liberal postulates guided by 'workfare' in their social and public policies, favouring privatization of social service production, social spending budget cuts and tightened benefit eligibility. This combination of labour market failure and tightening social security policy has caused difficulties for many people living precarious lives to achieve an adequate standard of living, including adequate food and nutrition. Income poverty, par excellence, is the primary cause of domestic hunger and increases the demand for food aid.

Charitable food banking as front line responses

Expansion and institutionalization

In the countries of initial comparison (Australia, Canada, New Zealand, the UK and the USA) the early 1980s and the rise of new conservatism precipitated the end of the period of expanding welfare states and urged a series of cutbacks in social expenditure. These cuts contributed to widespread hardship and impoverishment. One response to increasing social misery was the expansion and national institutionalization of private, charitable food aid which was nourished by its growing capacity to absorb and distribute edible, but unsaleable (e.g., expiring, cosmetically unfit or damaged) food for human consumption. This national consolidation has continued and, as Dowler notes, has been particularly marked in the UK since the 2007–2009 recession where charitable food banking has rapidly emerged as a divisive food and social policy issue. The motives behind philanthropic food aid delivery are social in the first place, but awareness of the environmental impacts of food waste has also been gaining significance.

The development in the other OECD countries (Estonia, Finland, Spain) as well as Hong Kong and the emerging economies (Brazil, South Africa and Turkey) has followed the same path with blatant similarities as well as certain differences. The starting point for the rise and institutionalization of charitable food aid is usually located in economic recession joined together with cuts in social budgets. However, the processes of institutionalization, the degree of corporatization and the relationship between private and public food aid vary depending on political and cultural underpinnings in each country.

Corporatization

The forerunners of the corporatization of food aid can be found amongst the Anglo-Saxon countries of the initial study with the USA, Canada and more recently Australia and New Zealand. The development in the other countries of this study lags more or less behind but, once again, parallels these earlier trends. There is little doubt that the founding of the European Federation of Food Banks (EFFB) in 1986 and the 2006 establishment of the Global Foodbanking Network (GFN) with transnational food corporation sponsorship have been significant influences in the development work of national charitable food banking.

The EFFB works in 22 countries including Estonia, Spain and the UK. The GFN is active in more than thirty countries and in two-thirds of those cited in this text including co-founders Canada and the USA, then Australia, the UK and also with development activities in four of the emerging economies – Brazil, Hong Kong, South Africa and Turkey. Yet, how appropriate is it that globalized corporate food charity seeks to twin the issues of hunger and food waste?

Certainly, food waste is a growing ethical and environmental problem all over the First World and the distribution of edible but unsaleable food as food aid is one way to reduce and control the waste. At the same time corporate social responsibility is a powerful motive in terms of product branding with corporate actors seeking to gain competitive advantages by participating in charity work. Benefits include the tax deductibility of donations as well as possibilities to reduce costs for storage, transport and landfill charges. In Turkey, donations to food banks in municipalities where the governing party has the majority can be a smart investment with the expectations of favourable results converting into government contracts. According to Koc this is how food may be used for political ends.

All the while corporate food industry sponsorship builds a public perception of efficiency, trust and good corporate citizenship connected to social and environmental responsibility by aligning themselves with charitable food delivery. For example in New Zealand corporate and charitable welfare have gradually become inseparable partners allowing the government to neglect its RTF obligations. The question is once again raised as to who is really benefitting from corporatized food charity, and in practice how effective is this food charity model?

Relationships between food charity and public food aid

Not surprisingly, the case studies reveal a complex set of relationships existing between charitable and public food aid and the institution-alization of food banking: usually publicly-funded food aid is supple-mented by donations from private sector actors like farmers, retailers, the food processing industry or individual citizens, and delivered by private sector operators or NGOs, such as civic or faith-based organiza-tions and churches. In those EU member countries (Estonia, Finland and Spain) which accepted food aid (in place between 1987 and the end of 2013) by participating in the EU's Food Distribution Programme for the Most Deprived Persons of the Community (MDP), this particular dona-tion of foodstuffs from the intervention stocks of agricultural products, accumulated as a result of over-production, offered an important basic stock for the distribution of charitable food. In this way publicly-funded emergency food (EU food aid) came, simultaneously, to be used by those countries participating in the scheme, as a safety valve for the EU's agri-cultural and trade policies as well as for poverty reduction policies, actu-ally facilitating and underpinning the expansion of charitable food aid distribution.

From this perspective and taking account of the testimony of the tight interrelatedness of agricultural policy, public food aid and social secu-rity in the USA, the connections between public food banks and the support of small scale farming in the *Zero Hunger* strategy in Brazil, and, for example, the corporatization of food aid in Canada, New Zealand and South Africa, charitable food aid should, in the future, definitely be understood and explored in the broader context of the typically discon-nected policies of social welfare, public health, agriculture, trade and environment.

This kind of contextualization exposes the dysfunctional results of prevailing policy mismatches by demonstrating the complex and often hidden relations between food, health, environment and society and by making those relations more explicit and democratically accountable – which, according to Lang et al. (2009, pp. 6–8), is the primary task of researching food policy. This will also open up new perspectives on the question of who, in fact, are benefitting from the increasing entrench-ment of charitable food aid? Obviously, it is not only, or even primarily, those vulnerable populations living in food poverty.

Further to the complex combination of public and charitable opera-tions, in Brazil there are three types of food banks: those run by private corporations as part of their social responsibility programmes; those run by NGOs; and next to these, those run and supported by the public sector as part of the *Zero Hunger* strategy. This public 'joined-up' food policy, including a central and significant role for *Bolsa Família* (the conditional cash transfer programme) is based on the understanding of food security as a public good. All food banks are governed by the same legislation concerning food safety and consumers' protection.

Against Brazil's history of high prevalence of extreme poverty, under-nourishment and child mortality, public intervention to address the food system and poverty policy in the form of food banks seems to be reasonable. Importantly, the intervention includes responsibility for the selection and evaluation of the needs of the client organizations, monitoring the proper use, handling and processing of the food as well as developing and providing nutrition education, for which purpose all public food banks must employ at least one nutritionist and a social worker. On the other hand, the sole existence of food banks is a sign of hunger and precarious food security for vulnerable population groups. As Rocha states, a 'truly food secure Brazil will be one without food banks'.

Historical, cultural and religious influences

There are historical, cultural and religious factors influencing in different ways the development, social reception and institutionalization of food aid distribution. Basically, prevailing welfare state models are grounded in different perceptions of family and public obligations in producing social security; in responding to social and material needs including the provision of welfare and social cohesion; and in acknowledging the position of women in the labour market. In Hong Kong, South Africa, Spain and Turkey there is a strong tradition of family solidarity that is supposed to meet social and material needs and provide welfare for family members. At the same time in Estonia, Kõre states families are obligated by law to help ascending as well as descending family members in need.

Practical forms of family solidarity and social care are often basically carried out by women. This arrangement is fragile in the face of modern ways of life: women's increasing labour market participation, high divorce rates, increasing co-habiting and complicated family relationships, not to mention feminized poverty, strike at the roots of the model based on care given by housewives or the double burden of working women. Consequently, in recent decades the function of the family as a social safety net has weakened throughout.

Yet, in Spain during the current economic recession family solidarity has reactivated, providing the main strategies facing the crisis and, hence, confining the need for charitable reactions although, as Pérez de Armiño writes, there is a strong tradition of charity and almsgiving within the

Catholic regime in Southern Europe, which could be understood as a form of 'uncritical solidarity' with the poor. Also as Tang, Zhu and Chen make clear, within Taoism and Buddhism, the beliefs by which many Hong Kong citizens are influenced, almsgiving is cherished, providing a strong cultural underpinning for food charity yet at the same time permitting government to avoid its public responsibility for addressing significant issues of food poverty. In Turkey, again, legalizing food banking in 2004 provided a legitimate venue for re-establishing traditional Islamic culture and the practice of almsgiving and, hence, contributed to charitable reaction to domestic hunger.

On the other hand, quotidian charity or voluntary work does not belong within the Lutheran cultural heritage (e.g., in Scandinavia). Instead there has been a long-standing and firm commitment to the public responsibility of society towards its citizens, based on a strong democracy and a determination to reduce poverty, inequality and vulnerability.

The intricacy and policy dilemmas of public–private partnerships in distributing food aid multiply, when taking account of different kinds of understandings of the nature and practice of the aid. In many of the case studies school meals, for example, are interpreted as food aid and they are directed especially at children living in vulnerable families. In Finland, Silvasti and Karjalainen note there has been universal free school lunch since 1948. Although the history of free lunches can be traced to the years of severe poverty after World War II, today free school meals are considered a universal entitlement without any connection to food aid, and with no talk of charitable food aid, unlike, for example, in Canada, New Zealand and the USA.

In Brazil, eradicating hunger is seen primarily as a government responsibility. Yet, food charity sustains some of the donations to NGO-based food banks. Strong public support of *'cidadania'*, roughly translated as 'participatory citizenship', drives the civic activity for participation in initiatives such as food banks. *'Cidadania'* means that to be part of Brazil, people have not only rights but also responsibilities. At the same time when people increasingly expect the government to protect their rights, they are also aware of a duty to participate. Hence, there is little reluctance to accept charity operations along with government intervention in the food system, particularly in addressing social inequities.

In the case of South Africa, Hendriks and McIntyre write that the African National Congress inherited in 1994 a country with a rapidly industrializing economy and deep inequality entrenched by long-term institutionalized racial discrimination. In addition, the social impact of HIV has produced a new variant of famine. The epidemic is a catastrophe to which resilience was weak after Apartheid's legacy: institutionalized inequality, gendered poverty, perpetuated deeply-rooted patriarchy, pernicious governance and transparency problems causing and exacerbating food insecurity and hunger. Although food security is enshrined in South Africa's constitution, the possibilities to claim the RTF are feeble. Food security policy puts forward food safety nets by focusing on food assistance in various forms, including cash transfers, subsidized feeding programmes and redistribution of wasted food. However, this has produced intertwined guises of social protection and 'corporate social responsibility' that encourage food charity responses.

To make the general view even more complicated, in the post-socialist transition countries such as Estonia, where organized charity, like faith-based care, was prohibited by law during the Soviet regime, there is an urgent pursuit to revive democracy and civil society, which of course includes charitable organizations. This kind of recent political history may favour charitable solutions beside or even at the expense of demands for public responsibility, especially in the context of globally prevailing neo-liberal economic hegemony.

The conclusion here is that the paths to addressing domestic hunger are multiple: different but increasingly enfeebled welfare state models; charitable and/or corporately sponsored food banks; community-based food provisioning; public–private food aid; and state dependence on degrees of family obligation or cultural or religious heritage. Yet whether 'joined-up' or acting alone such approaches cannot safeguard from hunger and food insecurity vulnerable people who are in severe economic distress. The key to avoiding hunger is not charitable food aid but the eradication of income poverty. Yet the emergent and converging trends favour food transfers in place of cash transfers.

Social construction of hunger as a matter for charity

Achieving a living wage policy and ensuring the adequacy of social security benefits when charitable food aid is on offer is enormously difficult. When charities win an increasing presence and ever more positive reception in the mass media, they are also gaining a stronger backing from public institutions including recognition and support from society. The media's role in constructing the public image of charity operations, for example by promoting massive charity rallies visibly supported by celebrities, is significant – the CBC, Canada's nationally-funded public broadcaster has for years sponsored food bank drives across the country.

When public funds are used in this way, little wonder that addressing domestic hunger is seen as a matter for charity.

Moreover, the present-day development in the UK offers an alarming example, when government denial of the hunger issue has turned not only to acceptance but to endorsing, enshrining and encouraging growing charitable emergency food systems without any signs of commitment to meeting the political obligations to respect, protect and fulfil social and economic human rights, such as the RTF. This trend contradicts strikingly with the widespread governmental denial of hunger: officially there seems to be no problem, but, nevertheless, there is a persistent tendency to accept charitable action as successfully managing the problem. This demonstrates the ways by which the food banking model familiar from North America is gaining an international foothold more generally, and as promoted by the GFN. Ironically, given that the United States has never ratified the ICESCR and the human right to adequate food, it is the US food charity model which is being exported to countries whose governments have committed themselves to progressively realizing the RTF.

Superficially, charitable and corporate food aid delivery appears to be effective. This ostensible effectiveness offers national governments a way to 'outsource' the political risk of domestic hunger. It does this in two ways by 'downloading' or 'downstreaming' its RTF obligations and responsibilities to lower levels of governments and local authorities; and secondly by supporting the neo-liberal social policy response to food poverty which pushes responsibilities for structural societal problems onto charities and individual citizens.

These developments have been promoted by the corporatization of charitable work and positive media attention with the result that hunger has been socially constructed as a matter for charity instead of an issue requiring the priority attention of the governments. At the moment there is no political will, except in the case of Brazil, or serious impulse for any large-scale public outrage about the stubborn and even increasing extent of food poverty in the rich First World countries. Hunger has been effectively de-politicized not only as an issue of fair income distribution but also as an issue of fundamental human rights. The effectiveness of charity in addressing the issue is assumed, but is this the case?

Effectiveness

The case studies clearly indicate that in spite of the positive image of the effectiveness of charitable food aid fed by the mass media and by the national and international central organizations of food banking there are, in practice, many problems: charitable responses are constrained by limited resources including the lack of donated food; ad hoc and uncoordinated provision; the continuous risk of withdrawal of corporate partners; dependence on the availability of volunteers and personnel; the accessibility and availability of food aid; geographical coverage and strategic directions; and frequently the lack of choice for food bank recipients.

Furthermore, food assistance is often provided based on more or less vague criteria decided by the charity agencies or even individual voluntary workers, not equally on the basis of a universal right for all citizens. Perhaps of most significance is the fact that food bank data underestimate the prevalence of domestic hunger or food insecurity in national settings, thereby undermining attempts to generate income security policies informed by the right to food.

In Australia, Canada, the UK and the USA, for example, emergency food services are unable to meet the growing demand for food: food banks run out of food. Although the high public profile of charity food aid gives the impression that charity is a sheet anchor for people in need, as Riches and Tarasuk remind us, in Canada only 20–30 per cent of people experiencing food insecurity seek food assistance. Even among people facing severe food insecurity, food bank usage is very low and when children are at risk of food deprivation, only one-third of families seek food bank assistance. There are several potential barriers to accessing charity food aid: limited operating hours, long queues, ineligibility for assistance, lack of information about available services and inadequate or unsuitable assistance. Also as noted by O'Brien in New Zealand, fear of degradation may hinder people to accept food aid as happens in New Zealand, when some parents ask their children not to attend free school breakfast because they experience it as stigmatizing.

From a public health perspective it is of the essence that many of those people receiving food aid have special dietary needs because of, for example, allergies, obesity and diseases like diabetes, arterial hypertension or cardiovascular diseases to say nothing of the scourge of HIV/Aids, particularly in the case of South Africa. Food charity is not designed to meet such dietary and nutritional requirements suggesting unaddressed public health issues of significant magnitude. Moreover the lack of possibility to choose one's own food may result in dependence on food of poor nutritional quality and thus be damaging for all recipients.

The ineffectiveness of food charity work is hidden by a growing degree of public legitimacy promoted by positive mass media attention. In the USA, charitable food banks, Poppendieck comments, are only a small part of the country's federally funded food assistance programmes, yet they command disproportionate public recognition in addressing the hunger problem. In the everyday realism of the general public, charitable operations are easily understood as practical, common sense responses, based on human compassion, to the immediate and every day issue of domestic hunger; and particularly so in times of tightening social budgets and gradually ever more damaged social security safety nets. As has been argued 'the ideology of philanthropy inhibits serious critique' (McMahon, 2011).

However, despite sincere intentions, charitable organizations cannot guarantee the universal right to adequate food and nutrition. In the end, in the quest for national food security, only the state is able to guarantee funds and resources and to ensure that these are, permanently and without stigmatization, available for all.

Public policy informed by the right to food

Possibility of RTF approaches and 'joined-up' food policy

The majority of authors express no hope for the possibility of progressive national politics and its capability to solve the hunger issue within the context of prevailing neo-liberal economic policy. Consequently, looking to and trusting the role of international human rights law and, hence, RTF approaches is not unexpected. Yet, the possibility of RTF approaches providing an alternative agenda for moral, legal and political action informing 'joined-up' food, agricultural, public health, income and social policy as a key strategy directed at resolving the issue of food poverty in wealthy first world societies, also seems to lie in the distant future.

There are few signs of serious political commitments to develop 'joined-up' food policy that might offer alternative approaches to achieve universal food security inclusive of disadvantaged and vulnerable populations. Brazil, though, offers some hope with the strength of political will demonstrated by their government. In most cases, however, as in Canada, Estonia and Finland, even a coherent national food policy is lacking and the domestic RTF approach is fairly unknown, being connected primarily with global hunger in public debate.

Alternative roles for key stakeholders in achieving just and sustainable food systems

As the case studies indicate, the increasing need for and supply of charity food aid underlines the crude non-compliance of the majority of wealthy states to 'respect, protect and fulfill' the right to food for vulnerable people.

All governments, which have ratified the ICESCR in their role as primary duty bearers, are required to act in domestic compliance with their obligations under international law to ensure food security in their own countries. Yet there is little or no evidence signalling such compliance.

The RTF implies a framework of national law which moves beyond policy guidelines to legislative action. It also implies the development and adoption of coordinated national plans, strategies and tools to advance and ensure the development of 'joined-up' food policy including the setting of targets, benchmarks and indicators, monitoring, justiciable remedies and all actions necessary to secure a just and sustainable food system. Governments have been continually reminded of these obligations not only through the periodic reviews undertaken by the UN's Committee on Economic and Social Rights but as a result of country missions undertaken by the UN Special Rapporteur on the Right to Food. The Special Rapporteur's work is primarily directed at the Global South but increasingly rich nation states would benefit from his advice.

The evidence of this book suggests governments first need to prioritize social protection policies in their national food policy, income security and social welfare debates. Critical for guaranteeing the RTF as a universal right is the political will to adopt the ICESCR into domestic law. While the right to food is a legal approach and basically an individual human right, the politics to ensure its advancement and enshrinement in domestic constitutional law necessitates engaging the political process and the politics of the public–private divide. Significantly, the RTF is also an economic, social and cultural right and, and as such, a collective right. It reflects a commitment to the universal, interdependent, indivisible and interrelated inseparability of all human rights and the obligations of government as the primary duty bearer to ensure its collective and progressive realization.

Despite the overall lack of willingness by governments to take charge and accept public accountability for widespread domestic hunger within their countries, the corporate sector and civil society, including vulnerable people themselves, are vital and relevant stakeholders in the processes which enable people to feed themselves with dignity within just and sustainable food systems.

The corporate sector is a particularly strong and, many would argue, dominant stakeholder in the field of food security. The current corporate food system produces huge amounts of waste, which reveals the unforgivable inefficiency of the system. However, the solution to the ethical and environmental problem of food waste should not be in organizing a secondary food market in forms of charitable food delivery to distribute wasted, unsaleable food free for residual citizens outside the primary market. Instead the primary market and prevailing food system needs to be rationalized, reorganized and made more effective.

As mentioned previously income poverty is the main reason for food poverty. In fact, as Dowler observes, the food system itself is infamous for its low wages, insecure part time jobs and zero-hour contracts affecting especially women as well as a tendency to promote unhealthy food at bargain prices. Moreover, in the USA the dependence of anti-hunger groups on philanthropic contributions from retailing giants has raised questions. For example, Walmart's pledge in food and cash grants is a small contribution compared to the billions that American taxpayers spend subsidizing Walmart, whose salaries are so small that many of the employees qualify for SNAP and Medicaid. Evidently, an end to hunger requires living wages, adequate benefits, and full employment. However, these policies are not in the immediate corporate self-interest.

The case studies do reveal, however, an emerging possibility for those civil society actors, both domestic and international, campaigning on food security and food poverty and justice issues, and those working for alternative affordable, ethical and sustainable food production to combine their forces. The key issue here is that people should be enabled to feed themselves in ways they see fit, so as to achieve wellbeing and potential for themselves and the planet. In any case, the present state of First World food insecurity is an indication of the unfortunate way capitalist markets meet the basic needs of human beings. There is no lack of food or even money, but lack of distributional justice.

Conclusion

The picture of First World hunger today as presented in the case studies reveals a number of converging general trends: increasing demand for and supply of food aid; the entrenchment of charitable food delivery and food banking in both high income and emerging economies; deepening and expanding corporatization of food charities through different kinds of partnerships; an increasing presence and unconditionally positive reception in the media producing, as a kind of side effect, increasingly stronger backing from public institutions including support from society for such charity; a failure to acknowledge the ineffectiveness of the food charity model; and a lack of political will for active public debate seeking collective and publicly accountable solutions to domestic hunger and food insecurity. The right to food does not appear to be on the agenda.

Only Brazil seems to be diverging from the general development by having clear politically set targets and benchmarks for the fight against hunger and is actively pursuing the development and practice of 'joined-up', integrated policies connecting food, public health, income and social policy, not to mention a progressive understanding of the meaning of agricultural policy. In the other countries, for example, serious shortages in data collection concerning hunger and food insecurity including general lack of official monitoring, reliable statistics and time series indicates not only neglecting the problem but also denying it.

Indeed, it seems that no one and nothing, not even the Scandinavian regime, can be safe from the mindset of the New Right. Consequently, despite all the effort and numerous international covenants the right to food is still a distant goal waiting to be fulfilled. Food charity, on the other hand, seems to be truly vigorous.

It is also evident that the pathways to domestic hunger and to charitable responses for food poverty are multiple. Individual case studies clearly prove that increasingly dismantled welfare state regimes, reliance on family solidarity/obligation or cultural/religious heritage as such cannot guarantee adequate food and nutrition to vulnerable people living in severe economic distress. There are naturally differences in stages of economic development between the OECD countries and emerging economies in light of different economic and political histories. In Brazil, South Africa and Turkey the socio-economic point of departure after the mid-1990s has been much more severe with high rates of extreme poverty, undernourishment and infant mortality for example. Yet, the rapid economic development measured by GNP growth, as seen also in Estonia and Hong Kong, has not benefitted all the people in these countries. Instead they are adopting, not to say eagerly, charitable food aid as a solution for the distress of the most vulnerable, indicative of convergence with the model entrenched in the First World.

The key to avoiding hunger, however, is not institutionalizing charitable or corporate food aid but the eradication of income poverty. Hence, a wealthy national economy by itself is not deliverance, whereas fair income distribution is. Eventually, only the state is able to guarantee funds and resources for basic social security and to ensure that it is permanently, universally and without stigmatization available for all people in real need.

In the future the multitude of understandings, practices and socio-political frameworks of public–private and third sector charitable activities and mixtures of them will offer important themes for studies in the field of the RTF. Also, in order to expose the dysfunctional results of prevailing policy mismatches, there is an urgent need, now and in the near future, to explore the hidden relationships and functions of food aid within the wider context of the typically disconnected policies of food policy, income security, social welfare, public health, agriculture, trade and the environment.

Further studies aside, the problem of First World hunger today is that it is both an immediate and long-term issue of distributional justice and human rights and a fundamentally political question demanding the priority attention of governments. The hungry poor deserve action now. To repeat the words of Louise Arbour, the former UN High Commissioner for Human Rights, 'there will always be a place for charity, but charitable responses are not an effective, principled or sustainable substitute for enforceable human rights guarantees' (2005, p. 8).

References

AAFC, 1998. *Canada's Action Plan for Food Security*. Agriculture and Agri-Food Canada, Ottawa.

ABS, 2011. *Consumer Price Index 2000–2010*. Australian Bureau of Statistics, Canberra.

ACOSS, 2012a. *Poverty in Australia*. Australian Council of Social Services, Strawberry Hills.

ACOSS, 2012b. *Welfare Groups and Human Rights Lawyers Appeal to UN to Prevent Sole Parent Payment Cuts*. [Online] Available: http://www.acoss.org.au/media/release/welfare_groups_and_human_rights_lawyers_appeal_to_un_to_prevent_damaging_so (Accessed 8 February 2012).

Adams, M., Cousins, B., Manona, S., 2009. Land Tenure and Economic Development in Rural South Africa, *Environment and Society: Advances in Research* 2(1), 87–105.

Ahola, E., Hiilamo, H. (eds), 2013. *Poverty in Helsinki. An analysis of social assistance recipients and use in 2008–2010*. Kela, Helsinki.

AHRC, 2009. *Review of Australia's fourth periodic report on the implementation of the International Covenant on Economic, Social and Cultural Rights*. Australian Human Rights Commission, Sydney.

AIHW, 2009. *Aboriginal and Torres Strait Islander Health Performance Framework 2008*, Report: Detailed Analysis. Australian Institute of Health and Welfare, Canberra.

Akgül, A., 2008. Yılda 24 Milyar YTL İsraf Ediliyor. *Türkiye İsrafı Önleme Vakfı*. Türkiye'nin Sorunlarına Çözüm Serisi, No 21, Ankara.

Alcock, P., Craig, G., 2009. *International Social Policy: Welfare Regimes in the Developed World*. Palgrave Macmillan, Houndmills.

Aldridge, H., Kenway, P., MacInnes, T., Parekh, P., 2012. *Monitoring Poverty and Social Exclusion 2012*. Joseph Rowntree Foundation, York.

Alence, R., 2004. Political Institutions and Developmental Governance in Sub-Saharan Africa. *The Journal of Modern African Studies* 42(2), 163–187.

Anderson, M., 2012. Beyond Food Security to Realizing Food Rights in the US. *Journal of Rural Studies* 29, 113–122.

Anderson, M.D., 2008. Rights-based Food Systems and the Goals of Food Systems Reform. *Agriculture and Human Values* 25(4), 593–608.

Andersson, S.A. (ed.), 1990. Core Indicators of Nutritional State for Difficult-to-Sample Populations. Life Sciences Research Office, *The Journal of Nutrition*, 120 (1557S–1600S).

ANU, 2009. *The HRA 2004 ACT: The First Five Years of Operation*. Australian National University, Canberra.

Aranha, A., 2010. A Project Turned into a Government Strategy. In: Graziano da Silva, J., Del Grossi, M.E., França, C.G. (eds), *The Fome Zero (Zero Hunger) Program: The Brazilian Experience*. Ministry of Agrarian Development, Brasilia.

Arbour, L., 2005. *Freedom From Want – From Charity to Entitlement*. La Fontaine-Baldwin Symposium Lecture, Quebec City.

ARIB, 2012. *European Union Food Aid. Food Aid to 2012*. Estonian Agricultural Registers and Information Board. [Online] Available: http://www.pria.ee/et/toetused/valdkond/euroopa_liidu_toiduprogrammid/toiduabi2012/ (Accessed 17 December 2013).

ARIB, 2013. *European Union Food Aid. Food Aid in 2013*. Estonian Agricultural Registers and Information Board. [Online] Available: http://www.pria.ee/et/toetused/valdkond/euroopa_liidu_toiduprogrammid/toiduabi2013/ (Accessed 17 December 2013).

Aricanli, T., Rodrik, D., 1990. *The Political Economy of Turkey: Debt, Adjustment and Sustainability*. New York, St. Martin's Press.

Ashoka Changemakers, 2013. *Food Bank SA*. [Online] Available: http://www.changemakers.com/project/FBSA-south-africa?ref=related-entry (Accessed 20 November 2013).

Attree, P., 2005. Low-income Mothers, Nutrition and Health: A Systematic Review of Qualitative Evidence. *Maternal and Child Nutrition* 1(4), 227–240.

Australian Government, 2010. *Australia's Human Rights Framework*. [Online] Available: http://www.ag.gov.au/humanrightsframework (Accessed 28 August 2013).

Australian Government, 2012. *National Food Plan Green Paper*. Department of Agriculture, Fisheries and Forestry, Canberra.

Ayton, D., Carey, G., Keleher, H., Smith, B., 2012. Historical Overview of Church Involvement in Health and Wellbeing in Australia: Implications for Health Promotion Partnerships. *Australian Journal of Primary Health* 18(1), 4–10.

Bacchi, C., 2009. *Analysing Policy: What's the Problem Represented to Be?* Pearson Education Australia, Frenchs Forest.

Baker, D., Fear, J., Denniss, R., 2009. *What a Waste: An Analysis of Household Expenditure on Food*, Policy Brief no.6. The Australia Institute.

Banco de Alimentos de Barcelona, 2012. *Memoria 2011*. Banco de Alimentos, Barcelona.

Banerjee, S.B., 2012. Corporate Social Responsibility: The Good, the Bad and the Ugly. *Critical Sociology* 34(1), 51–79.

Barling, D., Lang, T., Caraher, M., 2002. Joined-up Food Policy? The Trials of Governance, Public Policy and the Food System. *Social Policy and Administration* 36(6), 556–574.

Barrientos, S., Kritzinger, A., 2004. Squaring the Circle: Global Production and the Informalization of Work in South African Fruit Exports. *Journal of International Development* 16(1), 81–92.

Barros, R.P., 2009. *Sucessos e Desafios para a Política Social Brasileira* (apresentação). Instituto de Pesquisa Econômica Aplicada (IPEA), Brasília.

Battle, K., 2012. *Ottawa and Poverty*. Richard Splane lecture on Social Policy in November 2012. Cadelon Institute of Social Policy, Ottawa.

BDA Group, 2009. *The Full Cost of Landfill Disposal in Australia*. BDA Group, Melbourne.

Belik, W., 2010. Mobilization of Enterprises Around the Fight Against Hunger. In: Graziano da Silva, J., Del Grossi, M.E., França, C. (eds), *The Fome Zero (Zero Hunger) Program: The Brazilian Experience*. Ministry of Agrarian Development, Brasília.

Bentley, Christina, 2004. Women's Human Rights & the Feminisation of Poverty in South Africa. In: *Review of African Political Economy* 31(100), 247–261.

Berg, J., 2008. *All You Can Eat: How Hungry Is America?* Seven Stories Press, New York.

BI, 2012. *Towards a More Equal Canada*. Broadbent Institute, Ottawa.

Bilgic, A., Yen, S.T., 2013. Household Food Demand in Turkey: A Two-step Demand System Approach. *Food Policy* 43(C), 267–277.

Bonoli, G., 2005. The Politics of the New Social Policies: Providing Coverage Against New Social Risks in Mature Welfare States. *Policy & Politics* 33(3), 431–449.

Boratav, K., 1988. *Türkiye İktisat Tarihi* (1908–1985). Gerçek Yayınevi, Istanbul.

Bradsher, K., 2012. Hong Kong Retreats on 'National Education' Plan. *New York Times*, 9 September 2012.

Bradsher, K., 2013. In Hong Kong, a Budget with a Surfeit of Surpluses. *New York Times*, 28 February 2013.

Brazil – National Congress, 2005. *Projeto de le PL6047*. National Congress, Brasilia.

Bread for the World, 2013. *Fact Sheet: Churches and Hunger*. [Online] Available: www.bread.org/FactSheet.pdf (Accessed 1 August 2012).

Bugra, A., Candas, A., 2011. Change and Continuity Under an Eclectic Social Security Regime: The Case of Turkey. *Middle Eastern Studies* 47(3), 515–528.

Burity, V., Cruz, L., Franceschini, T., 2011. *Exigibilidade: Mechanisms to Claim the Human Right to Adequate Food in Brazil*. FAO, Rome.

Burlandy, L., Rocha, C., Maluf, R., 2013. Integrating Nutrition into Agricultural and Rural Development Policies: The Brazilian Experience of Building an Innovative Food and Nutrition Security Approach. In: Thompson, B., Amoroso, L. (eds), *Improving Diets and Raising Levels of Nutrition: Food-based Approaches* (Proceedings – International Symposium on Food and Nutrition Security: Food-Based Approaches for Improving Diets and Raising Levels of Nutrition). FAO, Rome.

Burns, C., 2004. *A Review of the Literature Describing the Link Between Poverty, Food Insecurity and Obesity with Specific Reference to Australia*. VicHealth, Melbourne.

Butler, P., 2013. Foodbanks surge leads to DEFRA inquiry. *The Guardian*. [Online] Available: http//www.guardian.co.uk/society/2013/feb/24/food-banks-increase-defra-inquiry/print (Accessed 26 February 2013).

CAFB, 1997. *Hunger Count 1997*. Canadian Association of Food Banks, Toronto.

CAISAN, 2009. *Subsídio para Balanço das Ações Governamentais de Segurança Alimentar e Nutricional e da Implantação do Sistema Nacional*. Câmara Interministerial de Segurança Alimenta, Ministério do Desenvolvimento Social e Combate à Fome, Brasilia.

Canada, n.d. *International Covenant on Economic, Social and Cultural Rights, Sixth Report of Canada 2005–2009*. Advanced Unedited Edition, Ottawa.

Cáritas, 2012. *De la coyuntura a la estructura. Los efectos permanentes de la crisis*, VII Informe del Observatorio de la Realidad Social. Cáritas Española, Madrid.

CBC, 2013. UN envoy scolds Ottawa's anti-poverty efforts. *CBC News* 3 March 2013, Toronto.

CBPP, 2011. Center for Budget and Policy Priorities, United States: TANF Caseload Factsheet, update September, 2011, http://www.cbpp.org/files/1–25–11tanf-USpdf.

CBO (Congressional Budget Office), 2012. *The Supplemental Nutrition Assistance Program*, April 2012.

CEC, 2004. Commission of the European Communities. *Social Inclusion in the New Member States. A Synthesis of the Joint Memoranda on Social Inclusion.* Commission Staff Working Paper. [Online] Available: http://ec.europa.eu/employment_social/ soc-prot/soc-incl/sec_04_848_en.pdf (Accessed 1 June 2014).

Census and Statistics Department, 2012. *Gini Coefficients for 2001, 2006 and 2011.* [Online] Available: http://www.census2011.gov.hk/ (Accessed 19 May 2012).

Centrelink, 2011. *A Guide to Commonwealth Government Payments,* March–July 2000–2010. Centrelink, Canberra.

Cerami, A., 2007. *Europeanization, Enlargement and Social Policy in Central and Eastern Europe,* Les Cahiers européens de Sciences Po, n° 01. Centre d'études européennes at Sciences Po, Paris. [Online] Available: http://www.cee.scienc- es-po.fr/erpa/docs/wp_2007_1.pdf (Accessed 3 September 2013).

CESCR, 1999. *General Comment No. 12,* Committee on Economic, Social and Cultural Rights, E/C.12/1999/5.

CESCR, 2012. *Consideration of Reports Submitted by States Parties under Articles 16 and 17 of the Covenant.* Forty-eighth Session, 30 April–18 May 2012. Concluding Observations of the Committee on Economic, Social and Cultural Rights, Spain, E/C.12/ESP/CO/5, Geneva.

CFHS, 2013. *Community Food and Health Scotland* [Online] Available: http://www. communityfoodandhealth.org.uk/ (Accessed 16 September 2013).

CFPA, 2010. *Food: A Recipe for a Healthy, Sustainable and Successful Future: Second Report from the Council of Food Policy Advisors.* Defra, London. [Online] Available: http://archive.defra.gov.uk/foodfarm/food/policy/council/reports. htm (Accessed 5 August 2013).

CFS, 2004. *Report of Intergovernmental Working Group for the Elaboration of a Set of Voluntary Guidelines on the Progressive Realisation of the Right to Food in the Context of National Food Security Committee on World Food Security.* Corporate Services, Human Resources, and Finance Department. [Online] Available: http://www.fao.org/docrep/meeting/008/J3345e/j3345e01.htm (Accessed 14 August 2013).

Chan, M., 2012. *Food Assistance in Hong Kong: Current situation, challenges and issues of concern* [Online] Available: http://www.poverty.org.hk (Accessed 22 October 2012).

Chilton, M., Rose, D., 2009. A Rights-based Approach to Food Insecurity in the United States. *American Journal of Public Health* 99(7), 1203–1211.

Chou, K.L., 2012. *Familial Effect on Child Poverty in Hong Kong Immigrant Families.* Social Indicators Research 113, 183–195.

Cinar, E.M., 1994. Unskilled Urban Migrant Women and Disguised Employment: Home-Working Women in Istanbul, Turkey. *World Development* 22(3), 369–380.

CIS, 2011. *Barómetro de Diciembre 2011.* Centro de Investigaciones Sociológicas, Madrid. [Online] Available: http://www.cis.es/cis/export/sites/default/-Ar- chivos/Marginales/2920_2939/2923/Es2923.pdf (Accessed 1 July 2013).

Colello, K.J., 2010. *Older Americans Act: Title III Nutrition Services Program.* [Online] Available: http://healthlegislation.blogspot.fi/2013/01/older-americans-act- title-iii-nutrition.html (Accessed 17 January 2013).

Coleman-Jensen, A., Nord, M., Andrews, M., Carlson, S., 2012. *Household Food Security in the United States in 2011.* Economic Research Report No. 141. USDA.

Coleman-Jensen, A., Nord, M., Singh, A., 2013. *Household Food Security in the United States in 2012.* Economic Research Report No. (ERR-155). [Online]

Available: http://www.ers.usda.gov/publications/err-economic-research-report/ err155.aspx#.Uskp8bSzL2s (Accessed 5 January 2014).

Commonwealth of Australia, 2006. *Common Core Document Forming Part of the Reports of State Parties – Australia.* Commonwealth of Australia, Barton.

Cooper, N., Dumpleton, S., 2013. *Walking the Breadline: The Scandal of Food Poverty in 21st Century Britain.* Oxfam, Oxford.

Cosar, S., Yegenoglu, M., 2009. The Neoliberal Restructuring of Turkey's Social Security System. *Monthly Review* 60(11). [Online] Available: http://monthlyreview.org/2009/04/01/the-neoliberal-restructuring-of-turkeys-social-security-system (Accessed 11 May 2014).

Cox, A., Black, R., 2012. *Window on Waikato Poverty: Food and Waikato School Communities.* Poverty Action Waikato, Hamilton.

CRA, 2013. *Seurakunnat jakoivat ruoka-apua vähävaraisille yli 3 miljoonalla eurolla.* http://www.kirkkopalvelut.fi/kirkkopalvelujen-uutiset/546-seurakunnat-jakoivat-ruoka-apua-vaehaevaraiselle-yli-3-miljoonalla-eurolla (Accessed 10 January 2014).

Craig, G., Dowler, E., 1997. 'Let them eat cake!' Poverty, Hunger and the UK State. In: Riches, G (ed.), *First World Hunger: Food Security and Welfare Politics.* Macmillan, Basingstoke.

CRC, 2001. *Initial and Second Report Submitted by Estonia under Article 44 of the Convention on the Rights of the Child.* [Online] Available: http://web-static.vm.ee/static/failid/487/CRC_report_Estonia_2001.pdf (Accessed 15 August 2013).

CSPC, 2012. *SNAP to Health: A Fresh Approach to Improving Nutrition in the Supplemental Nutrition Assistance Program.* Center for the Study of the Presidency and Congress, Washington, DC.

CSPI, 2013. *Selfish Giving: How the Soda Industry Uses Philanthropy to Sweeten its Profits.* Center for Science in the Public Interest, Washington, DC.

Dachner, N., Gaetz, S., Poland, B., Tarasuk, V., 2009. An Ethnographic Study of Meal Programs for Homeless and Under-housed Individuals in Toronto. *Journal of Health Care for the Poor and Underserved* 20(3), 846–853.

Dana, L.P., Dana, T.E., 1999. Fast Food in Istanbul. *British Food Journal* 101(5), 490–492.

Defra, 2006. *Food Security and the UK: An Evidence and Analysis Paper.* Defra, London. [Online] Available: http://archive.defra.gov.uk/evidence/economics/foodfarm/reports/documents/foodsecurity.pdf (Accessed 5 August 2013).

Defra, 2009. *UK Food Security Assessment: Our Approach.* Defra, London. [Online] Available: http://archive.defra.gov.uk/foodfarm/food/pdf/food-assess-approach-0908.pdf (Accessed 5 August 2013).

Defra, 2012. *Food Statistics Pocket Book 2011.* Defra, London.

Defra, 2013. *Food Statistics Pocket Book 2012.* Defra, London.

Del Grossi, M.E., 2010. Poverty Reduction: From 44 Million to 29.6 Million People. In: Giannotti, M.A. (ed.), *Desenvolvimento De Ontologies Para Sistemas De Apoio à Logística Humanitarian Baseados Em Serviços WEB De Informações Geográficas,* Doctoral Thesis. USP, São Paulo.

Dennis, M., Stewart, D., 2004. Justiciability of Economic, Social, and Cultural Rights: Should There Be an International Complaints Mechanism to Adjudicate the Rights to Food, Water, Housing, and Health? *The American Journal of International Law* 98(3), 462–515.

De Schutter, O., 2009. *The Right to Food and the Political Economy of Hunger.* 26th McDougall Memorial Lecture opening the 36th session of the FAO conference, Rome.

De Schutter, O., 2010. *Food Commodities Speculation and Food Price Crises. Regulation to Reduce the Risks of Price Volatility.* Briefing Note 02 September. [Online] Available: http://www.srfood.org/images/stories/pdf/otherdocuments/20102309_briefing_note_02_En_ok.pdf (Accessed 5 August 2013).

De Schutter, O., 2011. *Report of the Special Rapporteur on the Right to Food,* Nineteenth session, Agenda item 3. A/HRC/19/59/Add.3. UN Human Rights Council, Geneva.

De Schutter, O., 2012a. *Report of the Special Rapporteur on the Right to Food on his Mission to South Africa* (7–15 July 2011). UN, Human Rights Council, Geneva.

De Schutter, O., 2012b. *Report of the Special Rapporteur on the Right to Food on his Mission to Canada.* UN, Human Rights Council, Geneva.

De Waal, A., Whiteside, A., 2003. New Variant Famine: AIDS and Food Crisis in Southern Africa. *The Lancet* 362 (9391), 1234–1237.

DoHA, 2013. *National Aboriginal and Torres Strait Islander Health Plan* (NATSIHP) 2013–2023. Department of Health and Aging, Canberra.

Dökmeci et al., 2005. Informal Retailing in a Global Age: The Growth of Periodic Markets in Istanbul, 1980–2002. *Cities* 23(1), 44–55.

Dokmeci,V., Yazgi, B., Ozus, E. 2006. Informal Retailing in a Global Age: The Growth of Periodic Markets in Istanbul, 1980–2002. *Cities* 23(1), 44–55.

Donald, A., Mottershaw, E., 2009. *Poverty, Inequality and Human Rights – Do Human Rights Make a Difference?* Joseph Rowntree Foundation, London.

Dowler, E., 2003. Food and Poverty in Britain: Rights and Responsibilities. In: Dowler, E., Finer, C.J. (eds), *The Welfare of Food: Rights and Responsibilities in a Changing World.* Blackwell Publishing, Oxford.

Dowler, E., Caraher, M., 2003. Local Food Projects: The New Philanthropy? *The Political Quarterly* 74(1), 57–65.

Dowler, E., O'Connor, D., 2012. Rights-based Approaches to Addressing Food Poverty and Food Insecurity in Ireland and the United Kingdom. *Social Sciences and Medicine* 74(1), 44–51.

Dowler, E., Caraher, M., Lincoln, P., 2007. Inequalities in Food and Nutrition: Challenging 'Lifestyles'. In: Dowler, E., Spencer, N. (eds), *Challenging Health Inequalities: From Acheson to 'Choosing Health'.* Policy Press, Bristol. pp. 127–155.

Dowler, E.A., Kneafsey, M., Lambie, H., Inman, A., Collier, R., 2011. Thinking About 'Food Security': Engaging with UK Consumers. *Critical Public Health* 21(4), 403–416.

Drèze, J., Sen, A., 1989. *Hunger and Public Action.* Clarendon Press, Oxford.

Dumon, A., 2012. *Can South Africa Be Considered a Developmental State? The New Growth Plan and National Development Plan in Perspective.* [Online] Available: http://www.consultancyafrica.com/index.php?option=com_content&view=article&id=967:can-south-africa-be-considered-a-developmental-state-the-new-growth-path-and-national-developmental-plan-in-perspective&catid=87:african-finance-a-economy&Itemid=294 (Accessed 12 March 2013).

Duru, A., 2012. *Istanbul's Weekly Public Markets: Narratives of Access, Provisioning, and Governance.* PhD Dissertation, Carleton University, Department of Geography, Ottawa, Canada.

DWP, 2013. *Local Authorities and Advisers: Removal of the Spare Room Subsidy.* [Online] Available: https://www.gov.uk/government/organisations/depart-ment-for-work-pensions/series/local-authorities-removal-of-the-spare-room-subsidy (Accessed 16 September 2013).

EAG, 2012. *Solutions to Child Poverty in New Zealand. Evidence for Action.* Expert Advisory Group on Solutions to Child Poverty. Office of Children's Commissioner, Wellington.

EAPN, 2012. *Posicionamiento de EAPN-ES ante el Fondo de Ayuda a las Personas más Necesitadas de la Unión Europea* (Madrid: EAPN). [Online] Available: http://www.eapn.es/ARCHIVO/documentos/recursos/1/posicionamiento_alimentos_EAPNes.pdf (Accessed 20 June 2013).

EFFB, 2014. *European Federation of Food Banks.* [Online] Available: http://www.eurofoodbank.eu/portail/ (Accessed 6 January 2014).

Egeland, G.M., Pacey, A., Cao, Z., Sobol, I., 2010. Food Insecurity Among Inuit Preschoolers: Nunavut Inuit Child Health Survey, 2007–2008. *CMAJ* 182(3), 243–248.

Eide, A., 2005. The Importance of Economic and Social Rights in the Age of Economic Globalization. In: Eide, W.B., Kracht, U. (eds), *Food and Human Rights in Development.* Intersentia, Antwerpen–Oxford.

Eloglu, S.E., 2012. *Urban Agriculture in Istanbul: The Road to Food Security and Sustainability.* Department of Agroecology. Master's Thesis, Norwegian University of Life Sciences, Norway.

El País, 2013. El bocadillo mágico: pan con pan. *El País.* [Online] Available: http://elpais.com/ (Accessed 11 June 2013).

EMBRAPA/MDS, 2006a. *Boas práticas de manipulação em Bancos de Alimentos.* MDS, Brasilia. [Online] Available: http://www.mds.gov.br/segurancaalimentar/publicacoes/guias (Accessed 25 March 2013).

EMBRAPA/MDS, 2006b. *Orientações Alimentares – Contribuição para Banco de Alimentos.* Brasilia. [Online] Available: http://www.mds.gov.br/segurancaali-mentar/publicacoes/guias (Accessed 25 March 2013).

EMBRAPA/MDS, 2006c. *Preparo de frutas e hortaliças minimamente processadas em Banco de Alimentos.* Brasilia. [Online] Available: http://www.mds.gov.br/segur-ancaalimentar/publicacoes/guias (Accessed 25 March 2013).

EMBRAPA/MDS, 2006d. *Preparo de vegetais desidratados em Bancos de Alimentos.* Brasilia. [Online] Available: http://www.mds.gov.br/segurancaalimentar/publi-cacoes/guias (Accessed 25 March 2013).

Ergin, N., Neumann, C.K., Singer, A. (eds), 2007. *Feeding People, Feeding Power: Imarets in the Ottoman Empire.* Eren Yayıncılık, Istanbul.

ES, 2010. *Poverty in Estonia 2010.* Eesti Statistika. [Online] Available: http://www.stat.ee/publication-download-pdf?publication_id=21168 (Accessed 8 April 2013).

EUROSTAT, 2011. *Indicators of Immigrant Integration. A Pilot Study. EUROSTAT Methodologies and Working Papers.* [Online] Available: http://epp.eurostat.ec.europa.eu/cache/ITY_OFFPUB/KS-RA-11–009/EN/KS-RA-11–009-EN.PDF (Accessed 10 July 2013).

EUROSTAT database, 2013a. *In-Work at-Risk-of-Poverty Rate.* [Online] Available: http://epp.eurostat.ec.europa.eu/tgm/table.do?tab=table&init=1&plugin=1&language=en&pcode=tesov110 (Accessed 16 December 2013).

EUROSTAT database, 2013b. *People at Risk of Poverty or Social Exclusion.* [Online] Available: http://epp.eurostat.ec.europa.eu/statistics_Explained/index.php/People_at_risk_of_poverty_or_social_Exclusion (Accessed 9 December 2013).

Fangcaodi, 2012. Shenzhen Fangcaodi Social Work Center. [Online] Available: http://www.fangcaodi.org/ (Accessed 6 May 2013).

FAO, 1996. *Rome Declaration on World Food Security.* [Online] Available: http://www.fao.org/docrep/003/w3613e/w3613e00.HTM (Accessed 6 January 2014).

FAO, 2002. *Reducing Poverty and Hunger: The Critical Role of Financing for Food, Agriculture and Rural Development.* Paper Prepared for the International Conference on Financing for Development Monterrey, Mexico, 18–22 March 2002, FAO, Rome. [Online] Available: ftp://ftp.fao.org/docrep/fao/003/y6265E/Y6265E.pdf (Accessed 7 March 2010).

FAO, 2004. *Voluntary Guidelines to Support the Progressive Realization of the Right to Adequate Food in the Context of National Food Security.* Food and Agriculture Organisation of the United Nations, Rome.

FAO, 2005. *Voluntary Guidelines to Support the Progressive Realization of the Right to Adequate Food in the Context of National Food Security.* FAO, Rome.

FAO, 2006. *The Right to Food Guidelines.* Information Papers and Case Studies. FAO, Rome.

FAO, 2009. *Declaration of the World Food Summit on Food Security.* FAO, Rome.

FAO, 2010. *Turkey: Nutrition, Country Profile.* [Online] Available: http://www.fao.org/ag/agn/nutrition/tur_En.stm (Accessed 24 June 2013).

FAO, 2013a. *The State of Food Insecurity in the World 2013. The Multiple Dimensions of Food Security.* FAO, Rome. [Online] Available: http://www.fao.org/docrep/018/i3434e/i3434e00.htm (Accessed 6 January 2014).

FAO, 2013b. *Guidance Note: Integrating the Right to Adequate Food into Food and Nutrition Security Programmes.* FAO, Rome.

FareShare, 2013. *Fighting Hunger, Tackling Food Waste.* [Online] Available: http://www.fareshare.org.uk/work-with-us-2/corporate-partnerships/ (Accessed 16 August 2013).

FBA, 2012. *End Hunger in Australia Report 2012.* Foodbank Australia, New South Wales.

FBC, 2010. *Hunger Count 2010,* Food Banks Canada, Toronto.

FBC, 2012a. *Annual Report 2012.* Food Banks Canada, Toronto.

FBC, 2012b. *Hunger Count 2012.* Food Banks Canada, Toronto.

FBC, 2013. *Financial Statements,* Food Banks Canada, 31 March 2013. http://www.foodbankscanada.ca/FoodBanks/MediaLibrary/annual-reports/Audited-Financial-Statement-–2013 – Englis.pdf (Accessed 11 May 2014).

FBSA, 2010. *Food Bank Durban Hosts Unilever Team Building.* [Online] Available: http://fbsa.org.za/dbn/404-FBSA-durban-hosts-unilever-team-building-event (Accessed 12 March 2013).

FBSA, 2011a. *Massmart Continues Drive to Improve Food Security.* [Online] Available: http://www.fbsa.org.za/news/world/594-massmart-continues-drive-to-improve-food-security (Accessed 20 November 2013).

FBSA, 2011b. *Nestlé: Good Friend, Good Food.* [Online] Available: http://www.fbsa.org.za/news/world/580-nestle-good-friend-good-food (Accessed 20 November 2013).

FBSA, 2011c. *Pick n Pay and Sunday Times: Inspired by You.* [Online] Available: http://www.fbsa.org.za/news/world/623-pick-n-pay-and-sunday-times-were-inspired-by-you (Accessed 20 November 2013).

FBSA, 2011d. *Yum Yum YogoFun.* [Online] Available: http://www.FBSA.org.za/news/world/551-yum-yum-yogofun (Accessed 20 November 2013).

FBSA, 2011e. *Denny Does Good*. [Online] Available: http://www.fbsa.org.za/news/world/537-denny-does-good (Accessed 20 November 2013).

FBSA, 2012a. *Who We Serve*. [Online] Available: http://www.fbsa.org.za/who-we-serve (Accessed 20 November 2013).

FBSA, 2012b. *Newsletter* March/April. [Online] Available: http://www.fbsa.org.za/newsletters/640-marapr-2012-FBSA-grows (Accessed 3 December 2013).

FBSA, 2013. *FBSA at the Durban*. [Online] Available: http://fbsa.org.za/index.php/component/content/dbn/578-FBSA-at-the-durban-july (Accessed 20 November 2013).

FEC, 2010. *Food Justice: The Report of the Food and Fairness Inquiry*. Food Ethics Council, Brighton. [Online] Available: http://www.foodethicscouncil.org/node/465 (Accessed 12 July 2013).

FEC/DATAUFF, 2011. *Pesquisa de Avaliação do Programa Banco de Alimentos*. MDS, Brasilia.

Fell, M., Downing, E., Kennedy, S., 2013. *Food Banks and Food Poverty Commons Library*, Standard Note SN0665. [Online] Available: http://www.parliament.uk/brief-g-papers/SN06657 (Accessed 16 August 2013).

FESBAL, 2013a. *La labor de los bancos de alimentos en el año 2012*. [Online] Available: http://www.fesbal.org/ (Accessed 19 April 2013).

FESBAL, 2013b. *El derecho a la alimentación, ligado al derecho a la vida*. [Online] Available: http://www.fesbal.org/documentos/europa (Accessed 19 April 2013).

Fig, D., 2005. Manufacturing Amnesia: Corporate Social Responsibility in South Africa. *International Affairs* 81(3), 599–617.

FINA, 2013. *Tax Incentives for Charitable Giving in Canada*. Standing Committee on Finance, Ottawa.

Financial and Fiscal Commission, 2013. *Myths and Facts about the Economic Impacts of Child Support Grants*. [Online] Available: http://www.pmg.org.za/files/doc/2013/130731policybrief12.pdf (Accessed 26 November 2013).

Fisher, A., 2012. *Contradictions in the Anti-Hunger Movement*. [Online] Available: http://civileats.com/2012/03/06/contradictions-in-the-anti-hunger-movement/ (Accessed 3 June 2012).

FOESSA, 2012. *Exclusión y Desarrollo Social, Análisis y Perspectivas 2012*. Fomento de Estudios Sociales y Sociología Aplicada and Cáritas, Madrid.

FOESSA, 2013. *Desigualdad y derechos sociales. Análisis y perspectivas 2013*. Fomento de Estudios Sociales y Sociología Aplicada and Cáritas, Madrid.

Fonterra, 2013. *Supporting Our Communities*. [Online] Available: www.fonterra.co.nz/sustainability/community (Accessed 20 February 2013).

Foodcycle, 2013. *Impact*. [Online] Available: http://foodcycle.org.uk/what-we-do/impact/ (Accessed 16 September 2013).

Ford, J.D., Beaumier, M., 2011. Feeding the Family During Times of Stress: Experience and Determinants of Food Insecurity in an Inuit Community. *The Geographical Journal* 177(1), 44–61.

FRAC, 2013. *A Review of Strategies to Bolster SNAP's Role in Improving Nutrition as well as Food Security*. Food Research and Action Center.

Freire, P., 1996. *The Pedagogy of the Oppressed*. Penguin, London.

Fukuda-Parr, S., 2012. *Debate on the Right to Food in South Africa: Entitlements, Endowments and the Role of Economic and Social Policy: Event*. [Online] Available: http://www.communitylawcentre.org.za/projects/socio-economic-rights/

Research and Publications/ESR Review/ESR_Review13_2_2012.pdf (Accessed 20 November 2013).

Gallegos, D., Ellies, P., Wright, J., 2008. Still There's No Food! Food Insecurity in a Refugee Population in Perth, Western Australia. *Nutrition & Dietetics* 65(1), 78–83.

García, G., Barriga, L., Ramírez, J.M., Santos, J., 2013. *Índice de Desarrollo de los Servicios Sociales 2013*. Asociación Estatal de Directoras y Gerentes de Servicios Sociales de España. [Online] Available: http://www.directoressociales.com/images/documentos/idec%2007.06.2013.pdf (Accessed 30 June 2013).

GCIS, 2012. *Statement on Cabinet Meeting of 10 October 2012. Government Communications and Information Service.* [Online] Available: http://www.gcis.gov.za/content/newsroom/media-releases/cabstatements/11Ict2012 (Accessed 17 March 2013).

Get Up!, 2013. *Get Up! In Australia.* [Online] Available: https://www.getup.org.au/ (Accessed 31 July 2013).

GFN, 2011. *A Profile of Food Banking in Turkey*, November 2011. [Online] Available: http://www.foodbanking.org/site/PageServer?pagename=work_where_turkey_1011 (Accessed 17 March 2013).

GFN, 2013a. *The Global Food Banking Community*, Global FBSAing Network. [Online] Available: http://gfn.convio.net/site/PageServer?pagename=FBSAing_find&gclid=CJqouv7f9rUCFabLtAod8nEAYA#South_Africa (Accessed 12 March 2013).

GFN, 2013b. *What is Food Banking?* The Global FoodBanking Network. [Online] Available: www.foodbanking.org (Accessed 30 October 2013).

GLA, 2013. *A Zero Hunger City – Tackling Food Poverty in London*. [Online] Available: http://www.london.gov.uk/mayor-assembly/london-assembly/publications/a-zero-hunger-city-tackling-food-poverty-in-london (Accessed 5 August 2013).

Gobierno Vasco, 2012. *Encuesta de pobreza y desigualdades sociales 2012. Principales resultados.* Informe final: 15 de noviembre de 2012. Dpto. de Empleo y Asuntos Sociales, Vitoria-Gasteiz.

Goldberg, M., Green, D.A., 2009. *Understanding the Link Between Welfare Policy and the Use of Food Banks.* Canadian Centre for Policy Alternatives, Ottawa.

Goodstadt, L.F., 2009. *Politics and Poverty in Cash-rich Hong Kong.* Civic Exchange, Hong Kong.

Goodstadt, L.F., 2012. Myths About Poor Justify Hong Kong's 'Third World' Spending on Social Welfare. *South China Morning Post*, 30 November 2012.

Goulding, A., Grant, A.M., Taylor, R.W., Williams, S.M., Parnell, W.R., Wilson, N., Mann, J., 2007. Ethnic Differences in Extreme Obesity. *The Journal of Pediatrics* 151(5), 542–544.

Government of the Republic of South Africa v. Grootboom, 2000. 11 BCLR 1169 (CC).

Graziano da Silva, J., Del Grossi, M.E., França, C.G. (eds), 2010. *The Fome Zero (Zero Hunger) Program: The Brazilian Experience.* Ministry of Agrarian Development, Brasilia.

Griesse, M.A., 2007. The Geographic, Political, and Economic Context for Corporate Social Responsibility in Brazil. *Journal of Business Ethics* 73(1), 21–37.

Griffith, R., O'Connell, M., Smith, K., 2013. *Food Expenditure and Nutritional Quality over the Great Recession.* Institute of Fiscal Studies, London.

Grover, C., 2008. A Living Wage for London? *Benefits* 16(1), 71–79.

Guillén, A.M., León, M. (eds), 2011. *The Spanish Welfare State in the European Context*. Farnham, Ashgate.

Gundersen, C., 2008. Measuring the Extent, Depth, and Severity of Food Insecurity: An Application to American Indians in the USA. *Journal of Population Economics* 21(1), 191–215.

Gunther, M., 2012. *Anti-hunger, Pro-soda: Are You Kidding Me?* [Online] Available: http://sustainablebusinessforum.com/marcgunther/58801/anti-hunger-pro-soda-are-you-kidding-me (Accessed 21 June 2012).

Hamelin, A.-M., Beaudry, M., Habicht, J.-P., 2002. Characterization of Household Food Insecurity in Québec: Food and Feelings. *Social Science & Medicine* 54(1), 119–132.

Hamelin, A.-M., Mercier, C., Bédard, A., 2007. The Food Environment of Street Youth. *Journal of Hunger & Environmental Nutrition* 1(3), 69–98.

Hänninen, S., 1994. Nälästä. In: Heikkilä, M., Hänninen, S., Karjalainen, J., Kontula, O., Koskela, K. (eds), *Nälkä*. Stakes & STM: Raportteja 153.

Hänninen, S., 2010. Sosiaalioikeudet ja perustuslakiuudistus. In: Pajukoski, M. (ed.), *Pääseekö asiakas oikeuksiinsa?* THL, Helsinki.

Hänninen, S., Karjalainen, J., 1994. Jälkisanat. In: Hänninen, S., Karjalainen, J. (eds), *Kirjeitä nälästä*. Stakes, Helsinki.

Hansard, 2012a. *Social Security (Youth Support and Work Focus) Amendment Bill*. First Reading 678, 129.

Hansard, 2012b. *Food Prices and Food Poverty*, House of Commons, 23 Jan 2012: Column 38. [Online] Available: http://www.publications.parliament.uk/pa/cm201212/cmhansrd/cm120123/debtext/120123-0001.htm#12012313000001 (Accessed 12 August 2012).

Hansard, 2013. *Food: Food Banks*, House of Lords, Tuesday 2 July 2013: Column 1071. [Online] Available: http://www.publications.parliament.uk/pa/ld201314/ldhansrd/text/130702-0001.htm (Accessed 17 July 2013).

Hanson, K., 2010. *The Food Assistance National Input–Output Multiplier (FANIOM) Model and Stimulus Effects of SNAP*. USDA, Economic Research Report 103.

Hanson, K., Golan, E., 2002. *Issues in Food Assistance: Effects of Changes in the Food Stamp Expenditures across the U.S. Economy*. USDA, Economic Research Service.

Hanson, K., Oliveira, V., 2012. *How Economic Conditions Affect Participation in USDA Nutrition Assistance Programs*. USDA-ERS Economic Information Bulletin No. 100. [Online] Available: http://ssrn.com/abstract=2176939 or http://dx.doi.org/10.2139/ssrn.2176939 (Accessed 21 January 2014).

Health Canada, 2007. Canadian Community Health Survey, Cycle 2.2, Nutrition (2004): *Income-Related Household Food Security in Canada*. Health Canada, Ottawa.

Health Canada, 2010. Household Food Insecurity in Canada in 2007–2008: *Key Statistics and Graphics*. Health Canada, Ottawa.

Heikkilä, M., Karjalainen, J., 1998. *Leaks in the Safety Net. The Role of Civil Dialogue in the Finnish Inclusion Policy*. Stakes, Helsinki.

Hendriks, S.L., Olivier, N., 2013. *Review of the South African Agricultural Legislative Framework: Food Security Implications* (Unpublished Report to the Department of Agriculture, Forestries and Fisheries). Institute for Food, Nutrition and Well-being SADC Centre for Land-related, Regional and Development Law and Policy, University of Pretoria.

Hick, S., 2007. *Social Welfare in Canada: Understanding Income Security*. Thompson Education Publishing, Toronto.

Hickey, B., 1980. *No Charity There*. Nelson, West Melbourne.

Hirsch, D., 2013. *A Minimum Income Standard for the UK in 2013*. Joseph Rowntree Foundation, York. [Online] Available: http://www.jrf.org.uk/publications/ MIS-2013 (Accessed 5 August 2013).

HKCSS, 2012. *'Hotmail Canteen' Draws Food Recipients: Cutting Expenses and Fostering Integration*. [Online] Available: http://hkcss.organ.hk (Accessed 18 April 2013).

HKCSS, 2013. *Press release on latest estimate of poverty*. [Online] Available: http:// hkcss.organ.hk (Accessed 26 January 2013).

HLPE, 2012. *Social Protection for Food Security*. A Report by the High Level Panel of Experts on Food Security and Nutrition of the Committee on World Food Security. FAO, Rome.

HMT, 2010. *Spending Review 2010 Summary*, CM7942. The Stationery Office, London.

Hodge, P., 1980. *Social Planning Models and Their Application*. In: Proceedings of the 20th International Conference on Social Welfare. Hong Kong Council of Social Service, Hong Kong, pp. 1–22.

Hodgson, L., 2004. Manufactured Civil Society: Counting the Cost. *Critical Social Policy* 24(2), 139–164.

Hopgood, T., Asher, I., Wall, C.R., Grant, C.C., Stewart, J., Muimuiheata, S., Exeter, D., 2010. Crunching the Numbers: The Affordability of Nutritious Food for New Zealand Children. *Nutrition & Dietetics* 67(4), 251–257.

Hossain, N., Byrne, B., Campbell, A., Harrison, E., McKinley, B., Shah, P., 2011. *The Impact of the Global Economic Downturn on Communities and Poverty in the UK, Findings*. Joseph Rowntree Foundation, York.

HRC, 2013a. *Report of the Special Rapporteur on the Right to Food*, Oliver De Schutter, Mission to Canada. Human Rights Council, Geneva.

HRC, 2013b. *Country Response to the Special Rapporteur on the Right to Food Statement by the Delegation of Canada*. Human Rights Council, Geneva.

Hürriyet Daily News, 2012. Turkish Economy a Miracle, says EU Vice President Rehn, 17 May 2012. [Online] Available: http://www.hurriyetdailynews.com/ turkish-economy-a-miracle-says-eu-vice-president-rehn.aspx?pageID=238&nI D=20933&NewsCatID=344 (Accessed 20 May 2012).

IBGE, 2011. *Censo Demográfico 2010*. Instituto Brasileiro de Geografia e Estatística, Rio de Janeiro.

ICESCR, 1976. International Covenant on Social, Economic and Cultural Rights ratified by Canada in 1976, United Nations. [Online] Available: http://tbinternet. ohchr.org/_layouts/TreatyBodyExternal/Treaty.aspx?Treaty=CESCR&Lang=en (Accessed 19 January 2014).

ICESCR, 2001. Implementation of the *International Covenant on Economic, Social and Cultural Rights*. Initial and second report submitted by the Republic of Estonia under articles 16 and 17 of the Covenant. [Online] Available: http:// www.vm.ee/?q=node/10128 (Accessed 9 April 2013).

ICESCR, 2008. Implementation of the *International Covenant on Economic, Social and Cultural rights*. Second periodic report of Estonia concerning articles 1 and 15 of the covenant. [Online] Available: http://www.vm.ee/?q=node/10128 (Accessed 9 April 2013).

Ife, J., 2008. *Human Rights and Social Work: Towards Rights-Based Practice.* Cambridge University Press, Sydney.

IFPRI, 2011. Global Hunger Index. *The Challenge of Hunger: Taming Price Spikes and Excessive Food Price Volatility.* IFPRI, Bonn, Washington, DC, Dublin.

IFPRI, 2012. Global Hunger Index 2012. International Food Policy Research Institute, New York.

IFS, 2010. Presentation following Spending Review 2010. [Online] Available: http://www.ifs.org.uk/projects/17/346 (Accessed 5 August 2013).

INE, 2012. *Encuesta de Población Activa, tercer trimestre de 2012.* Instituto Nacional de Estadistica. [Online] Available: http://ines.es (Accessed 1 July 2013).

INE, 2013. *Encuesta de condiciones de vida 2012* (resultados provisionales). [Online] Available: http://www.ine.es (Accessed 7 July 2013).

International Human Rights Clinic, 2013. *Nourishing Change: Fulfilling the Right to Food in the United States.* International Human Rights Clinic, New York.

ISMMMO, 2009. Yardım Ekonomisi Yaklaşık 8 Milyar TL.İSMMMO, 2009/2, 11 January 2009. [Online] Available: http://archive.ismmmo.org.tr/docs/basin/2009/bulten/11012009_YARDIMEKONOMISI.pdf (Accessed 29 December 2013).

Jacobs, D., 2000. Low Public Expenditures on Social Welfare: Do East Asian Countries have a Secret? *International Journal of Social Welfare* 9(1), 2–16.

JCHR, 2004. The Implementation of the International Convention on Economic, Social and Cultural Rights. The Stationery Office, Joint Committee on Human Rights, London.

Johnson, A., 2013. *She'll Be Right. A State of the Nation Report from the Salvation Army.* Salvation Army, Wellington.

Kaldjian, P., 2004. Istanbul's Bostans. *The Geographical Review* 94(3), 284–304.

Karjalainen, J., 2008. Nälkä-äläkästä Nälkäryhmään. Tutkimus, ruokapankit ja politiikka lehdistössä. In: Hänninen, S., Karjalainen, J., Lehtelä, K.-M., Silvasti, T. (eds), *Toisten Pankki. Ruoka-apu hyvinvointivaltiossa.* Stakes, Helsinki.

Karvelas, P., 2012. No Special Deals for Single Mums. *The Australian*, 13 October 2012.

Kavanagh, A., Thornton, L., Tattam, A., Thomas, L., Jolley, D., Turrell, G., 2007. *Place Does Matter to Your Health: A Report of the Victorian Lifestyle and Neighbourhood Environment Study.* University of Melbourne, Carleton.

Keles, R., 1983. *100 Soruda Türkiye'de Kentleşme, Konut ve Gecekondu.* Gerçek Yayınevi, Istanbul.

Kelsey, J., 1995. *The New Zealand Experiment.* Auckland University Press, Auckland.

Kent, G., 2005. *Freedom from Want – The Human Right to Adequate Food.* Georgetown University Press, Washington. No-cost download available at http://press.georgetown.edu/book/georgetown/freedom-want.

Kent, G., 2008. *Global Obligations for the Right to Food.* Rowman and Littlefield, Lanham.

Kettings, C., Sinclair, A.J., Voevodin, M., 2009. A Healthy Diet Consistent with Australian Health Recommendations is too Expensive for Welfare-dependent Families. *Australian and New Zealand Journal of Public Health* 33(6), 566–572.

Key, J., 2013. *Funding Boosts to Help Vulnerable Children.* Press release 28 May 2013. [Online] Available: http://www.beehive.govt.nz/release/funding-boosts-help-vulnerable-children-pm (Accessed 7 July 2013).

Kiggundu, M.N., 2012. Anti-poverty and Progressive Social Change in Brazil: Lessons for Other Emerging Economies. *International Review of Administrative Sciences* 78(4), 785–808.

Kim, S., 2010. Collaborative Governance in South Korea: Citizen Participation in Policy Making and Welfare Service Provision. *Asian Perspective* 34(3), 165–190.

Kimber, C.J.M., 1996. Equality or Self-Determination. In: Gearty, C., Tomkins, A. (eds), *Understanding Human Rights*. Mansell Publishing, London.

King, R.F., 1999. Welfare Reform: Block Grants, Expenditure Caps, and the Paradox of the Food Stamp Program. *Political Science Quarterly* 114(3), 359–385.

Kirkpatrick, S.I., McIntyre, L., Potestio, M.L., 2010. Child Hunger and Long-term Adverse Consequences for Health. *Archives of Pediatrics & Adolescent Medicine* 164(8), 754–762.

Kneafsey, M., Cox, R., Holloway, L., Dowler, E., Venn, L., Tuomainen, H., 2008. *Reconnecting Consumers, Producers and Food: Exploring Alternatives*. Berg, Oxford.

Kneafsey, M., Dowler, E., Lambie, H., Inman, A., Collier, R., 2012. Consumers and Food Security: Uncertain or Empowered? *Journal of Rural Studies* 28, 1–12.

Koc, M., 1994. Globalisation as a Discourse. In: Bonanno, A., Busch, L., Friedland, W.H., Gouveia, L., Mingione, E. (eds), *Colombus to Conagra: Globalisation of Agriculture and Food*. University of Kansas Press, Lawrence, KS.

Koc, M., 2013. Discourses of Food Security. In: Karaagac, B. (ed.), *Accumulations, Crises, Struggles: Capital and Labour in Contemporary Capitalism*. LIT Verlag, Berlin, London.

Koc, M., Koc, H., 1999. From Staple Stores to Supermarket: The Case of Tansas in Izmir, Turkey. In: Koc, M., MacRae, R., Mougeot, L., Welsh, J. (eds), *For Hunger Proof Cities: Sustainable Urban Food Systems*. Ottawa, International Development Research Centre.

Kodutud Tallinnas, 2012. *Uuringu aruanne*. Tallinna Sotsiaaltöö keskus. 39 lk. [Online] Available: http://www.swcenter.ee/site/data/10_kodutuuringuaruanne_1302.12. pdf (Accessed 9 April 2013).

Koelble, T.A., 2004. Economic Policy in the Post-colony: South Africa Between Keynesian Remedies and Neoliberal Pain. *New Political Economy* 9(1), 57–78.

Koivupuro, H.-K., Jalkanen, L., Katajajuuri, J., Reinikainen, A., Silvennoinen, K., 2010. *Elintarvikeketjussa syntyvä ruokahävikki*. MTT, Jokioinen.

Kok, P., O'Donovan, M., Bouare, O., Van Zyl, J., 2003. *Post Apartheid Patterns of Internal Migration in South Africa*. Human Sciences Research Council.

Kong, K.Y., 2009. The Right to Food for All: A Rights-Based Approach to Hunger and Social Inequality. *Suffolk Transnational Law Review* 32(3), 525–566.

Kong, K.Y., 2013. Personal communication with lawyer Kong, 10 June 2013.

Kontula, O., Koskela, K., 1993. *Taloudellisen laman terveysvaikutuksia 1992–1993*. STM, Helsinki.

Kõre, J., 1998. The Social Protection System in Estonia. In: *Social Protection in Estonia. Handbook and Dictionary*. Phare Programme.

Kõre, J., 2010. *Social NGOs in Estonia, Latvia, Lithuania*. Conference report, Riga, 12 April 2010.

Kõre, J., Karpuskiene, V., 2010. *Analysis of the National Action Plans of Social Inclusion 2004–2006, 2006–2008, 2008–2010*. Vilnius University Publications, 4/2010.

Kõre, J., Kiik, R., Boswinkel, E., 2006. Homelessness in Estonia – Problem of the Individual or the Society? *European Journal of Housing Policy* 6(3), 297–312.

Kotz, N., 1984. The Politics of Hunger. *New Republic*, 30 April 1984.

Kurban, D., Hatemi, K., 2009. *Bir Yabancılaştırma Hikâyesi: Türkiye'de Gayrimüslim Cemaatlerin Vakıf ve Taşınmaz Mülkiyet Sorunu*. TESEV Yayınları, İstanbul.

Kutsar, D., Trumm, A., 1999. *Vaesuse leevendamine Eestis: taust ja sihiseaded*. Tartu Ülikool, Sotsiaalministeerium, ÜRO Arenguprogramm Eestis (UNDP), Tartu, 89 lk.

Kuvaja, S., 2002. *Ruokapankeista vaikuttamisen foorumeille. Näkökulmia kirkon yhteiskuntavastuuseen*. Kirkkopalvelut, Helsinki.

Labadarios, D., Mchiza, Z.J., Steyn, N.P., Gericke, G., Maunder, E.M.W., Davids, Y.D., Parker, W., 2011. *Food Security in South Africa: A Review of National Surveys*. Bulletin of the World Health Organization. [Online] Available: http://www. who.int/bulletin/volumes/89/12/11–089243.pdf. (Accessed 20 August 2012).

Labadarios, D., Swart, R., Maunder, E.M.W., Kruger, H.S., Gericke, G.J., Kuzwayo, P.M.N. et al., 2005. Executive Summary of the National Food Consumption Survey Fortification Baseline (NFCS-FB-I). *South African Journal of Clinical Nutrition* 21(2), 247–300.

Laes, T.-L., 2013. *The Individual and Social Nature of Poverty*. 1/13. Quarterly Bulletin of Statistics Estonia. [Online] Available: www.stat.ee/dokumendid/68625 (Accessed 14 August 2013).

Lambie-Mumford, H., 2013. 'Every Town Should Have One': Emergency Food Banking in the UK. *Journal of Social Policy* 42(1), 73–89.

Lambie-Mumford, H., Crossley, D., Jensen, E., Verbeke, M., Dowler, E., 2014. *Household food security: A review of Food Aid*. Report to Defra, Available at: https://www.gov.uk/government/publications/food-aid-research-report.

Lang, T., 2007. Food Control or Food Democracy? Re-engaging Nutrition with Society and the Environment. *Public Health Nutrition* 8(6A), 730–737.

Lang, T., Heasman, M., 2004. *Food Wars: the Global Battle for Mouths, Minds and Markets*. Earthscan, London.

Lang, T., Barling, D., Caraher, M., 2009. *Food Policy: Integrating Health, Environment and Society*. Oxford University Press, Oxford.

Laparra, M., 2010. *El impacto de la crisis en la cohesión social o el surf de los hogares españoles en el modelo de integración de la 'sociedad líquida'*. Documentación social 158, 97–130.

Laparra, M., 2012. Conclusiones. In: Laparra, M., Pérez, B. (eds), *Crisis y Fractura Social En Europa. Causas y Efectos En España*. Obra Social la Caixa, Barcelona.

Lawlor, D.A., 2013. The Vienna Declaration on Nutrition and Non-communicable Diseases. *British Medical Journal* 347, f4417.

Lee, K., 2007. China and the International Covenant on Civil and Political Rights: Prospects and Challenges. *Chinese Journal of International Law* 6(2), 445–474.

Leubolt, B., 2013. Institutions, Discourse and Welfare: Brazil as a Distributional Regime. *Global Social Policy* 13(1), 66–83.

Lezberg, S., 1999. *Finding Common Ground Between Food Security and Sustainable Food Systems*. Paper presented at the 1999 Joint Meetings of the Agriculture, Food and Human Values Society and the Association for the Study of Food and Society. [Online] Available: http://ftp.foodshare.net/resource/show.cfm?id=354 (Accessed 6 January 2014).

Lloyd, S., Lawton, J., Caraher, M., Singh, G., Horsley, K., Mussa, F., 2011. A Tale of Two Localities: Healthy Eating on a Restricted Income. *Health Education Journal* 70(1), 48–56.

Lockie, S., Pietsch, J., 2012. *Food Security: What are the Real Issues for Australia.* National Institute of Rural and Regional Australia, University of Australia, Canberra.

Loevinsohn, M., Gillespie, S.R., 2003. *HIV/AIDS, Food Security and Rural Livelihoods: Understanding and Responding.* IFPRI, Washington, DC.

Loopstra, R., Tarasuk, V., 2012. The Relationship Between Food Banks and Household Food Insecurity among Low-income Toronto Families. *Canadian Public Policy* 38(4), 497–514.

Mackay, R., 1995. Foodbank Demand And Supplementary Assistance Programmes: A Research And Policy Case Study. *Social Policy Journal of New Zealand* 2(5), 129–141.

MacMillan, T., Dowler, E., 2012. Just and Sustainable? Examining the Rhetoric and Potential Realities of UK Food Security. *Journal of Agricultural and Environmental Ethics* 25(2), 181–204.

MacRae, R., 1999. Policy Failure in the Canadian Food System. In: Koc, M., MacRae, R., Mougeot, L.A.J., Welsh, J. (eds), *For Hunger Proof Cities: Sustainable Urban Food Systems.* International Development Research Center, Ottawa.

MacRae, R., 2011. A Joined-Up Food Policy for Canada. *Journal of Hunger & Environmental Nutrition* 6(4), 424–457.

Malkavaara, M., 2002. Nälkä ja köyhyys kirkon asiaksi. Näkökulmia laman ja markkinakilpailun aikaan. In: Mäkinen, V. (ed.), *Lasaruksesta leipäjonoihin. Köyhyys kirkon kysymyksenä.* Atena, Jyväskylä.

Maluf, R.S., 2010. CONSEA's Participation in Building the National Food and Nutrition Security System and Policy. In: Graziano da Silva, J., Del Grossi, M.E., França, C.G. (eds), *The Fome Zero (Zero Hunger) Program: The Brazilian Experience.* Ministry of Agrarian Development, Brasilia.

Maney, A., 1989. *Still Hungry After All These Years: Food Assistance Policy from Kennedy to Reagan.* Greenwood Press, New York and Westport, CT.

Margulies, R., Yildizoglu, E. (1988). Austerity Packages and Beyond: Turkey Since 1980. *Capital & Class* (12), 141–162.

Marks, S., 2002. An Epidemic Waiting to Happen? The Spread of HIV/AIDS in South Africa in Social and Historical Perspective. *African Studies* 61(1), 13–26.

Martin, K.S., Rogers, B.L., Cook, J.T., Joseph, H.M., 2004. Social Capital is Associated with Decreased Risk of Hunger. *Social Science & Medicine* 58(12), 2645–2654.

Martinson, M., 2013. Vaesuses elevate inimeste arv Tallinnas on kasvanud. http://www.delfi.ee/news/paevauudised/eesti/merike-martinson-vaesuses-elavate-inimeste-arv-tallinnas-on-kasvanud.d?id=65682960 (Accessed 17 December 2013).

Maslen, C., Raffle, A., Marriott, S., Smith, N., 2013. *Food Poverty: What Does The Evidence Tell Us?* Bristol City Council, Bristol. [Online] Available: http://bristolfoodpolicycouncil.org/wp-content/uploads/2013/08/Food-Poverty-Report-July-2013-for-publication.pdf (Accessed 16 September 2013).

Mavi, 2010. *EU:n ruoka-apu yhteisön vähävaraisimmille.* Hakuopas. Maaseutuvirasto, Helsinki.

Mavi, 2012a. *Suomi osallistuu EU:n elintarvikeapu ohjelmaan.* [Online] Available: http://www.mavi.fi (Accessed 31 August 2012).

Mavi, 2012b. *Elintarviketukea jakavat järjestöt 1996–2009.* [Online] Available: http://www.mavi.fi (Accessed 21 June 2012).

McFadden, P., 2001. *Cultural Practice as Gendered Exclusion, Discussing Women's Empowerment.* SIDA Studies 3, 58.

McIntyre, L., Connor, S.K., Warren, J., 2000. Child Hunger in Canada: Results of the 1994 National Longitudinal Survey of Children and Youth. *Canadian Medical Association Journal* 163(8), 961–965.

McIntyre, L., Bartoo, A.C., Pow, J., Potestio, M.L., 2012a. Coping With Child Hunger in Canada: Have Household Strategies Changed Over a Decade? *Canadian Journal of Public Health* 103(6), 428–432.

McIntyre, L., Williams, J.V.A., Lavorato, D.H., Patten, S., 2012b. Depression and Suicide Ideation in Late Adolescence and Early Adulthood are an Outcome of Child Hunger. *Journal of Affective Disorders.* [Online] Available: doi: 10.1016/j.jad.2012.11.029 [Epub ahead of print].

McKenzie, M., 2012. *South Africa Generates over 9 Million Tonnes of Food Waste Annually.* [Online] Available: http://urbanearth.co.za/articles/south-africa-generates-over-9-million-tonnes-food-waste-annually. (Accessed 13 March 2013).

McMahon, M., 2011. Personal correspondence (16 October). Food Sovereignty Versus Global Philanthropy Conference, University of British Columbia, Vancouver. 10 October 2011.

McNeill, K., 2011. *Talking With Their Mouths Half Full: Food Insecurity in the Hamilton Community.* PhD thesis, University of Waikato.

McPherson, K., 2006. *Food Insecurity and the Food Bank Industry: Political, Individual and Environmental Factors Contributing to Food Bank Use in Christchurch.* GeoHealth Library, University of Canterbury, Christchurch.

MDS, 2007. *Banco de Alimentos por Banco de Alimentos,* Ministério do Desenvolvimento Social e Combate à Fome. MDS, Brasilia. [Online] Available: http://www.mds.gov.br/segurancaalimentar/publicacoes/guias (Accessed 25 March 2013).

MDS, 2009a. *Programa Banco de Alimentos – Lista de Equipamentos e Móveis Sugerida.* Ministério do Desenvolvimento Social e Combate à Fome, Brasilia. [Online] Available: http://www.mds.gov.br/segurancaalimentar/publicacoes/guias (Accessed 25 March 2013).

MDS, 2009b. *Programa Banco de Alimentos – Lista de Utensílios e Equipamentos de Proteção Individual* (EPI). Ministério do Desenvolvimento Social e Combate à Fome, Brasilia. [Online] Available: http://www.mds.gov.br/segurancaalimentar/publicacoes/guias (Accessed 25 March 2013).

MDS, 2011. Edital MDS/SESAN No 02/2011 – Seleção Pública de Propostas para Apoio à Implantação ou Modernização de Bancos de Alimentos. Ministério do Desenvolvimento Social e Combate à Fome, Brasilia.

MDS, 2013a. Bolsa Família website. [Online] Available: http://www.mds.gov.br/bolsafamilia (Accessed 7 July 2013).

MDS, 2013b. Banco de Alimentos. Ministério do Desenvolvimento Social e Combate à Fome, Brasilia. [Online] Available: http://www.mds.gov.br/segurancaalimentar/equipamentos/bancosdealimento (Accessed 3 October 2012).

MDS, 2013c. *Modelo de Regimento Interno para Banco de Alimentos.* Ministério do Desenvolvimento Social e Combate à Fome, Brasilia. [Online] Available: (Accessed 25 March 2013).

Menezes, F., 2010. Social Participation in the Zero Hunger Program – The Experience of CONSEA. In: Graziano da Silva, J., Del Grossi, M.E., França, C.G. (eds), *The Fome Zero (Zero Hunger) Program: The Brazilian Experience.* Ministry of Agrarian Development, Brasilia.

Mert, M., 2010. *Yoksulluk ve Açlık*. Yeni Ümit. No. 88. [Online] Available: file:///K:/Aclik/Yeni %C3%9Cmit Dergisi – Konular – yoksulluk-ve-aclik.htm#. UqbC8OLm4ZF (Accessed 2 June 2011).

Messer, E., Cohen, M.J., 2009. *US Approaches to Food and Nutrition Rights, 1976–2008*. [Online] Available: http:/www.worldhunger.org/articles/08/hrf/messer. htm. (Accessed 8 February 2009).

Midgley, J., 1997. *Social Welfare in Global Context*. SAGE, Thousand Oaks.

Miewald, C., Ibanez-Carrasco, F., Turner, S., 2010. Negotiating the Local Food Environment: The Lived Experience of Food Access for Low-income People Living With HIV/AIDS. *Journal of Hunger & Environmental Nutrition* 5(4), 510–525.

Ministry of Public Works, 2009. Social Protection Cluster Targets Food Security in Rural Areas. Sabinet Law. [Online] Available: http://www.sabinetlaw.co.za/social-affairs/articles/social-protection-cluster-targets-food-security-rural-areas (Accessed 12 March 2013).

MIS, 2013. Minimum Income Standards website. [Online] Available: http://www.lboro.ac.uk/research/crsp/mis/ (Accessed 16 September 2013).

Mitrunen, M., 2013. *Työmarkkinoiden polarisaatio Suomessa*. Vatt, Helsinki.

Monroe, 2013. 'Dear Richard Littlejohn – here are all the things you got wrong about me' *The Guardian*. [Online] Available: http://www.theguardian.com/commentisfree/2013/nov/01/richard-littlejohn-wrong-about-jack-monroe-daily-mail (Accessed 1 November 2013).

Moreno, L., 2009. NURSOPOB: Presentación, contexto del bienestar y nuevos riesgos sociales. In: Moreno, L. (ed.), *Reformas De Las Políticas Del Bienestar En España*. Siglo XXI, Madrid.

Moreno, L., 2012. *La Europa asocial. Crisis y estado del bienestar*. Península, Barcelona.

Morgan, K., Sonnino, R., 2008. *The School Food Revolution: Public Food and the Challenge of Sustainable Development*. Earthscan, London.

Morvaridi, B., 2013. The Politics of Philanthropy and Welfare Governance: The Case of Turkey. *European Journal of Development Research* 25(3), 305–321.

MSA, 1999. *Poverty Reduction in Estonia: Background and Guidelines*. University of Tartu, Ministry of Social Affairs, United Development Programme, Tartu.

MSA, 2008. *Estonia in European Comparison*. Series of the Ministry of Social Affairs No 3. [Online] Available: http://www.sm.ee/fileadmin/meedia/Dokumendid/V2ljaanded/Toimetised/2008/03.pdf (Accessed 3 September 2013).

MSA, 2012a. *Employment and Working Life in Estonia 2010–2011*. Series of the Ministry of Social Affairs, No 2, p. 66. [Online] Available: http://www.sm.ee/fileadmin/meedia/Dokumendid/V2ljaanded/Toimetised/2012/series_20122eng.pdf (Accessed 9 April 2013).

MSA, 2012b. Day Centre Services 2007–2011. Ministry of Social Affairs. [Online] Available: http://www.sm.ee/meie/statistika/sotsiaalvaldkond/sotsiaalhoolekanne/paevakeskuse-teenused.html (Accessed 2 November 2013).

MSD, 2012. The Statistical Report for the Year Ending June 2011, Table HA.5. Ministry of Social Development, Wellington.

Mullany, G., Bradsher, K., 2013. Leader Issues Populist Vows in Hong Kong. *New York Times*, 17 January 2013.

Mywaste, 2013. *SA Retailer First to Adopt Cooked Food Composting Method*. [Online] Available: http://www.mywaste.co.za/articles/view/36 (Accessed 27 March 2013).

NACLC, 2009. *Freedom Respect Equality Dignity: Action – Executive Summary: Australia.* National Association of Community Legal Centres, Sydney, Melbourne and New South Wales.

Nahman, A., De Lange, W., Oelofse, S., Godfrey, L., 2012. The Costs of Household Food Waste in South Africa. *Waste Management* 32(11), 2147–2153.

National Council of Welfare, 2010. *Welfare Incomes 2009.* National Council of Welfare, Ottawa.

NHRCC, 2009. National Human Rights Consultation Report. Commonwealth of Australia, Barton ACT.

Nicholson, A., Behrendt, L., Vivian, A., Watson, N., Harris, M., 2009. *Will They Be Heard? A Response to the NTER Consultations June to August 2009.* Jumbunna Indigenous House of Learning, New South Wales.

Nord, M., Coleman-Jensen, A., Andrews, M., Carlson, S., 2010. *Household Food Security in the United States, 2009.* Economic Research Report No. (ERR-108). [Online] Available: http://www.ers.usda.gov/publications/err108/ (Accessed 10 October 2013).

NPC, 2011. *National Development Plan.* Office of the Presidency, Pretoria.

NT, 2011. *Intergovernmental Fiscal Review.* National Treasury, Pretoria.

NTSARS, 2012. *2012 Tax Statistics.* National Treasury and the South African Revenue Service, Pretoria.

Nussbaum, M.C., 2000. *Women and Human Development: The Capabilities Approach.* Cambridge University Press, Cambridge.

NZCCSS, 2005. *Forgotten Poverty? Poverty Indicator Project: Foodbank Study.* Final Report. New Zealand Council of Christian Social Services, Wellington.

O'Brien, M., 2012. Lone Parents Working for Welfare in New Zealand. *Local Economy* 27(5–6), 577–592.

O'Brien, M., 2013. Welfare Reform in New Zealand: From Citizen to Managed Worker. *Journal of Social Policy & Administration* 47(6), 729–748.

OECD, 2013. Social Expenditure – Aggregated Data. [Online] Available: http://stats.oecd.org/Index.aspx?QueryId=4549 (Accessed 2 December 2013).

Oelofse, S.H., Nahman, A., 2013. Estimating the Magnitude of Food Waste Generated in South Africa. *Waste Management & Research* 31(80), 80–86.

OHCHR, 2012. *Special Rapporteur on the Right to Food: Visit to Canada –End of Mission Statement.* United Nations Office of the High Commissioner for Human Rights, Geneva.

Ohisalo, M., 2013. EU:n ruoka-apuohjelman vaikutus ruoka-avun vakiintumiseen Suomessa. In: Niemelä, M., Saari, J. (eds), *Huono-osaisten hyvinvointi Suomessa.* Kela, Helsinki.

Oliveira, V., 2012. *The Food Assistance Landscape:* FY 2011 Annual Report. USDA, Economic Research Service, Economic Bulletin EIB-93, March.

ONG Banco de Alimentos, 2011. *Cardápio de Atividades – Relatório 2011.* ONG Banco de Alimentos, São Paulo. [Online] Available: http://www.bancodealimentos.org.br/nossos-numeros/ (Accessed 20 March 2013).

Öniş, Z., 2004. Turgut Özal and His Economic Legacy: Turkish Neo-Liberalism in Critical Perspective. *Middle Eastern Studies* 40(4), 113–134.

Oxfam HK, 2011a. Press Statement: Oxfam Hong Kong Response to the 2011 Policy Address.

Oxfam HK, 2011b. *Survey on the Impact of Soaring Food Prices on Poor Families in Hong Kong.* Oxfam Hong Kong, Hong Kong.

Oxfam HK, 2012a. *Poverty Report: Employment and Poverty in Hong Kong Families (2003–2012)*. Oxfam Hong Kong, Hong Kong.

Oxfam HK, 2012b. *Oxfam Calls on New Administration to Consider Subsidies for Poor Workers' Families*. Oxfam Hong Kong, Hong Kong.

Oxhorn, P., 2010. Cidadania como consumo ou cidadania como agência: uma comparação entre as reformas de democratização da Bolívia e do Brasil. *Sociologias* 12(24), 18–43.

Pajunen, T., 2012. *EU-ruokakasseja jaettiin ennätysmäärä.* [Online] Available: http://www.kirkkopalvelut.fi/ (Accessed 21 February 2013).

Patel, R.C., 2012. Food Sovereignty: Power, Gender, and the Right to Food. [Online] Available: *PLoS Med* 9(6): e1001223. doi:10.1371/journal.pmed.1001223.

Patton, M.J., 2006. The Economic Policies of Turkey's AKP Government: Rabbits from a Hat? *Middle East Journal* 60(3), 513–536.

Peix, J., 2009. El Banc dels aliments, destí prioritari dels aliments no vendibles. TECA: Tecnologia i Ciència dels Aliments 11(2), 36–40.

Peix, J., 2012. Blog. [Online] Available: http://bancoalimentoscatalunya.blogspot.com.es/ (Accessed 13 November 2012).

Perry, B., 2012. *Household Incomes in New Zealand. Trends in Indicators of Inequality and Hardship 1982 to 2011*. Ministry of Social Development, Wellington.

PFSN, 2004. Primer on People's Food Sovereignty and Draft People's Convention on Food Sovereignty, People's Food Sovereignty Network Asia Pacific and Pesticide Action Network, Asia and the Pacific. [Online] Available: www.panap.net/docs/campaign/primer.pdf (Accessed 1 September 2013).

Phillips, B., Nepal, B., 2012. *Going Without: Financial Hardship in Australia*, National Centre for Economic Modelling. Centre for Economic Modelling, University of Canberra.

Pitts III, J.W.I., 2002. First U.N. Social Forum: History and Analysis. *Journal of International Law and Policy* 31(2), 297–324.

Pollan, M., 2009. *Food Rules: An Eater's Manual*. Penguin Books, London.

Poppendieck, J., 1986. *Breadlines Knee-Deep in Wheat: Food Assistance in the Great Depression*. Rutgers University Press, New Brunswick, NJ. Revised, updated and republished by University of California Press, Spring, 2014.

Poppendieck, J., 1997. The USA: Hunger in the Land of Plenty. In: Riches, G. (ed.), *First World Hunger: Food Security and Welfare Politics*. Macmillan, Basingstoke.

Poppendieck, J., 1998. *Sweet Charity? Emergency Food and the End of Entitlement*. Penguin Books, London.

Poppendieck, J., 2000a. Hunger in the United States: Policy Implications. *Nutrition* 16(6–7), 651–653.

Poppendieck, J., 2000b. Want Amid Plenty: From Hunger to Inequality. In: Magdoff, F., Bellamy Foster, J., Buttel, F. (eds), *Hungry for the Profit. The Agribusiness Threat to Farmers, Food and the Environment*. Monthly Review Press, New York.

Poppendieck, J., 2010. *Free for All: Fixing School Food in America*. University of California Press, Berkeley.

Posel, D., Rogan, M., 2009. Women, Income and Poverty: Gendered Access to Resources in Post-Apartheid South Africa. *Agenda* 23(81), 25–34.

Powell, A., 2013. *The Myth of Labour's Excessive Borrowing: Why it's Time to Fight Back*. Fabian Review online, 7 March 2013. [Online] Available: http://www.fabians.org.uk/the-myth-of-labours-excessive-borrowing-why-its-time-to-fight-back/ (Accessed 18 July 2013).

Power, E., Riches, G., Tarasuk, V., 2012. Corporate Tax Breaks Are Not the Answer to Hunger in Canada. *The Toronto Star*, 19 November 2012.

Puttergill, C., Bomela, N., Grobbelaar, J., Moguerane, K., 2011. The Limits of Land Restitution: Livelihoods in Three Rural Communities in South Africa. *Development Southern Africa* 28(5), 597–611.

Quintal, G., 2013. DA questions ANC conduct in Tlokwe. *IOL News*. [Online] Available: http://www.iol.co.za/news/politics/da-questions-anc-conduct-in-tlokwe-1.1579591 (Accessed 12 April 2013).

Radikal, 2009. Yardım Ekonomisi 7 Milyar Lira. Radikal 12 January 2009. [Online] Available: http://www.radikal.com.tr/radikal.aspx?atype=haberyazdir&articleid =916570 (Accessed 29 December 2013).

Rahigh-Aghsan, A., 2011. Turkey's EU Quest and Political Cleavages under AKP. *Review of European Studies* 3(1), 43–53.

Rainville, B., Brink, S., 2001. *Food Insecurity in Canada, 1998–1999*. Human Resources Development Canada, Hull (Quebec).

Ramsey, R., Giskes, K., Turrell, G., Gallegos, D., 2011. Food Insecurity Among Australian Children: Potential Determinants, Health and Developmental Consequences. *Journal of Child Health Care* 15(5), 401–16.

Rangan, H., Gilmartin, M., 2002. Gender, Traditional Authority, and the Politics of Rural Reform in South Africa. *Development and Change* 33(4), 633–658.

REDES, 2006. *Pesquisa de Avaliação do Programa Bancos de Alimentos*. Rede Desenvolvimento Ensino e Sociedade, MDS, Brasilia.

Reid, S., 2013. *Mythbusters: Strivers Versus skivers*. [Online] Available: http://www.neweconomics.org/blog/entry/mythbusters-strivers-versus-skivers (Accessed 12 August 2013).

Resmî Gazete, 2013. *Genelge*. Başbakanlıktan: Ekmek İsrafını Önleme Kampanyası. Sayı : 28606, Nisan 2013 Salı.

Riches, G., 1986. *Food Banks and the Welfare Crisis*. Canadian Council on Social Development, Ottawa.

Riches, G. (ed.), 1997a. *First World Hunger: Food Security and Welfare Politics*. Macmillan, Basingstoke.

Riches, G., 1997b. Hunger in Canada: Abandoning the Right to Food. In: Riches, G. (ed.), *First World Hunger: Food Security and Welfare Politics*. Macmillan, Basingstoke.

Riches, G., 1997c. Hunger and the Welfare State: Comparative Perspectives. In: Riches, G. (ed.), *First World Hunger. Food Security and Welfare Politics*. Macmillan, Basingstoke.

Riches, G., 1999. Advancing the Human Right to Food in Canada: Social Policy and the Politics of Hunger, Welfare, and Food Security. *Agriculture and Human Values* 16(2), 203–211.

Riches, G., 2002. Food Banks and Food Security: Welfare Reform, Human Rights and Social Policy. Lessons from Canada? *Social Policy and Administration* 36(6), 648–669.

Riches, G., 2011. Thinking and Acting Outside the Charitable Food Box: Hunger and the Right to Food in Rich Societies. *Development in Practice* 21(4–5), 768–775.

Riches, G., Buckingham, D., MacRae, R., Ostry, A., 2004. *Right to Food Case Study: Canada*. Food and Agricultural Organization of the United Nations, Rome.

Ripley, R.B., 1969. Legislative Bargaining and the Food Stamp Act, 1964. In: Cleveland, F.N. Associates (eds), *Congress and Urban Problems, A Casebook on the Legislative Process*. The Brookings Institute, Washington, DC.

Robinson, M., 2004. *Ethics, Globalization and Hunger: In Search of Appropriate Policies*. Keynote Address. Cornell University, 18 November 2004.

Rocha, C., 2007. Food Insecurity as Market Failure: A Contribution from Economics. *Journal of Hunger and Environmental Nutrition*, 1(4), 5–22.

Rocha, C., 2009. Developments in National Policies for Food and Nutrition Security in Brazil. *Development Policy Review* 27(1), 51–66.

Rocha, C., Bandy, L., Maluf, R., 2012. Small Farms and Sustainable Rural Development for Food Security: The Brazilian Experience. *Development Southern Africa* 29(4), 519–529.

Roett, R., 2011. *The New Brazil*. The Brookings Institute, Washington, DC.

Rogers, 2011. England Riots: Was Poverty a Factor? Reading the Riots: Investigating England's Summer of Disorder. *The Guardian and London School of Economics*. [Online] Available: http://www.theguardian.com/news/datablog/2011/aug/16/riots-poverty-map-suspects (Accessed 5 August 2013).

Royston, S., Rodrigues, L., 2013. *Nowhere to Turn? Changes to Emergency Support*. The Children's Society, London. [Online] Available: http://www.childrens-society.org.uk/sites/default/files/tcs/nowhere-to-turn-final.pdf (Accessed 12 August 2013).

RPH, 2011. *Food Costs for Families*. Regional Public Health Information Paper, Lower Hutt.

RSA, 1996. The Bill of Rights of the Constitution of the Republic of South Africa. Government Gazette No.17678.

RSA, 2013. *National Food and Nutrition Security* Strategy. Available from: www.nda.agric.za/docs/media/NATIONAL%20POLICYon%20food%20and%20nutririton%20security.pdf (Accessed 3 March 2014).

RT I, 1995. Sotsiaalhoolekande seadus. RT I 1995, 21, 323. [Online] Available: http://www.estlex.ee/tasuta/?id=7&aktid=13907&fd=1&leht=3 (Accessed 9 May 2013).

RT I, 2009. Perekonnaseadus. RT I, 2009, 60, 395. [Online] Available: http://www.estlex.ee/tasuta/?id=7&aktid=118317&fd=1&leht=1 (Accessed 15 August 2013).

RT II, 2006. Article 24 of the Convention on the Rights of the Child (Lapse õiguste konventsioon. RT II 1996, 16, 56). [Online] Available: https://www.riigiteataja.ee/akt/24016 (Accessed 21 August 2013).

Runnels, V., Kristjansson, E., Calhoun, M., 2011. An Investigation of Adults' Everyday Experiences and Effects of Food Insecurity in an Urban Area in Canada. *The Canadian Journal of Community Mental Health* 30(1), 157–172.

Ruotsalainen, P., 2011. Jäävätkö tuloerot pysyvästi suuriksi? *Hyvinvointikatsaus* 1/2011. Tilastokeskus, Helsinki.

Russell, D., Parnell, W., Wilson, N., Faed, J., Ferguson, E., Horwarth, C., 1999. *NZ food: NZ people. Key Results of the 1997 National Nutrition Survey*. Ministry of Health, Wellington.

SACOSS, 2011. Cost of Living Update no. 6, May 2011. South Australian Council of Social Service, Adelaide.

Santos, V.F., Vieira, W.C., Reis, B.S., 2009. Effects of Alternative Policies on Income Redistribution: Evidence from Brazil. *Development Policy Review* 27(5), 601–616.

Satman, I. et al., 2013. Twelve-year Trends in the Prevalence and Risk Factors of Diabetes and Prediabetes in Turkish Adults. *European Journal of Epidemiology* 28, 169–80.

Saul, N., Curtis, A., 2013. *The Stop*. Random House Canada, Toronto.

Schanbacher, W.D., 2010. *The Global Conflict between Food Security and Food Sovereignty*. Praeger, Santa Barbara.

Schott, L., Cho, C., 2011. *General Assistance Programs: Safety Net Weakening Despite Increased Need*. Center on Budget and Policy Priorities.

Sen, A., 1992. *Inequality Reexamined*. Oxford University Press, Oxford.

Sen, A., 2004. Elements of a Theory of Human Rights. *Philosophy and Public Affairs* 32(4), 315–356.

Service Unit of the Church, 2013. *Seurakunnat jakoivat ruoka-apua vähävaraiselle yli 3 miljoonalla eurolla*. [Online] Available: http://www.kirkkopalvelut.fi (Accessed 9 March 2013).

SESC, 2013. *O Mesa Brasil SESC*. Serviço Social do Comércio. [Online] Available: http://www.sesc.com.br/mesabrasil/omesabrasil.html (Accessed 25 March 2013).

Sevenhuijsen, S., Bozalek, V., Gouws, A., Minnaar-McDonald, M., 2003. South African Social Welfare Policy: An Analysis Using the Ethic of Care. *Critical Social Policy* 23(3), 299–321.

SFFA, 2013. *Working Towards Food Security and Sustainable Food Systems*. The Sydney Food Fairness Alliance. [Online] Available: http://sydneyfoodfairness. org.au/ [Accessed 31 July 2013).

Shamir, R., 2008. Corporate Social Responsibility: Towards a New Market-Embedded Morality? *Theoretical Inquiries in Law* 9(2), 371–94.

Sharpe, A., Capeluck, E., 2012. *The Impact of Redistribution on Income Inequality in Canada and the Provinces, 1981–2010*. Centre for the Study of Living Standards, Ottawa.

Shisana, O., Labadarios, D., Rehle, T., Simbayi, L., Zuma, K., Dhansay, A., Reddy, P., Parker, W., Hoosain, E., Naidoo, P., Hongoro, C., Mchiza, Z., Steyn, N., Dwane, N., Makoae, M., Maluleke, T., Ramlagan, S., Zungu, N., Evans, M., Jacobs, L., Faber, M., Team, S.-1, 2013. *South African National Health and Nutrition Examination Survey*. HSRC Press, Cape Town.

Silvasti, T., 2008. Elintarvikejärjestelmä globalisoituu – ruokaturvasta yksityinen liikesuhde? In: Hänninen, S., Karjalainen, J., Lehtelä, K., Silvasti, T. (eds), *Toisten pankki. Ruoka-apu hyvinvointivaltiossa*. Stakes, Helsinki.

Silvasti, T., 2014. Participatory Alternatives for Charity Food Delivery? Finnish Development in International Comparison. In: Matthies, A.-L., Uggerhöj, L. (eds), *Participation, Marginalization and Welfare Services – Concepts, Politics and Practices Across European Countries*. Ashgate, London.

Síndic de Greuges de Catalunya, 2013. Informe sobre la malnutrición infantil en Cataluña, agosto. Síndic de Greuges de Catalunya, Barcelona.

Singer, A., 2006. Soup and Sadaqa: Charity in Islamic Societies. *Historical Research* 79(205), 1468–2281.

SK, 2013. *Statistikat kodanikuühiskonnast*. Siseministeerium. [Online] Available: https://www.siseministeerium.ee/kodanikuuhiskonna-statistika/ (Accessed 22 November 2013).

Skinner, C., Mersham, G., 2008. Corporate Social Responsibility in South Africa: Emerging Trends. *Society and Business Review* 3(3), 239–255.

Smith, C., Parnell, W., Brown, R., 2010. *Family Food Environment: Barriers to Acquiring Nutritious Food in New Zealand Households*. Blue Skies, Families Commission, Wellington.

SNS, 2012. New Report Shows the Importance of Food Relief. *Newswire*, Canberra.

Sotsiaaltrendid, 2013. *Sotsiaaltrendid. 6. Social Trends.* Eesti Statistika, Tallinn.

Statistics Estonia, 2013. *Poverty and Material Deprivation Rate by Type of Household.* [Online] Available: http://pub.stat.ee/px-web.2001/Dialog/varval.asp?ma=H HS03&ti=POVERTY+AND+MATERIAL+DEPRIVATION+RATE+BY+TYPE+OF +HOUSEHOLD&path=../I_Databas/Social_life/13Social_Exclusion_Laeken_ indicators/003Poverty_and_inequality/&lang=1 (Accessed 9 December 2013).

Statistics New Zealand, 2013. *New Zealand in Profile: 2013.* [Online] Available: http://www.stats.govt.nz/browse_for_stats/snapshots-of-nz/nz-in-profile-2013/ exports.aspx (Accessed 14 May 2013).

StatsSA, 2012. *General Household Survey 2011.* Statistics South Africa, Pretoria.

StatsSA, 2013. *Latest key statistics.* [Online] Available: http://www.statssa.gov.za/ keyindicators/keyindicators.asp (Accessed 12 November 2013).

Steinhauer, J., 2012. Dole Appears, but G.O.P. Rejects a Disabilities Treaty. *New York Times*, 4 December 2012.

Stephens, B., 1992. Budgeting with the Benefit Cuts. In: Boston, J., Dalziel, P. (eds), *The Decent Society? Essays in Response to National's Economic and Social Policies.* Oxford University Press, Auckland.

Stephenson, M.A., Harrison, J., 2011. *Unraveling Equality: A Human Rights and Equality Impact Assessment of the Public Spending Cuts on Women in Coventry.* Coventry Women's Voices and Centre for Human Rights in Practice, Coventry.

Strayer, M., Eslami, E., Leftin, J., 2012. *Characteristics of Supplemental Nutrition Assistance Program Households: Fiscal Year 2011.* USDA, Food and Nutrition Service, Office of Research and Analysis.

Stuart, T., 2009. *Waste: Uncovering the Global Food Scandal.* Penguin Books, London.

Stuttaford, M., Harrington, J., Lewando-Hundt, G., Dowler, E.A., O'Connor, D., 2012. Rights-based Approaches to Addressing Food Poverty and Food Insecurity in Ireland and UK. *Social Science & Medicine* 74(1), 44–51.

Sunstein, C., 2010. *Social and Economic Rights? Lessons from South Africa.* Working paper. The University of Chicago Law School. [Online] Available: http://www. law.uchicago.edu/Lawecon/index.html (Accessed 2 July 2013).

Super, D.A., 2004. Quiet Welfare Revolution: Resurrecting the Food Stamp Program in the Wake of the 1996 Welfare Law. *New York University Law Review* 79, 1271–1397.

Sustain, 2013. *The Alliance for Better Food and Farming.* [Online] Available: http:// www.sustainweb.org/ (Accessed 16 September 2013).

SUT, 2012. *Statistiline ülevaade Tartu 2011.* Tartu Linnavalitsus, Tartu. [Online] Available: http://www.tartu.ee/data/tartu_stat_aastaraamat_2011_veeb.pdf (Accessed 3 April 2013).

SWD, 2012. Social Welfare Department. [Online] Available: http://www.swd.gov. hk/en/index/ (Accessed 15 November 2012).

Tang, K., Midgley, J., 2002. Social Policy After the East Asian Financial Crisis: Forging a Normative Basis for Welfare. *The Journal of Comparative Asian Development* 1(2), 301–318.

Tang, K.L., 1996. Marginalization of Social Welfare in Developing Countries: The Relevance of Theories of Social Policy Developments, *Journal of Sociology and Social Welfare* 23(2), 41–57.

Tang, K.L., 2000. The Leadership Role of International Law in Enforcing Women's Rights: The Optional Protocol to the Women's Convention. *Gender and Development* 8(3), 65–73.

Tang, K.L., 2011. Colonial Policy and Social Welfare: The Case of Hong Kong. In: Midgley, J., Piachaud, D. (eds), *Colonialism and Welfare – Social Policy and the British Imperial Legacy*. Edward Elgar, London.

Tarasuk, V., 2001. A Critical Examination of Community-based Responses to Household Food Insecurity in Canada. *Health Education & Behavior* 28(4), 487–499.

Tarasuk, V., 2005. Household Food Insecurity in Canada. *Topics in Critical Nutrition* 20(4), 299–312.

Tarasuk, V., Davis, B., 1996. Responses to Food Insecurity in the Changing Canadian Welfare State. *Journal of Nutrition Education* 28(2), 71–75.

Tarasuk, V., Eakin, J.M., 2003. Charitable Food Assistance as Symbolic Gesture: An Ethnographic Study of Food Banks in Ontario. *Social Science and Medicine* 56(7), 1505–1515.

Tarasuk, V., Eakin, J.M., 2005. Food Assistance Through 'Surplus' Food: Insights from an Ethnographic Study of Food Bank Work. *Agriculture and Human Values* 22(2), 177–186.

Tarasuk, V., Dachner, N., Poland, B., Gaetz, S., 2009. Food Deprivation is Integral to the 'Hand to Mouth' Existence of Homeless Youths in Toronto. *Public Health Nutrition* 12(9), 1437–1442.

Tarasuk, V., Mitchell, A.N., Dachner, N., 2013. Household Food Insecurity in Canada, 2011. Toronto: Research to Identify Policy Options to Reduce Food Insecurity (PROOF).

TBMM, 2004. Gidalarin Üretimi, Tüketimi ve Denetlenmesine Dair Kanun Hükmünde Kararnamenin Değiştirilerek Kabulü Hakkinda Kanun. Kanun No. 5179, Kabul Tarihi : 27 May 2004. [Online] Available: http://www.tbmm.gov.tr/kanunlar/k5179.html (Accessed 28 December 2013).

TCU, 2005. *Relatório de Avaliação de Programas – Programa Banco de Alimentos*, Tribunal de Contas da União. TCU, Brasilia.

Temple, J.B., 2008. Severe and Moderate Forms of Food Insecurity in Australia: Are They Distinguishable? *Australian Journal of Social Issues* 43(4), 649–668.

The Poverty Initiative, 2013. [Online] Available: http://www.povertyinitiative.org (Accessed 12 March 2013).

THL, 2011. *Perusturvan riittävyyden arviointiraportti*. THL, Helsinki.

Toidupank, 2012. [Online] Available: http://www.delfi.ee/teemalehed/toidupank (Accessed 22 November 2013).

Toth, J., 2003. Islamism in Southern Egypt: A Case Study of a Radical Religious Movement. *International Journal of Middle East Studies* 35(4), 547–572.

Trisi, D., Pavetti, L., 2012. *TANF Weakening As A Safety Net for Poor Families*. Center for Budget and Priorities.

Trumm, A., Kasearu, K., 2011. *Toimetulekutoetuse kasutamine ja mõjud leibkonna vaesusele aastatel 2005–2010*. Uuringu lõpparuanne, Sotsiaalministeerium, Resta 90 lk. [Online] Available: http://www.sm.ee/fileadmin/meedia/Dokumendid/Sotsiaalvaldkond/kogumik/Toimetulekutoetuse_uuringu_lopparuanne_LÕPLIK.pdf (Accessed 8 April 2013).

Trussell Trust, 2013. UK Foodbanks. [Online] Available: http://www.trusselltrust.org/foodbank-projects (Accessed 16 August 2013).

TSU, 2008. *Food Matters: Towards a Strategy for the 21st Century*. Cabinet Office: The Strategy Unit, London.

Tudge, C., 2011. *Good Food for Everyone Forever*. Pari Publishing, Grosseto.

TUIK, 2012. *Gelir ve Yaşam Koşulları Araştırması, 2012*. [Online] Available: http://tuik.gov.tr/PreHaberBultenleri.do?id=13594 (Accessed 23 September 2013).

Turan, N., 2010. Towards an Ecological Urbanism for Istanbul. In: Sorensen, A., Okata, J. (eds), *Megacities: Urban Form, Governance, and Sustainability*. Springer, London and New York, pp. 223–242.

Turk-Is, 2011. *Ocak 2011 Açlık Ve Yoksulluk Sınırı*. [Online] Available: www.turkis.org.tr (Accessed 11 May 2014).

UN, 2011. *Human Development Reports*. United Nations. [Online] Available: http://hdr.undp.org/en/statistics/ (Accessed 15 August 2012).

UNCESCR, 1999. *General Comment 12: The Right to Adequate Food* (Article 11), UN Doc E/C.12/1999/5. United Nations Committee on Economic, Social and Cultural Rights. [Online] Available: http://www.unhchr.ch/tbs/doc.nsf/0/3d02758c707031d58025677f003b73b9 (Accessed 22 March 2013).

UNCESCR, 2006. Concluding Observations of the Committee on Economic, Social and Cultural Rights, Canada, United Nations Economic and Social Council, Geneva.

UN-Habitat, 2008. *Harmonious Cities Report*. United Nations, New York.

UNICEF, 2012a. *La infancia en España 2012–2013. El impacto de la crisis en los niños*. UNICEF, Madrid.

UNICEF, 2012b. *Committing to Child Survival: A Promise Renewed – Progress Report*. UNICEF, New York.

UOMH, 2011. *A Focus on Nutrition: Key Findings of the 2008/2009 New Zealand Adult Nutrition Study*. Ministry of Health, Wellington.

USDA, 2009. Economic Research Service. *Food Security in the United States: Measuring Household Food Security*. United States Department of Agriculture. [Online] Available: http://www.ers.usda.gov/Briefing/FoodSecurity/measurement.htm (Accessed 6 January 2014).

USDA, 2012. *Building A Healthy America: A Profile of the Supplemental Nutrition Assistance Program*. Food and Nutrition Service, Office of Research and Analysis.

Uttley, S., 1997. Hunger in New Zealand: A Question of Rights? In: Riches, G. (ed.), *First World Hunger: Food Security and Welfare Politics*. Macmillan, Houndmills.

Valente, F.L.S., 2003. Fome, desnutrição e cidadania: inclusão social e direitos humanos. *Saude e sociedade* 12(1), 51–60.

Valente, F.L.S., Immink, M.D.C., Coitinho, D.C., 2001. How Political and Social Activism Lead to a Human Rights Approach to Food and Nutritional Security in Brazil. *Ecology of Food and Nutrition* 40(6), 619–633.

Van der Berg, S., 1997. South African Social Security Under Apartheid and Beyond. *Development Southern Africa* 14(4), 481–503.

VGs, 2005. *Voluntary Guidelines to Support the Progressive Realization of the Right to Adequate Food in the Context of National Food Security*. Food and Agricultural Organisation, Right to Food Unit, Rome. [Online] Available: http://www.fao.org/righttofood/publl_01-en-.htm (Accessed 6 January 2014).

Via Campesina, 2012. *What is the Via Campesina?* [Online] Available: http://viacampesina.org/en/index.php?option=com_content&view=category&layout=blog&id=27&Itemid=44 (Accessed 6 January 2014).

Vozoris, N.T., Tarasuk, V.S., 2003. Household Food Insufficiency is Associated With Poorer Health. *The Journal of Nutrition* 133(1), 120–126.

WACOSS, 2012. *Cost of Living Report 2012*. Western Australian Council of Social Service Inc, Perth.

WADH, 2010. *Food Access and Cost Survey*. Western Australia Department of Housing. [Online] Available: http://www.public.health.wa.gov.au/cproot/4115/2/Food%20Access%20and%20Costs%20Survey%202010.pdf (Accessed 15 February 2013).

Wang, Y.T., Lyu, L.C., 2013. The Emergence of Food Bank/Voucher Programs in Taiwan: A New Measure for Combating Poverty and Food Insecurity? *Asia Pacific Journal of Social Work and Development* 23(1), 48–58.

Ward, P.R., Verity, F., Carter, P., Tsourtos, G., Coveney, J., Wong, K.C., 2013. Food Stress in Adelaide: The Relationship Between Low Income and the Affordability of Healthy Food. *Journal of Environmental and Public Health 2013*. [Online] Available: http:77dx.doi.org/10.1155/2013/968078 (Accessed 17 July 2013).

Warshawsky, D.N., 2011. *Urban Food Insecurity and the Advent of Food Banking in Southern Africa*. Urban Food Security Series No 6. African Food Security Urban Network, Johannesburg.

WHO, 2012. *Health Behavior in School-aged Children*, HBC study: International Report from the 2009/2010 survey. [Online] Available: http://www.euro.who.int/__data/assets/pdf_file/0003/163857/Social-determinants-of-health-and-well-being-among-young-people.pdf (Accessed 10 July 2013).

Wilding, P., 2007. Social Policy. In: Lam, W.M., Lui, P., Wong, W., Holliday, I. (eds), *Contemporary Hong Kong Politics: Governance in the Post-1997 Era*. HKU Press, Hong Kong.

Wilkins, J.L., 2005. Eating Right Here: Moving from Consumer to Food Citizen. *Agriculture and Human Values* 22(3), 269–273.

Wilkinson, R., Pickett, K., 2009. *The Spirit Level: Why More Equal Societies Almost Always Do Better*. Allen Lane, London.

Williams, G., 2007. A Charter of Rights for Western Australia, *The New Critic*, Issue 6. [Online] Available: http://www.ias.uwa.edu.au/new-critic/six/rifhtsforwa (Accessed 14 February 2013).

Willows, N.D., Veugelers, P., Raine, K., Kuhle, S., 2009. Prevalence and Sociodemographic Risk Factors Related to Household Food Security in Aboriginal Peoples in Canada. *Public Health Nutrition* 12(8), 1150–1156.

Wilson, J., 1997. Australia: Lucky Country/Hungry Silence. In: Riches, G. (ed.), *First World Hunger: Food Security and Welfare Politics*. Palgrave Macmillan, Houndmills.

Windfuhr, M., 2006. *The Code of Conduct on the Right to Adequate Food: A Tool for Civil Society*. [Online] Available: www.worldhunger.org (Accessed 22 June 2013).

Wittman, H., 2011. Food Sovereignty: A New Rights Framework for Food and Nature? *Environment and Society: Advances in Research* 2(1), 87–105.

Women's Budget Group, 2010. *Impact on Women of the Coalition Spending Review, 2010*. Women's Budget Group, London.

Women's Budget Group, 2012. *Impact on Women of the Budget 2012*. Women's Budget Group, London.

Wong, C.K., 2003. More people are being forced to seek meals from charities. *South China Morning Post*, 27 October 2003.

Woolworths, 2013. *Our Good Business Journey.* [Online] Available: http://www. woolworths.co.za/Home/Our-Good-Business-Journey/People-Transformation/ What-are-we-doing-/cat320478.cat (Accessed 26 March 2013).

World Bank, 2012. Data. [Online] Available: http://data.worldbank.org (Accessed 28 December 2012).

Wuhan Agape Foodbook, 2010. [Online] Available: http://www.whfoodbank. com/ (Accessed 6 May 2013).

WWG, 2011. *Reducing Long-Term Benefit Dependency: Recommendations.* Welfare Working Group, Wellington.

Wynd, D., 2005. *Hard to Swallow: Foodbank Use in New Zealand.* Child Poverty Action Group, Auckland.

Wynd, D., 2011. *Hunger for Learning. Nutritional Barriers to Children's Learning.* Child Poverty Action Group, Auckland.

Ziegler, J., Golay, C., Mahon, G., Way, S., 2011. *The Fight for the Right to Food: Lessons Learned.* Palgrave Macmillan, Geneva.

Zürcher, E.J., 2007. *Turkey: A Modern History.* I.B. Tauris, London.

Zwartz, B., 2010. Sex Scandals 'To Diminish Catholic Church'. *The Age,* 1 April 2010. [Online] Available: http://www.theage.com.au/national/sex-scandals-to-diminish-catholic-church-20100331-rewc.html (Accessed 5 April 2013).

Index

Printed and bound by CPI Group (UK) Ltd, Croydon, CR0 4YY